Revising Eternity

Figure 1. Eric and Lorey Robeck, July 2001, Salt Lake City, Utah

Eric writes, "After our wedding, we paused for a moment, hands clasped, next to the statue on Temple Square of Joseph and Emma Smith. Our shared faith in the church they founded is the reason we met and fell in love. In our innocence, we could never have imagined my loss of faith that would occur years later, nor the challenges that our marriage would endure as a result. Yet while we no longer share that faith, the love we feel for each other has only deepened over the years."

Revising Eternity

27 Latter-day Saint Men Reflect on Modern Relationships

Edited by Holly Welker

Foreword by Patrick Q. Mason

UNIVERSITY OF ILLINOIS PRESS
Urbana, Chicago, and Springfield

An earlier version of "An Apology I've Been Working on for a While" by Joey Franklin was originally published in *Dialogue: A Journal of Mormon Thought*, vol. 43, no. 3, 2010, pp. 94–99.

Manufactured in the United States of America
1 2 3 4 5 C P 5 4 3 2 1
♾ This book is printed on acid-free paper.

Cataloging data available from the Library of Congress
ISBN 9780252044359 (hardcover)
ISBN 9780252086427 (paperback)
ISBN 9780252053344 (ebook)

For all the Mormon men
who have been my friends,
including contributors to this collection,
and especially MJD

Contents

Foreword

Mormon American Masculinities,
Ideal and Actual

Despite appearances from the outside and perhaps even the view from the inside, masculinity and marriage within Mormonism have never been altogether stable nor entirely monolithic.

This is most obvious when we look at the history of marriage within The Church of Jesus Christ of Latter-day Saints. In the space of only sixty years, from 1830 to 1890, the religion's ideal marital structure went from monogamy to polygamy (technically, polygyny) and back again. Even during the roughly four decades when plural marriage was preached from the pulpit and practiced openly, the majority of Mormons remained monogamist. In the twentieth century, Latter-day Saints came to portray themselves as the paragons of heterosexual monogamy; for boundary maintenance purposes, the LDS Church assiduously expelled those who maintained commitments to polygamy. Modern Mormons embraced Victorian domesticity and the nuclear family as their ideal in heaven as it is on earth. The religion's most sacred ceremony literally "seals" one man, one woman, and their children as a family unit for all eternity. But the theological and cultural ideal never fully encompassed the community's very real internal diversity. The church was always home to singles, divorcées, widowers, blended families, homosexuals, childless couples, single parents, and those who for one reason or another were married civilly—till death do you part—rather than eternally in one of the church's temples.

Mormon masculinity has also developed substantially over time. Latter-day Saints have typically conformed to broader cultural notions of manhood and masculinity while emphasizing and magnifying particular gendered norms. For instance, polygamy exacerbated masculinist patriarchy; part of the theological justification for marital plurality was that each additional wife added to the expansion of a man's eternal kingdom, glory, perfection, and exaltation. In the twentieth century, Latter-day Saints defined marriage relationships through the lens of gender complementarianism, which often manifest in a kind of benevolent patriarchy.[1] Mormon men were counseled to be attentive and kind to their wives and their children, but they were still mandated to "preside" in the home by virtue of their priesthood, which the church bestowed exclusively on men. The church told Mormon men that nothing else they did would replace the work they did within the home—but then instructed those men that they had a sacred duty to work full time while their wives stayed home with the children and called those men to spend upward of twenty hours per week outside the home to staff each congregation's lay priesthood leadership and run the church's extensive ecclesiastical, social, youth, and athletic programs.

This century-long construction of Latter-day Saint marital and gender norms found its fullest and most authoritative expression in the church's 1995 seminal document, "The Family: A Proclamation to the World." The Family Proclamation, as it is sometimes known, is inescapable in modern Mormonism. Church leaders and members alike quote it reverentially; many Latter-day Saint homes have a framed copy hung on the living room wall. The Proclamation declares that "gender is an essential characteristic of individual premortal, mortal, and eternal identity and purpose" and that "marriage between man and woman is essential" to God's plan. Eternal gender dictates marital and domestic roles. "By divine design," the Proclamation pronounces, "fathers are to preside over their families in love and righteousness," while "mothers are primarily responsible for the nurture of their children." At the same time, "fathers and mothers are obligated to help one another as equal partners." In simultaneously affirming complementarian and egalitarian models of marriage without resolving the real tensions between them, the Proclamation represented both the culmination of twentieth-century Mormonism and a signal toward the emergence of something new.

If the Family Proclamation represented the apex of modern Mormon ideas about gender and marriage, then those ideals became embodied in the public eye in the person of Mitt Romney, particularly in 2012, when he became the Republican Party's presidential nominee. Professionally successful, a former church hierarch, well-educated, always put-together, confident but not brash, conservative but not extreme, once and happily (and eternally) married, the father of five successful and put-together sons, impeccably faithful to church, family, and country—here was peak Mormon masculinity on display. For some, Romney's persona was a laudable ideal to aspire to; for others, it was a little too perfect, a little too *Leave It to Beaver.* Through it all, single men, divorced men, civilly married men, childless men, unemployed men, and (often closeted) gay men have been there in the pews, right alongside those men and families that seemingly better matched the Proclamation's ideals. It's not that these men broke the mold of Mormon masculinity and marriage; their perpetual presence proved that there was never just one mold to begin with.

Enter Holly Welker's invaluable new collection of essays, *Revising Eternity: 27 Latter-day Saint Men Reflect on Modern Relationships*. What you are holding in your hands is a rare and important accomplishment: getting a bunch of Latter-day Saint men to talk (or at least write) openly, authentically, and intimately about marriage, sex, masculinity, and all of the messiness inherent in human relationships. We know a fair bit about how Mormon men thought about and practiced plural marriage; we know far less about how they do it today. The rise of women's history has belatedly brought female voices and experiences out of obscurity, but the scholarly literature contains precious little about Mormon men *as men*.[2]

This phenomenon is not unique, of course, to the study of Mormonism. "Gender studies" has too often been equated with "women's studies." To a degree this is understandable, insofar as gender studies has been part of the necessary corrective to academic androcentrism. The older assumption had been that if men are the primary (or only) agents in history and culture, then it is not particularly important to consider their gender. And so, somewhat ironically, our understanding of women as gendered beings has outpaced our understanding of men in similar terms. Thankfully, that has begun to change, although maleness still retains a residual normativity in a similar way that whiteness does when we talk of race.

Revising Eternity places men's lived experiences front and center. This book is not about what General Conference talks and church magazines say about what men are *supposed* to think and do and be—although those norms matter—but instead about what men *actually* think and do and are. Mormon men aren't *supposed* to masturbate, or struggle with addictions, or be polyamorous, or cross-dress; in real life it turns out that some *actually* do. There may be a broader tolerance these days for the fact that Latter-day Saint men actually face erectile dysfunction, loss of faith, mental illness, and confusion over what feminism and #MeToo mean for them, but in Mormon culture there is currently almost no space to talk about those things, even in private conversations and especially in official church settings. These articulate, vulnerable, and smart essays give us a singular gift, granting us a peek into the minds (and bodies) of modern Mormon men in all their variety.

To be sure, this is not a representative sample of all Latter-day Saint men, nor is it meant to be. What would representativeness even look like? The Book of Mormon prophet Lehi implored his sons to "arise from the dust . . . and be men" (2 Nephi 1:21). If the admonition to "be men" was ever straightforward, it certainly isn't in twenty-first-century America, where seemingly the one thing we know about masculinity is that it is in transition or, depending on who you listen to, in crisis. The singer-songwriter Jason Isbell captures this sentiment in his lyric, "I used to want to be a real man / I don't know what that even means."[3] *Revising Eternity* opens a window onto what it means to be a man in contemporary Mormonism. Scholars will long refer to the essays here as data in building larger theories about Mormon men and manhood. Every reader will come away realizing that there is no single way to inhabit or perform Mormon masculinity, especially in relationship with others.

Welker's selection of authors and subjects shows that she is fully attuned to the often-unspoken struggle, even pain, that accompanies Mormon manhood. Part of this is just what it means to be human; we all encounter loss and bereavement, setbacks and unfulfilled dreams. But what we see here is the particularity of what it means to inhabit a male body in a modern American Mormon culture. It's one thing to encounter hardship when you're operating in foreign territory, so to speak—a context or culture that isn't natively yours. What does it feel like when a system that you know was engineered by and for people like you—mostly white, American, middle-class, religiously attuned men—doesn't always work for you? The very structures and strictures that give us meaning can also leave us cold.

As always, there is more work to be done. The varieties of American Mormon masculinities and marriages on display here should alert us to the need to map out the contours of gender and relationships in Latter-day Saint communities around the globe. If American Mormon men sometimes struggle to conform to American Mormonism's cultural expectations, what does that look like for Mexican, Nigerian, Filipino, Korean, and Russian Mormon men? How have certain presentations of masculinity and marriage traveled with Latter-day Saint missionaries throughout the world, and how have these ideas and practices been received, interpreted, adapted, reformed, and/or rejected?

Revising Eternity significantly advances the conversation about Mormon men, marriage, and relationships and in some areas practically begins it. Maybe most importantly, twenty-first-century Mormons wrestling with what it means to "be men" will know they are not alone.

Patrick Q. Mason
Logan, Utah

Notes

1. For an articulation of gender complementarianism within Mormon belief, see Hudson, "The Two Trees" (www.fairlatterdaysaints.org/conference/august-2010/the-two-trees). See also McDannell 83–85, 159–166.

2. A major recent exception is Hoyt and Petrey.

3. Jason Isbell and the 400 Unit, "Hope the High Road."

Acknowledgments

I must first thank the contributors to this volume for their candor, generosity, time, and hard work. I must also thank the men who discussed their marriages with me but whose work, for one reason or another, is not included here. It is always a privilege and an honor to learn about the lives of others through the writing they entrust to me.

Thanks to the contributors and spouses who generously allowed their photographs to be included in this book.

Thanks to Donna Banta, Carol Hamer, and Mary Ellen Robertson for feedback on the manuscript. Thanks to Ellen Decoo and Carol Hamer for connecting me to contributors whose work is essential to this collection.

Thanks to friends and family who provided support and encouragement as I worked on this project, especially Doe Daughtrey, Elizabeth Graham, Tanya Hughes, LoraLee Jesperson, Joan Marcus, Melissa Offutt, and my father, Dudley Welker.

Thanks to my agent, Linda Roghaar, whose wise guidance and steadfast support of my work have been invaluable.

Thanks to the University of Illinois Press for connecting me to not one but two exceptionally insightful and supportive editors, Dawn Durante and Alison Syring. Thanks also to the rest of the press's highly professional staff. I grew up in a house full of books, including my father's extensive collection of Mormon studies titles, and I couldn't help but notice how many such titles were published by UIP. Given the press's long-standing centrality and commitment to Mormon studies, I'm very proud to be among the scholars whose work it has chosen to publish.

Revising Eternity

Introduction

Personal, Contingent, and Incomplete Views on Eternal Marriage

HOLLY WELKER

If you're unsure of the importance of marriage in American culture, consider this statement from Supreme Court Justice Anthony Kennedy's opinion in *Obergefell v. Hodges*, the case that legalized gay marriage in 2015: "No union is more profound than marriage, for it embodies the highest ideals of love, fidelity, devotion, sacrifice, and family. In forming a marital union, two people become something greater than once they were. As some of the petitioners in these cases demonstrate, marriage embodies a love that may endure even past death" (28).

This ideal of marriage as ennobling and enduring beyond death aligns neatly with that expounded by The Church of Jesus Christ of Latter-day Saints, with the caveat that for Latter-day Saints, marriage is also "a commandment, an absolutely necessary prerequisite for salvation and exaltation. Marrying 'for time and all eternity'—which happens when a couple is 'sealed' in an LDS temple in a special ordinance that yokes people together in a covenanted relationship intended to survive death—is both the reward for living a righteous life and a primary method by which righteousness is demonstrated," as I've noted previously (Welker, "Attempting" 2–3). Consequently, admonishments and entire sermons from the church's male leadership abound about the importance of "temple marriage" (as it's commonly referred to in Latter-day Saint discourse) and how to succeed at it.

But when, in the wake of my mother's death, I wanted to read not pronouncements from pulpits by important men but candid accounts of what modern marriage means to individual Latter-day Saint women, I found very little, in print or even on the Internet. Blogging, for instance, fits right in with Latter-day Saint encouragement to keep a journal and chronicle important events in our lives, as many of us realized when the blogosphere took off.[1] You might think blogs would therefore provide a rich trove of information about what modern

Mormon marriage means to its participants. But while carefully curated depictions of happy families in Mormon mommy blogs have sometimes attracted huge readerships, their obvious veneer of cheerful wholesomeness obscures difficulties and thus any insight into how to deal with them.[2] Moreover, marriage and motherhood are typically so conflated for Latter-day Saint women that the emphasis on spousal relationships I sought was surprisingly rare.

Consequently, I decided to put together the sort of book I wanted to read, the result being *Baring Witness: 36 Mormon Women Talk Candidly about Love, Sex, and Marriage*. Even before that collection was published, I began imagining a companion collection—this one—because *Baring Witness* was merely one way of discussing marriage in The Church of Jesus Christ of Latter-day Saints, and nothing like the last word.

In both collections, I haven't been concerned with orthodoxy but with "a writer's willingness to scrutinize how Mormon belief and practice shaped [their] ideas and experiences of marriage, regardless of whether [they] remained active and devout" (Welker, "Attempting" 14), so writers collected here provide a range of commitment to and belief in the church. A question I got frequently when I told Latter-day Saints about *Baring Witness* was "Is it pro- or anti-Mormon?" with the clear implication that it must be one or the other. But my answer was always simply "no." The juxtaposition of devout affirmations of the church's inherent goodness and truthfulness with accounts of the church's failings and falseness doesn't constitute an endorsement of either position, though I will point out that the collection begins and ends with essays written by active Latter-day Saints. While individual contributors express very different views of the church and its beliefs, the goal of the book is not to persuade anyone to see the church or its members in any particular way but to demonstrate the varieties of Latter-day Saint experience and to help readers both in and out of the church apprehend and appreciate the complexity of that experience.

The essays in each collection can be understood as addressing this question: "Given that a particular emphasis on marriage is one of the things distinguishing The Church of Jesus Christ of Latter-day Saints, what distinguishes LDS marriages for the [people] in them?" (Welker, "Attempting" 4). The answers the essays provide are, of course, personal, contingent, and incomplete, but it's clear that a frequent distinguishing feature is concern about gender roles, sometimes for reasons unique to Latter-day Saint belief and other times because of broader trends in society at large.

It's important to understand the extent to which "broader trends in society at large" regarding gender and marriage both influence and threaten behavior and belief in The Church of Jesus Christ of Latter-day Saints. Consider, for instance, the church's support of California's Proposition 8 in 2008, which amended the state's constitution to make gay marriage illegal: the vigor of its support suggested that the church perceived gay marriage as an existential threat. As I noted in one of my early discussions of the church's approach to marriage, "It is no surprise that people so invested in a social structure would want to make sure that it remain stable, familiar, and under their control" (Welker, "From Here"). In February 2020, pushing back against gender fluidity and the growing visibility of trans Latter-day Saints, the church released an updated *General Handbook* stating, "Gender is an essential characteristic of Heavenly Father's plan of happiness," gender being *"biological sex at birth"* (38.6.21, emphasis in original); the document also discourages any medical or social transition away from biological sex. It's therefore useful, I think, to provide a brief overview of developments in gender expectations and marriage, especially since the 1950s, as change accelerated and as the church became influential enough to wield significant political clout in situations it deemed crucial to its well-being.

* * *

The story of one person in a marriage is typically, to some extent, the story of their spouse. This has long been true for women, who for centuries in Anglo-American law ceased to exist upon marrying thanks to the concept of coverture, the legal fiction asserting that a husband and wife are a single entity, that entity being the husband, so that a woman's existence is subsumed or covered by her husband's. Consider, for example, the lives of Catherine of Aragon, Anne Boleyn, Jane Seymour, Anne of Cleves, Catherine Howard, and Catherine Parr: they are the wives of Henry VIII of England, and that's the primary thing they're remembered for. But Henry's biography is likewise bound up in the ways that marriage, both the institution and the individual marriages with each of his wives, shaped his life. Furthermore, his desire for a particular type of marriage (one that gave him a son) had repercussions for the entire world: it's why he broke with Roman Catholicism and created the Church of England.

Admittedly, biographies of other important men—and I do mean men—have been written that pay scant attention to their wives. Sometimes, as with the Buddha or Mahatma Gandhi, a wife is important primarily in that she is something a man must abandon to achieve his destiny. But even in such cases, questions remain that can illuminate the overall context of an individual's life. How did these two people come to marry? How did the marriage expand or limit the opportunities available to them? Was the marriage a support or a hindrance in achieving their goals? Did the marriage alter or accelerate the trajectory of someone's life? Did it blight or brighten their happiness? Could the life's course have differed had the marriage been more joyous or miserable, calmer or stormier?

Let's begin with the first question: How did these two people come to marry? Justice Kennedy could draw on a long history when claiming that "in forming a marital union, two people become something greater than once they were" (28), but that doesn't mean that marital unions today mean what they did long ago. Historically, for powerful men, marriage was a way to create alliances and consolidate power; for ordinary men, it was a matter of survival. As Stephanie Coontz demonstrates in *Marriage, a History*, "For millennia, one reason people married was that an individual simply could not survive trying to do everything on his or her own" (30). As "the most important marker of adulthood and respectability as well as the main source of social security, medical care, and unemployment insurance" (7), marriage was, for most of history, "far too vital an economic and political institution to be left entirely to the free choice of the two individuals involved, especially if they were going to base their decision on something as unreasoning and transitory as love" (5).

By the early twentieth century, marriage was no longer vital to economic *survival* in the United States: average people could and did support themselves, though opportunities to do so were significantly more limited for women, because fewer professions were open to them. But marriage remained vital to economic and social *prosperity* if for no other reason than it was expected of respectable adults, especially since sex outside of marriage was still strenuously condemned. The rub was that adults were expected not merely to marry but also to strive for a particular type of marriage: one in which husbands assumed most if not all responsibility for supporting the family financially while wives labored unpaid to maintain the home and rear children.

This type of marriage, although frequently characterized as "traditional" marriage, is both a recent innovation and an option available only to society's more affluent members, as even a cursory inquiry into the topic reveals. That does little to weaken religious enthusiasm for it. For example, in 1995, as part of its campaign against same-sex marriage, The Church of Jesus Christ of Latter-day Saints published a document officially titled "The Family: A Proclamation to the World" (more colloquially known as the Proclamation on the Family) that asserts that "by divine design, fathers are to preside over their families in love and righteousness" while also protecting and providing for them, while women "are primarily responsible for the nurture of their children."[3]

Having decided what type of life was optimal, society went about confirming the validity of its assessment not only by religious decree but by scientific dictum: "By the 1950s and '60s psychiatry had developed a massive weight of theory establishing that marriage—and, within that, the breadwinner role—was the only normal state for the adult male. Outside lay only a range of diagnoses, all unflattering" (Ehrenreich 15), such as homosexuality, pathological immaturity, effeminacy, and infantile fixations. But among the many problems with both religious decrees and scientific "proof" that breadwinner was the only natural—and therefore only acceptable—role for adult men was the fact that rebelling against it "did have a certain seductive appeal" (23), especially since the 1950s marriage model couldn't deliver what it promised. Furthermore, "two of its defining features—separate spheres and togetherness—are virtually incompatible. In retrospect, it seems bizarre that people sought to build an institution that separated husbands and wives more than ever before while simultaneously expecting them to serve as each other's primary source of intimacy and emotional support" (Finkel 65).

Andrew J. Cherlin notes that since its beginning, "the United States has [had] one of the highest levels of both marriage and divorce of any Western nation. . . . The most distinctive characteristic of American family life, then, the trait that more clearly differentiates it from family life in other Western countries, is sheer movement: frequent transitions, shorter relationships" (*Marriage-Go-Round* 4–5). Among the reasons for this, he suggests, are "the contradictory emphases on marriage and individualism found only in the United States" (24). It's not surprising that citizens of a country whose founding document, the Declaration of Independence, affirms that "life, liberty, and the pursuit of happiness" are "unalienable rights" would believe that they should retain the freedom to make choices and pursue actions they deem most likely to result in their happiness.

Barbara Ehrenreich asserts in *The Hearts of Men* that in the twentieth-century battle against oppressive gender roles, it was men who proclaimed their liberation first. Many American men found the postwar cult of conformity soul-killing and the demands of their workplaces crushing; these pressures were bound up in marriage and the responsibilities of providing for and presiding over a family. Still, forgoing marriage hurt women more than men, economically and sexually; single women earned far less than men and were punished more for sex outside of marriage. Consequently, "women were more insistent on marriage than men" and therefore "could be blamed for the entire male predicament" (39). *Playboy*, the first issue of which was published in December 1953, was, if you will, a declaration of social and sexual independence. It told men that there was absolutely nothing wrong with them for wanting a career, a pleasant home, and plenty of sex—without getting married. The message found a receptive audience, especially among feminists, who saw no reason why men should be obligated to support women. Feminists noted that freeing men from that onerous burden would necessitate empowering women to support themselves. This fact, the logic of which is evident, no doubt surprises many who've accepted caricatures of feminists as interested primarily in oppressing men, not in freeing both sexes from rigid gender roles they believe have harmed women.

Given that both men and women felt oppressed by fixed gender expectations, you might wonder why anyone opposed men's liberation—or women's liberation—when it became a movement. There were several objections. First, however painful and taxing breadwinning might be, it still conferred significant prestige and privilege, which many men were loath to relinquish. Beyond the issue of privilege and prestige was the question of power. As Ehrenreich pithily puts it, "Men had nothing to lose but their authority over women" (116), and many decided they'd just as soon retain that.

Furthermore, if gender roles are divinely decreed, as the Proclamation on the Family preaches, any battle to free people from them is not only folly but sin. That rationale helps explain the church's continued opposition to the Equal Rights Amendment (Jacobs). I remember Sunday school lessons in the late 1970s about the evils the ERA would unleash, including women in combat, same-sex marriage, and unisex bathrooms, all of which arrived without the ERA's inclusion in the Constitution. But Ehrenreich notes that for women happy with female dependency, "what was at stake in the battle over the ERA was the *legitimacy* of women's claim on men's incomes" (146, emphasis in original) and that "at bottom, the antifeminists accepted the most cynical assessment of the heterosexual bond: that men are at best half-hearted participants in marriage and women are lucky to get them" (149).

Today, however, marriage is optional in ways that two incomes for one family frequently are not.[4] In fact, one reason both individuals and committed couples delay marriage is the sense that it's economically risky, especially for poorer Americans, who "aspire to marriage at similar or higher rates than their higher-income counterparts, according to a 2012 U.C.L.A. study. But when they do marry, their marriages are much more likely to end in divorce" in part because financial difficulties are such "a powerful source of marital stress" (Yarrow). One culprit, Victor Tan Chen argues, is "the disappearance of good jobs for people with less education." This disappearance "has made it harder for [the poor] to start, and sustain, relationships," while "the U.S.'s relatively meager safety net makes the cost of being unemployed even steeper than it is in other industrialized countries—which prompts many Americans to view the decision to stay married with a jobless partner in more transactional, economic terms" (Chen).

Thus, it's unavoidable that the reasons people marry and what marriage means—to the spouses themselves, to their families and friends, to their governments and employers and insurance companies—have also evolved. As Claire Chambers notes in *Against Marriage*, "Couples may marry so as to obtain various practical benefits, but a key aspect of most marriages is the statement the couple make about their relationship. For the marrying couple and for society in general, the symbolic significance of marriage is at least as important as its practical aspects, as demonstrated in debates about same-sex marriage" (27).

In the late 1990s in graduate school, I joined a dissertation support group. I've forgotten the other participants' projects, with one exception: a queer scholar's dissertation explored reasons same-sex couples should not seek the legal right to marry. I'd been a supporter of marriage equality since the fight over it grew heated in Hawai'i earlier that decade, and the only opposition to gay marriage I'd encountered had been from social conservatives fighting to preserve the status quo. I found the scholar's arguments compelling and insightful. Some were pragmatic: any legal battle would require significant expenditures of time, energy, and money, which he argued could be better used elsewhere. Some were philosophical: heterosexual marriage oppressed both men and women in different ways, so why would gay couples want to opt into an outdated institution when they could fundamentally reimagine and reinvent relationships as more egalitarian and liberating? If they chose to innovate beyond marriage instead of focusing within its legal parameters, they might well create superior models for relationships they could gift to society as a whole, much to the benefit of all families.

Obviously, my friend lost this debate; the winners were those gay couples who "respect [marriage] so deeply that they seek to find its fulfillment for themselves" (Kennedy 28). And my friend's desire to see queer couples reimagine and reinvent relationships might still be realized, since researchers have found that same-sex couples already set examples that can benefit different-sex couples:

> Gays and lesbians who discussed a disagreement with their partner did so in less belligerent, domineering and fearful ways than different-sex individuals, possibly because they did not bring the same history of power inequalities to the table. . . . Even in ordinary daily interactions, people in same-sex unions use more positive methods of influencing a partner, studies find, than individuals in different-sex partnerships, offering encouragement and praise rather than criticism, lectures or appeals to guilt. (Coontz, "How")

When granted the right to marry, many same-sex couples did so with alacrity: a Gallup poll from 2017 "estimates that 61% of same-sex, cohabiting couples in the U.S. are now married, up from 38% before the Supreme Court legalized same-sex marriage in June 2015, and 49% [in 2016]" (Jones).[5] Cherlin asks why so many couples would marry "after living, presumably happily, as cohabiting unmarried partners?" ("Marriage Has"). Given the extent to which same-sex relationships have been disparaged as immoral and a fundamental threat to stability and order, it's perhaps no wonder that, as Clyde Kunz's essay here describes, same-sex couples who had cohabitated happily for years if not decades deemed marriage "a public marker of their successful union, providing them the opportunity to display their love and companionship to family and friends" ("Marriage Has").

And that reason for marrying, Cherlin notes, is common among couples both gay and straight: "For many people, regardless of sexual orientation, a wedding is no longer the first step into adulthood that it once was, but, often, the last. It is a celebration of all that two people have already done, unlike a traditional wedding, which was a celebration of what a couple would do in the future" ("Marriage Has"). This trend is lamented by the brethren in Salt Lake City, who admonish single members not to "postpone the blessings of marriage" (Carroll). But whether couples marry early or late, the underlying values celebrated include stability and commitment.

As marriage evolves, as our culture rethinks gender roles and even gender itself—which the Proclamation posits as "eternal"—and as the church maintains its opposition to premarital sex, cohabitation, same-sex marriage, transsexuality, and the ERA, it's likely that tension around the church's ideals will not merely persist but intensify for Latter-day Saints who must accommodate openly queer loved ones and a society that, dire predictions notwithstanding, hasn't self-destructed now that gay couples can be legally married.

✴ ✴ ✴

For reasons I can't entirely explain, I still own a 1970s textbook called *Achieving a Celestial Marriage* from a course I took at the LDS Institute of Religion at the University of Arizona in the mid-1980s. It's chock-full of statements like this:

> *The most important things that any member of The Church of Jesus Christ of Latter-day Saints ever does in this world are: 1. To marry the right person, in the right place, by the right authority; and 2. To keep the covenant made in connection with this holy and perfect order of matrimony—thus assuring the obedient persons of an inheritance of exaltation in the celestial kingdom.* (McConkie 118, qtd. in *Achieving* 132, emphasis in original)

Keep in mind that "the right person" doesn't necessarily refer to a partner with compatible interests, temperament, or libido—especially not libido, since even today, the church warns members not to fall for the "'sexual chemistry' paradox," or the "distorted . . . belief that one needs to test sexual chemistry within a relationship—that the couple shouldn't move to later stages of commitment until they've tested and made sure that the chemistry is a strong and compatible part of their relationship" (Carroll). Instead, the reference is to righteousness: "The right person is someone for whom the natural and wholesome and normal affection that should exist does exist. It is the person who is living so that he or she can go to the temple of God and make the covenants that we there make" (McConkie, in Conference Report 13). But other discourse asserts that almost anyone can be the right person and promises that "almost any good man and any good woman can have happiness and a successful marriage if both are willing to pay the price," which is to "love the Lord more than their own lives and then love each other more than their own lives, working together in total harmony with the gospel program as their basic structure" (Kimball, "Oneness") without acknowledging what a tall order that is. Attitudes like that are among the reasons that for decades, the church aggressively encouraged gay Latter-day Saints to enter different-sex marriages: it was a way to keep both spouses righteous, and other issues of compatibility didn't matter. This policy created plenty of misery for most everyone involved, as Joseph Broom, Kelland Coleman, and Boyd Jay Petersen discuss in their essays here, though as Scott Blanding asserts, rare exceptions are relatively successful marriages.[6]

Given the disparity between the Latter-day Saint ideal of joyous marriages and the reality of mismatched couples trying to endure miserable marriages they covenanted to stay in for eternity, it's unsurprising that not every Latter-day Saint is eager to marry. In a 2015 book offering straight people ways to improve their chances of finding a spouse, author John Birger discusses articles contrasting Latter-day Saint men reluctant to marry with "Mormon women who want to marry but cannot find a good Mormon man" (127). In particular, Birger references a *Salt Lake Tribune* article blaming the problem on such things as social media (a twenty-two-year-old man complains that after seeing someone's Facebook posts, he can find nothing to discuss on a first date) and "a 'modern nonchalance' about marriage" (127). Both Birger and the *Tribune* article include this 2011 statement from Elder Richard G. Scott: "If you are a young man of appropriate age and are not married, don't waste time in idle pursuits. Get on with life and focus on getting married. Don't just coast through this period of life."[7]

Birger asserts that lopsided gender ratios in certain places (too many single men in Silicon Valley vs. too many single women in New York City and within both The Church of Jesus Christ of Latter-day Saints and communities of Orthodox Jews) make it hard for marriage-minded young singles to find a spouse. But when it comes to older people, women are less likely than men to want to remarry. Canadian census data show that "more than 68 percent of seniors residing alone in 2016 were women"; of such women, "72 percent [reported] they were highly satisfied living on their own." Whereas, according to Zosia Bielski, "for a generation of older men, traditional, live-in relationships remain important because female partners meet so many of their social, emotional, health and domestic needs." To put it bluntly, older men frequently want to remarry because they require a wife to care for them. Consequently, it's hardly surprising that

> marriage increases the gender inequality of housework. . . . Scott South and Glenna Spitze compare six different kinds of households in the USA: never married and living with parents, never married and living independently, cohabiting, married, divorced, and widowed. They find that women do more housework than men across the board, but that "the gender gap is highest among married persons." Men's hours of housework remain consistent whether married or single (they increase where men are divorced or widowed), but women's hours are higher when cohabiting and higher still when married. The authors argue that wives'

increased housework is not explained by children or reduced hours of paid work, and attribute it instead to the increased power of the normative requirements to "display gender" that marriage brings. (Chambers 21)

Several contributors to this collection discuss their desires for and efforts at establishing equitable divisions of labor, so there's reason to hope that the tendency just discussed can change—sooner rather than later. The Pew Research Center provides data showing that fathers in 2016 spent more than triple the number of hours on child care than they spent in 1965—which sounds impressive until closer inspection reveals that the increase is from two and a half hours a week to eight (Livingston and Parker). Nonetheless, change that starts small is still change.

There's also the problem of equitable division of emotional labor. Principle number 4 of *The Seven Principles for Making Marriage Work* from renowned marriage researcher John Gottman is "Let Your Partner Influence You," advice directed especially toward men for the simple fact that they often avoid doing so. Gottman notes:

It's certainly important for wives to treat their husbands with honor and respect. But my data indicate that the vast majority of wives—even in unstable marriages— already do that. This doesn't mean that they don't get angry and even contemptuous of their husbands. It just means that they let their husbands influence their decision making by taking their opinions and feelings into account. But too often, the men do not return the favor. . . . Our study didn't really find that men should give up all of their personal power and let their wives rule their lives. But we did find that the happiest, most stable marriages in the long run were those in which the husband did not resist sharing power and decision making with the wife. (116)

I think the essays here demonstrate that Latter-day Saint husbands can be as willing as anyone to accept, learn, and grow from the influence of their spouse. In *A History of the Wife*, Marilyn Yalom writes, "The notion that husband and wife should make each other better people does not resonate with the most visible goals of contemporary American society. How many young people marry with the conscious expectation that they will become kinder and wiser by virtue of choosing a decent, generous mate? Happier, richer, more successful. Yes! But better human beings?" (156).

I would answer that within Latter-day Saint culture, the answer is, as often as not, yes, and the expectation of moral influence is frequently fulfilled—though not necessarily in ways newlyweds expect, as many of these essays explicitly underscore. This is one reason the collection's first part is called "Revised Expectations," though it should be noted that basically every essay in the collection deals with that theme. In particular I must call attention to T. Kay Browning's essay, which grapples with issues raised by the #MeToo movement. Given that

I was working on this collection in 2017 as the #MeToo movement gained widespread attention, I was anxious to include an essay that confronted various issues #MeToo highlighted. I'm grateful that Browning did so, with considerable self-awareness and generosity.

The men who wrote essays for me were far more willing than their female counterparts in *Baring Witness* to discuss sex—so much so that sex is the unifying theme of Part II, "Sex and Its Consequences." The emphasis on sex fits a stereotype but still surprised me—I thought Mormon men might be more reticent on a topic about which Latter-day Saints are frequently reticent. I'm glad to be wrong and grateful for these writers' candor on topics including cross-dressing, sterilization, erectile dysfunction, pornography, promiscuity, infidelity, polyamory, polygamy, and masturbation.

The topic of masturbation requires further commentary. An early reader of this work wondered how Scott Blanding could grow up thinking masturbation was inconsequential, given that David Nicolay was explicitly told that masturbating made him unworthy to serve a mission or advance in the priesthood. The answer is timing: Blanding was already married before the church began its aggressive campaign against adolescent masturbation. Some sermons on this topic, such as "To Young Men Only" by Boyd K. Packer (1976) and "Steps in Overcoming Masturbation" (often attributed to Mark E. Petersen, ca. 1970), are so notorious and so widely ridiculed that the church ceased making them available.[8] In any event, I think a comparison of Blanding's and Nicolay's essays reveals that the shame the church deliberately created around masturbation blighted lives in ways masturbation itself never could, especially when coupled with a tendency for religious scrupulosity.[9]

Another reader was confused by the second part and complained that several essays in it were "not really about sex, but about belief and belonging." I would underscore that Part II is actually titled "Sex and Its Consequences"; those consequences can encompass a great many things. The sexual code of The Church of Jesus Christ Latter-day Saints is called the law of chastity; living by it is crucial to belonging, and violating it is grounds for excommunication (which the church renamed "withdrawal of membership" in 2020), a painful process involving an ecclesiastical trial (likewise renamed "Church membership councils") (Curtis). I also remember a seminary teacher (seminary being religious instruction for high school students every weekday) expounding on Matthew 16:4—"A wicked and adulterous generation seeketh after a sign"—and informing my class that sexual immorality would destroy our ability to recognize truth or have faith. In other words, in religious contexts, sex is often fully bound up in issues of belonging and belief; it's missing the point to try to separate them.

I was surprised at how many men discuss bereavement. Five essays discuss death in some detail; two others mention it tangentially. In fact, illness and death are such frequent themes that the final part of the book is titled "In Sickness and in Health." Given that I began *Baring Witness* as a way to help me mourn my mother's death, I was disappointed that only one contributor (Anita Tanner) discussed being widowed. Rather than attempting to draw any conclusion about why bereavement was such a common topic here, I'll simply be grateful that a lacuna in the previous collection has been addressed, especially with the sensitivity and generosity displayed by Joseph Broom, Scot Denhalter, Thomas W Murphy, Robert Raleigh, and Robert A. Rees.

As is too often the case, the discussion of race here is anything but straightforward. I'm grateful for Thomas W Murphy's thoughtful, complicated discussion of race, ancestry, colonization, and DNA, especially given his expertise on the topic of DNA and its relevance to Latter-day Saint teachings.[10] I was lucky in *Baring Witness* that one of the contributors was Gina Colvin, a Māori scholar of race whose essay nonetheless didn't mention race. After fretting about how to discuss this fact, I simply requested Colvin's advice. She replied that a discussion of race was "superfluous to her response to the subject at hand."[11] This gave me the confidence to use the same approach when Robert Raleigh, who is Native American, and Andrew Spriggs, who is Black, likewise contributed essays that didn't mention race. I asked each about the omission. Spriggs replied that discussing race in the context of his marriage "would say more about the depth of my unconscious socialization into whiteness than I have ever attempted to untangle because I suspect it would make me more vulnerable than I could stomach."[12] Raleigh's comment addressed not only his race but that of his wife:

> Even though I'm half Native American, being adopted by a white Mormon family meant I wasn't particularly conscious of race, especially since my parents taught me that God meant for us to be together from the preexistence. It's only recently that, through DNA testing, I've learned that my Native American relatives are Yakama. I'm only now making connections to the Native American side of my heritage, as I've started to meet Native people closely related to me by blood.
>
> Juanita, on the other hand, was very conscious and proud of her status as Chicana or Latina. In many ways, she helped me think more about the relationship between race and culture, obviously very different things. For this I will always be grateful.[13]

It will take someone with more expertise and understanding on the topic of race to tease out the implications of these situations, and I welcome the insights such analysis will provide.

I asked nearly every unmarried Latter-day Saint man I know to write an essay about being single, but only Nicholas Don Smith agreed; he also obliged me by writing humor. As in *Baring Witness*, I wanted to showcase a variety of styles—including the decided irreverence of someone whose profession involves "yelling jokes at a sea of strange faces."

Speaking of being single, I'll discuss my own situation. As a spinster, I obviously have less stake in marriage. This doesn't mean I feel particularly excluded or think I'm missing something crucial; I recognize myself when I read, for instance, that single people generally "are far more connected to the social world around them. On average, they provide more care for their siblings and aging parents. They have more friends. They are more likely to offer help to neighbors and ask for it in return. This is especially true for those who have always been single, shattering the myth of the spinster cat lady entirely" (Catron). But the fact is, I'm simply interested in marriage, in the force it exerts on our choices and narratives. My attitude is similar to my attitude about the church itself, which I served a mission for but stopped attending in my twenties. I once wrote that "if the church somehow lost all its members tomorrow and existed only as a historical relic, I would still be concerned with scrutinizing and puzzling out how my present life has been shaped by my past, including the twenty-six years I spent as a devout Mormon, obeying the commandments, participating in the culture and passionately studying the doctrines of the church" (Welker, "Why I Go"). Likewise, if marriage disappeared, I'd still be interested in why people had married, what their marriages had meant to them, and how they felt about and adjusted to any change.

It should be noted that there are people who want to abolish marriage. In *Against Marriage*, Claire Chambers asserts that the state shouldn't be in the business of regulating people's most intimate relationships, noting that "the very function that marriage serves within both a society and a state is to legitimate and prioritize certain sorts of relationships, to demarcate them as worthy of special consideration, validity and respect" (60). She asks, "What is it about marital relationships that makes them valuable and worthy of state recognition?" (34). I hadn't asked this question until I read it, but I think it's worth considering, especially since marriage, at least in the United States, doesn't make relationships more durable: "Children born to married parents in the United States were more likely to experience their parents' breakup than were children born to cohabiting parents in Sweden" (Cherlin, *Marriage-Go-Round* 3). It's a question I hope people will ask as they read this book; I likewise hope that they will not arrive at a single definitive answer but discover instead a wealth of insight.

A couple of recent significant changes in Latter-day Saint practice require comment. In January 2019, without fanfare, the church altered the temple sealing ceremony, in that spouses began to give themselves reciprocally to each other.[14] Previously, it was only the wife who gave herself to her husband. This clear-cut case of female subordination and the pain it caused is discussed here in "The Highest" by T. Kay Browning and has been something feminists invoked to underscore sexism in the church. I believe this change demonstrates that addressing injustice and inequality in its beliefs and practices increases rather than diminishes the church's moral integrity.

Despite its celebrated separation of church and state, the United States recognizes private religious marriages as legally binding, as does Canada. Many countries, however, do not, either because clergy aren't deputized to act on behalf of the state or because legal proceedings like marriages must be open to the public. In countries where these legal restrictions apply, Latter-day Saints desiring a temple wedding ceremony must first have a civil ceremony, which all their friends and loved ones can be invited to. Consequently, it matters less that the subsequent ceremony in the temple can be attended only by Latter-day Saints who are adults and possess something called a temple recommend, obtained via a worthiness interview. (Thomas W Murphy, for instance, discusses in his essay his young daughter's exclusion from her parents' marriage sealing; the child was brought in only for a secondary ceremony in which she was sealed to her parents.) The situation was very different in countries where closed religious ceremonies are recognized by the state—which, as mentioned, include the United States and Canada, countries with relatively large Latter-day Saint populations. At some point after World War II, the church began requiring Latter-day Saint couples in these countries to choose between a civil and a religious ceremony— they couldn't have both. If they chose to have a civil ceremony, they had to wait a year to be sealed in the temple. The delay was problematic, because forgoing a temple marriage was both strenuously discouraged by the church and often perceived as evidence that the couple had been denied temple recommends (usually for sexual immorality) and weren't worthy to enter the temple, which, as several essays here mention, is deeply shameful. Consequently, couples with family members who weren't members of the church essentially had to choose between the church and their loved ones. Nonmember parents were often understandably flummoxed and heartbroken at being told they couldn't attend their child's wedding, though couples sometimes tried to skirt the dilemma by having a ring ceremony after the temple sealing, as rings aren't exchanged in the temple, but even that was often discouraged. People found the policy hurtful, divisive, and completely antithetical to the church's professed profamily stance. Early this century, groups began petitioning the church to change the policy; it finally did so in May 2019.[15]

I must also discuss the name of the church. Although his two most recent predecessors, Gordon B. Hinckley and Thomas S. Monson, embraced the term "Mormon," President Russell M. Nelson declared it verboten in 2018 because "if we allow nicknames to be used or adopt or even sponsor those nicknames ourselves, [the Savior] is offended. . . . To remove the Lord's name from the Lord's Church is a major victory for Satan."

In this introduction, I've retained the word "Mormon" in quotations for the sake of accuracy but have otherwise avoided it. The church's official style guide states, "When referring to Church members, the terms 'members of The Church of Jesus Christ of Latter-day Saints,' 'Latter-day Saints,' 'members of the Church of Jesus Christ' and 'members of the restored Church of Jesus Christ' are preferred." Given that "The Church of Jesus Christ" is the legal name of an entity headquartered in Monongahela, Pennsylvania, I'm uncomfortable using it to refer to one headquartered in Salt Lake City, Utah, and have consistently added "of Latter-day Saints" in order to be accurate. Since "Latter-day Saint" is deemed acceptable for referring to people, that's the term I've used most often when doing so. However, I haven't asked writers to delete the term "Mormon" from their essays, especially when they were written, in good faith and thorough compliance with a belief system and an identity, before President Nelson made his statement.

I'll conclude with a brief note on form. My training is in literature and creative writing; that's what I asked contributors to this collection to produce. Since its creation by Michel de Montaigne in the sixteenth century, the personal essay has been characterized by a willingness to follow a train of thought where it leads, which some people characterize as "meandering" (academics often prefer the term "discursive"); for scholars and fans of the personal essay, this trait can be a highly prized feature, not a bug. Montaigne called his discursive considerations of things that interested or confused him *essais*, which is French for "attempts," because they were merely attempts at understanding, not definitive last words. This has proven true for several contributors to *Baring Witness*, as I'm aware of nine who changed their marital status: seven who were married divorced; one who had never married got married; one who was divorced remarried. So I expect that changes will ensue for contributors to this collection as well, but I hope it won't diminish the worth of their insights here. If nothing else, change provides the opportunity for something the *Wall Street Journal* said was important for the sort of "successful family-storytelling" that can help children develop a sense of family history and identity: "Be open to reframing old stories to find new meaning" (Shellenbarger). It seems to be true of churches as well as individuals.

Notes

1. The corner of the blogosphere occupied by faithful Latter-day Saints is called the bloggernacle, after the Tabernacle on Temple Square in Salt Lake City. Regarding journal keeping, see Kimball, "The Angels," in which the prophet of the church encourages Latter-day Saints to "get a notebook, a journal that will last through all time, and maybe the angels may quote from it for eternity."

2. For discussions of the popularity and problems of blogs by Mormon women, see Aronowitz, Gregory, Kiesling, and Matchar.

I will add that as a missionary in Taiwan in 1986, I attended a conference in which a visiting general authority told us that we must never include anything negative in our journals or our letters home, that it was important to portray our missions in exclusively positive terms. I was temperamentally incapable of following such advice, but I understand well why others felt obliged to heed similar exhortations.

3. For discussions of how this document shapes Latter-day Saints' perceptions of their marriages, see Carter, "Transgressors," and Morris, "Pie Month," in this collection.

4. See Livingston and Parker about families with two incomes: "As of 2016, about a quarter of couples (27%) who live with children younger than 18 were in families where only the father works. This marked a dramatic change from 1970, when almost half of these couples (47%) were in families where only the dad worked. The share of couples living in dual-earner families has risen significantly and now comprises the majority of two-parent families with children."

5. This doesn't mean that 61 percent of gay people are married; most LGBT people are single. Jeffrey Jones further notes that "LGBT Americans are still more likely to be married to an opposite-sex spouse (13.1%) than a same-sex spouse (10.2%), but the gap is narrowing. According to prior research on LGBT identification, roughly half of those who self-identify as LGBT are bisexual, helping explaining the high proportion of LGBT individuals who are married to opposite-sex partners. Gallup's question does not probe specifically for whether LGBT individuals are lesbian or gay or bisexual or transgender."

6. See my analysis of mixed-orientation marriages ("Cleanshaven").

7. For Birger's discussion, see 127–28. For Scott's statement, see "The Eternal Blessings of Marriage." For the article in *Salt Lake Tribune*, see Peggy Fletcher Stack, "Why Young LDS Men Are Pushing Back Marriage."

8. Regardless of who wrote "Steps in Overcoming Masturbation: A Guide to Self-Control," the text has circulated on the web for at least twenty-five years. Consider its recommendation that teens train themselves in the art of aversion therapy: "If you associate something very distasteful with your loss of self-control it will help you to stop the act. For example, if you are tempted to masturbate, think of having to bathe in a tub of worms, and eat several of them as you do the act."

9. See, for instance, Matsuura. The article notes that there's some evidence that Latter-day Saints have higher levels of religious scrupulosity. See also Michael Carpenter's essay in this volume, "Never Good Enough," which illustrates some of the traits of religious scrupulosity.

10. See Murphy, "Lamanite Genesis, Genealogy, and Genetics" as an example of his scholarly work.

11. See Welker, "Attempting"(10), and personal email dated 13 February 2016.

12. Personal email dated 2 November 2019.

13. Personal email exchange dated 2 December 2019 and 3 December 2019.

14. For more information on this change, see Welker, "Changes."

15. For some background and history on this policy and on efforts to change it, see Welker, "Sorry." On its recision, see Welker, "LDS Church Rescinds."

PART I

Revised Expectations

Figure 2. Kirsten Andersen Morris and Scott Russell Morris, November 2013, Lubbock, Texas

Scott writes, "This picture is the first time Kirsten made caramel apple pie, which has since become a favorite recipe. Besides how happy we look in the picture, it's one of our favorites because it's evidence of what we love about our marriage: we support each other in new adventures—whether that's a new recipe or a new career or a new country—and we just really like hanging out together."

Transgressors

STEPHEN CARTER

My six-year-old trots down the stairs of the gymnastics studio and heads toward the snack room. She grabs something carby and brings it to the counter.

"What's your name?" asks the woman behind the computer.

My daughter tells her; the woman taps a few buttons.

"And what's your mom's name?"

"Stephen," she chirps.

I feel a familiar pang of awkwardness as the woman looks up.

"She means that the snack account is under my name," I say.

But my daughter has a point.

* * *

"By divine design, fathers . . . are responsible to provide the necessities of life and protection for their families," reads "The Family: A Proclamation to the World." "Mothers are primarily responsible for the nurture of their children."

This quote has haunted me my entire marriage. And even more since my daughter was born.

A framed copy of the Proclamation on the Family hangs in the living room of many a Mormon household, and it's frequently quoted in church meetings. So when a male Mormon and a female Mormon get married, there's no question who should be the provider and who should be the nurturer. The Proclamation explicitly connects these two roles to gender, which it states is "an essential characteristic of our premortal, mortal, and eternal identity and purpose." And the roles should not be taken lightly. People who "fail to fulfill family responsibilities will one day stand accountable before God."

Early in our marriage, Noelle and I both worked outside the home. Since we didn't have children to nurture, provide for, or protect, those sentences from the

Proclamation didn't feel relevant. And even after our first child was born, we still seemed to have some wiggle room because Noelle worked writing online college courses from home and could therefore still be our child's "nurturer."

But then another child arrived, and soon thereafter we agreed to provide day care for three little nieces. Noelle suddenly had her hands full—and we had a mortgage. So, being the good Proclamation follower I was, I worked three jobs to keep our finances above water.

One of my jobs was being a news reporter (back when you could make money at it), so I was running around Utah Valley attending meetings, chasing down interviews, and turning in three articles a day. My other two jobs were at Utah Valley State College. When I think back on the sheer energy I expended during that time in my early twenties, my head spins. It was simultaneously thrilling and exhausting.

But soon we realized we couldn't maintain our family on my current earning power. It was time for graduate school.

I researched academic programs with the idea that further education would enhance my providing ability, leaving Noelle free to nurture. But one night, after I told her about a few schools I was considering, Noelle said she would attend graduate school as well.

My first thought was, "What?" But my second thought was, "Of course."

Noelle, after all, had taken pretty much every AP class in high school (while I was about as middle-of-the-pack as you could get) and had earned some great scholarships at BYU (while all I ever got were Pell Grants). She was perfect grad school material. And, as it turned out, one of the schools that accepted both of us, the University of Alaska–Fairbanks, offered her an assistantship *and* a scholarship, while I just got waitlisted for an assistantship (though I did get one soon after arriving).

So we moved to Alaska and did the Tetris-like work of arranging our schedules so one of us could be with our two children when the other was gone.

On one hand, it seemed we had most certainly regressed in our adherence to the Proclamation: Noelle was no longer at home being a full-time nurturer, and I wasn't out being a full-time provider. But on the other hand, there was one part of the Proclamation we could still hide behind: "Fathers and mothers are obligated to help one another as equal partners." If pressed, though, we would have to admit that those words are immediately followed by qualifiers: "Disability, death, or other circumstances may necessitate individual adaptation." Could we interpret that to mean "disability, death, or graduate school"?

We *were* the personification of "equal partners," though. Being in the same program, Noelle and I had exactly the same number of classes to attend and exactly the same graduation requirements. So by necessity, we shared the child-care/school load fifty-fifty.

And the extra time I spent with my children had its effect. Recently I found a book of photos from that time that I hadn't seen in years. Looking through it, I was astonished at how beautiful our children were, how purely their personalities showed through, how endearingly proportioned their bodies were, and how many memories the images called up.

And not just family-vacation-type memories, or even weekend memories, or even putting-the-kids-to-bed memories, but mundane, everyday-life memories, the kind that can only be made when you're around your kids a *lot*. Playing in the sandbox on the last day of summer, already in our long-sleeve shirts; trick-or-treating in (literally) zero-degree weather; watching a moose and her calf grazing in our flowerbeds.

After years of this balancing act, Noelle and I earned our master's degrees and doctorates. Our family then moved from Alaska to its warmer but windier cousin, Wyoming, where we both took jobs as schoolteachers. It worked out well because our children were the right age to attend the elementary school Noelle taught at. She even arranged for our oldest to be placed in her fourth-grade class. Meanwhile, I taught sophomore English to kids who would make twice my salary right out of high school working on the oil rigs—no knowledge of Greek tragedy required.

The Proclamation seemed placated during those two years, since Noelle and our children kept essentially the same schedule, though it rumbled a bit about who should be the primary provider.

Then I landed a job editing a magazine from home. I actually struggled with the decision to take the job. I enjoyed teaching more than I'd expected. I also worried about the stability of a small nonprofit job versus a state-sponsored job. But the magazine seemed like the thing to do.

And I guess it was, because a few months after I took the position, Noelle and I found that we were expecting a baby. It was a surprise. We'd been thinking that two kids were enough, and our youngest was ten. Suddenly we had to wrap our heads around the fact that we'd soon start all over again with the sleep deprivation, projectile pooping, and Sisyphean laundry cycles.

As we considered the impending change, we realized that in many ways, we were perfectly set up for it. I worked from home, so I could be the baby's main caretaker while Noelle continued to teach. Had I still been a teacher, we would have had to make the difficult decision of losing half our income or hiring someone else to take care of our child.

Though I was nervous about taking on this responsibility, I already had some experience under my belt, not just with my own children but with my eight younger brothers and sisters, many of whom I helped raise. I remembered how much fun it was to watch them grow up—how much I enjoyed their company. And I realized that I was excited to meet this new little soul, too.

But the day Noelle returned to school from maternity leave was the day the Proclamation started banging down my door. I felt like Adam when he realizes not only that he is naked but that God is coming to visit. I had nothing to hide behind—not a single shred of verbiage that I could muster in defense of my new role. Even if I was helping to provide for my family, I had become a full-time nurturer. And it wasn't just *my* soul I was worried about, it was my baby's. Was I starving her in a way I couldn't see? Was my male spirit simply unequipped to provide her an essential form of nurture?

That tension increased when we moved to Utah for Noelle's new job at an educational software company. In Wyoming, she was home by four o'clock on a regular basis, and she had summers off. But in Utah she worked all year and usually didn't get home until much later.

Our ward in Orem had no idea what to make of us. Our home teacher laughed out loud when I told him I was a stay-at-home dad. The women in the ward were simultaneously awed and frightened by Noelle, who, much to our surprise, found that she had a knack for management and started moving up the corporate ladder. Through years of watchfulness, suffering, and practicing, she learned to navigate with authority and grace through a company loaded with male executives (most of whom are bishops and former mission presidents and therefore used to being obeyed, especially by women). She has built a grounded, trustworthy ethos that makes her a natural leader.

Our new setup became a lasting one, and our roles blended together. Despite my day managing the children and maintaining the house, it was a matter of course for me to start my work around six o'clock at night—after getting everyone fed—and push through until two in the morning. And despite a long day at work, Noelle would spend her evenings helping with homework, getting kids ready for bed, and calming the baby in the middle of the night.

About six years after our baby was born, I was sitting in a priesthood meeting where the teacher grew misty-eyed as he held forth about how wonderful mothers are, how their role as nurturer was the most important and fulfilling job in the world, how he could *never* do it himself. Everyone nodded along, offering their own platitudes.

Their words called up memories of staring at my baby for hours as her eyes explored the room, as she auditioned her voice, as her arms conducted silent orchestras. But also memories of watching the DVD menu of *Bear in the Big Blue House* repeating over and over again for hours as I held the sleeping baby in my lap—because if I moved, the baby would wake up, and if I turned the sound down, the baby would wake up. (Sartre would have written a very different play about hell had he seen my plight.) They called up memories of the many hours I spent following my little fire sprite down streets, across yards, and through play equipment; watching her patrol the earth—examining skies and pebbles, talking with dogs and the wind, testing gravity and my heart. Memories of waking every morning with the inescapable knowledge that the day was in no way mine, that my will did not matter, that the small things of the earth were in control—and feeling that desolation instantly evaporate at the sight of my daughter's impish smile. Only to return a few minutes later.

Suddenly, a fire ignited in me.

"You guys have no idea what you're talking about," I said. "I'm here to tell you: for the past six years I've been the primary caretaker for my daughter, and it has changed me to the core. Nothing in my entire life, not even my mission, has affected me so deeply. To spend endless tracts of inescapable time with my child, day in and day out for years, has been the most joyful, despair-ridden, heart-expanding, soul-sucking experience I've ever had. I've never felt so utterly alone; I've never felt so completely connected. My being is larger and stronger and wiser in ways I never could have imagined when I was just a provider. I've been you. I've said those same words. And they are empty. If you ever have the chance to become your child's full-time nurturer, *take it*. Of *course* you can do what your wives do! These are your children, too! If you believed all the platitudes you've been spewing, you'd be begging for the chance. But instead, you're hiding behind your role, missing a profound opportunity."

You could definitely call the silence that followed stunned. But the teacher soon moved on to the next topic, and, as far as I can tell, the incident sank into the morass of ward history like a diaper into a laundry bucket.

* * *

When introducing Eve and Adam to the Garden of Eden, God gave them two commandments. First, don't eat the fruit of the tree of knowledge of good and evil. Second, multiply and replenish the earth. But as Mormon theology interprets it, these two commandments were mutually exclusive—Eve and Adam's procreative mechanisms wouldn't kick in until *after* they ate the fruit of the tree. So they could only keep *one* of the commandments.

Eve finally broke the lower commandment (don't eat the fruit) in order to obey the higher commandment (bear fruit). It was a choice that came with a lot of consequences. The couple lost their paradise; they wandered in a lone and dreary world; they labored and suffered for their bread and for their children. But it was the only way humanity could ever start progressing.

For making this frightening but generative choice, Mormonism honors Eve.

It seems to me that the role assignment in the Proclamation may be like "don't eat the fruit." It's a useful commandment: it keeps things efficient; it staves off messy decisions; it gives us a role to master. But does it ever impede the expansion of our humanity? Does it ever make us into unproductive soil that rejects good seeds because we consider them outside our role? Does it ever keep us in a naive state, never entering each other's lone and dreary world—the only place our souls can be built?

Mormon discourse tells us that Eve did not "break" that commandment, she "transgressed" it: she crossed a boundary in order to enter a more expansive, demanding learning space.

Noelle and I have become transgressors, too, and we have found that the world can indeed be lone and dreary. At times we feel forgotten by God, the church, and the ideals of our upbringing. We sometimes wonder how our children may have suffered because of our choices. When things go badly, we guiltily trace the problem's roots to see if they lead back to our transgression.

These fears can never be resolved. We made a choice. Its consequences—good and bad—will always attend us.

The only comfort we have is the undeniable growth of these seeds within us.

By the Drinking Fountain

ERIC ROBECK

I was one of those missionaries who fell head over heels in love with the culture and people I encountered on my mission. Although—or perhaps because?—I had never traveled outside the continental United States and Canada before my Spanish-speaking mission to Southern California, I became deeply enamored with the culture and charm of the Latin communities I was immersed in. I had always been socially awkward and introverted—painfully so—but on my mission I became much more confident, and my newfound personality developed some of the characteristics I admired in the people I met. As my language became more Hispanic, so did I. I didn't know how much this culture had become part of me until I left it.

After I returned to BYU in the fall of 2000, my social awkwardness and loneliness returned too. I missed the families who had shared their homes and lives with me. I missed their language, food, music, and marvelous sense of humor. I realized that I felt more comfortable in Hispanic culture than in the American college lifestyle surrounding me in Provo, so I signed up for an online LDS pen pal service with a Spanish-speaking group. On Thanksgiving weekend in 2000—ironically, while in California to visit my mission families—I received an email from a young Mormon woman living in Chihuahua, Mexico. Lorey had seen my profile and felt I was oddly familiar, as if we had known each other before. She was surprised to see how much we had in common and was curious to learn more.

What began as a friendship based on shared interests, including a deep love of the gospel, quickly developed into something more, despite limited contact and the border between us. Our relationship initially consisted primarily of emails and the occasional online chat. Before Skype and before I owned a mobile phone, calls were rare. Usually, my calling card ran out of minutes before we finished talking. In those days, packages were often lost in the mail between our countries, so after a few failed attempts we gave up trying to send each other gifts. A few grainy, scanned photos were the only glimpses we had of each other for the first five months of our relationship.

The following spring, Lorey obtained a tourist visa to attend General Conference in Salt Lake City, an hour north of Provo. I was ecstatic. We agreed to meet Friday evening at the reflecting pool on Temple Square when her bus arrived. Yet the bus never came. After several hours at the edge of the pool, I left, disheartened. I didn't know the phone number or location where she was staying, and she had no access to email, so I couldn't contact her to set up a new meeting. She had called my apartment, but my roommates didn't speak Spanish and weren't able to get a callback number. There were no further calls or email that night.

* * *

After an anxious night, I arrived at Temple Square the following morning, hoping beyond hope that I could recognize, out of a crowd of thousands, a face I had never seen in real life. I wandered, scanning the throngs of people, increasingly depressed. At one point, I bent down to drink water from a fountain. Someone called out, "Eric!" I continued drinking, only to hear the voice again. "Eric!" I looked up—and there she was! I could hardly believe it.

We talked as we waited in line to enter the Conference Center. During one of the talks, Lorey reached out and took my hand. I don't remember anything that was said in that conference session, but I'll never forget how I felt. It may not have been the most romantic of settings, but I was overwhelmed. At that moment, I realized I had fallen in love.

Our parting the next day was bittersweet, but as Lorey boarded the bus, I promised to visit her. When the semester ended a few weeks later, I flew to Chihuahua and stayed with her family for a week. Before I left, I asked her to marry me, and she accepted. We would not see each other for another three months, only two weeks prior to our wedding.

In the meantime, I kept busy. After a six-week geology field camp, I returned to my family's home in northern Washington State, where my father had just purchased a dilapidated caboose. We remodeled it, first stripping interior and exterior walls down to the steel frame, then building new walls, windows, floors, and interior furnishings. I attacked the project with zeal. I felt like an early pioneer, building a home for the woman who would soon be my wife and who would share this home with me for the first months of our marriage. The work was grueling but made the weeks pass quickly.

Finally, we wrapped up work and prepared for a trip to Mexico. My parents and a couple of siblings joined me in Chihuahua to meet my future in-laws and attend our first wedding reception. A few days later, we returned to Utah.

We were married in the Salt Lake Temple next to the drinking fountain where we first met. The wedding was a simple affair. Few of our family members made the trip, and even fewer could enter the temple. After the ceremony, we walked out, hand in hand, and posed for wedding photos around the temple. In one photo, we stand with hands clasped, looking into each other's eyes, while behind us stand statues of Joseph Smith and his first wife, Emma, also depicted holding hands and gazing happily at one another. This photo distills how we viewed our marriage: ordained by God, sealed by his prophet, and sanctified by love.

We spent the first months of our marriage in the caboose, like two grown-up boxcar children, as the days shortened and the mountain air cooled. It was quite an adventure. We had no television, phones, or electronic devices of any kind. Yet there were other sources of entertainment. On warm fall afternoons, we would sit on the caboose porch and scatter sunflower seeds. Up to a dozen chipmunks would emerge from the rocks for the fall harvest, returning to their dens with full cheeks. The bravest chipmunks would climb into our hands and laps. While I worked in town, Lorey passed afternoons playing with the chipmunks, cats, dogs, horses, and a baby yak.

Despite the minor inconveniences (lack of plumbing among them), I loved the experience. The same was not true of Lorey, however. Having grown up in the city, she found the sudden absence of all traffic noise a shock. There was something reassuring about street lights and the background city sounds that she never noticed until they were gone. She bore the culture shock and loneliness well, but it was a relief when, in January 2002, we returned to civilization and rented an apartment in Provo.

I continued pursuing my geology degree at BYU. I was fascinated by the sciences, particularly the concepts of evolution and geological time. Neither was compatible with the fundamentalist Mormon worldview I was raised with. I struggled with doubts. One doubt led to another, and the pillars of my testimony began eroding. As I grew more skeptical, it became difficult to reconcile my studies with the beliefs I treasured most in the gospel: the Book of Mormon, the atonement of Jesus Christ, and life after death. Unlike most of my scientific colleagues at BYU, I could not compartmentalize religion and science or shelve my doubts when the two conflicted. By the time I graduated, little of my testimony remained.

A year later, I was offered a job in Mongolia. For two months I lived in a remote yurt camp near the Siberian border, drilling and mapping a large coal deposit. In that remote environment, for the first time in my life, I found myself

completely outside the church's influence. I observed the influence of the dominant Tibetan Buddhist religion everywhere, participated in a few Mongolian
shamanistic rituals, and worked with colleagues raised during the Soviet oc-
cupation who had grown up without any sort of religious orthodoxy. It struck
me how out of place the Mormon worldview felt in this context.

I returned to the United States and continued geological consulting, spending
weeks at remote drilling projects in Utah and Colorado. This provided plenty
of time for study and contemplation. I began reading books by authors critical
of religion in an attempt to understand my own evolving beliefs. What little
remained of my testimony quickly vanished. One night at camp, I had one of
the most profound and spiritual experiences of my life. It was the moment I
realized that I no longer believed in God.

Yet I could not bring myself to tell Lorey. I continued to pray with my family, sit through church meetings, and pay tithing, behaving as if nothing had
changed. My hope was that months or years later, whenever I worked up the
courage, I could casually break the news, pointing to my Mormon lifestyle as
proof that losing my faith had not fundamentally changed me.

The following year, I was offered a full-time expatriate job in Mongolia. This
time, Lorey and our children came along. The adventure began well. There was
the culture shock and brutal winter to confront, and we were isolated from
Lorey's mother and sister, who shared our home in Provo. Yet the novelty of
the experience was exciting, and we adapted as best we could.

To my surprise, my interest in the conflict between science and religion didn't
end the day I lost my faith. While in Mongolia, I joined a worldwide community
of post-Mormon bloggers and joined discussions critical of LDS doctrine and
practice. My new interests didn't go unnoticed. One night, as we lay in bed,
Lorey turned her head toward mine on the pillow and asked, "Honey, do you
believe in God?" The question caught me off guard. This was not how I planned
to break the news. But time had run out; I could no longer kick this can down
the road. Her question required an honest answer.

I hesitated. "No," I answered. I tried to reassure her that nothing else had
changed, that I would still be the same husband I'd been before. We hugged,
then fell asleep.

The next morning, I could see that the full impact of the news was sinking in.
Lorey was deeply hurt that I hadn't trusted her enough to say anything earlier.
Her dreams for the future—having a righteous priesthood holder in the home,
fulfilling our church callings, seeing our children married in the temple, serving a mission together—all had been shattered. Most importantly, what would
become of our eternal family now that I no longer honored my covenants?

I became increasingly angry toward the church. A dam had burst. For years,
I'd gone through the motions, forced myself to sit in church while wishing I

were elsewhere, and withheld comment while listening to doctrine I disagreed with. Feelings long repressed—so deeply I wasn't even aware of them—erupted. I blamed the church for making my loss of faith so hard on our marriage. The doctrine of eternal families is one of the most beautiful teachings in Mormonism. But it comes with a cost. Much of what cements Mormon marriages is the promise of an eternity together, but that can only happen if both spouses are fully obedient and keep all their covenants. This is why one spouse's loss of faith is so devastating to Mormon marriages. Cement that once bound the spouses together instead becomes a wedge driving them apart and often results in divorce.

We argued constantly, and Lorey became depressed. During one particularly difficult moment, I realized that she needed the comfort and reassurance only a priesthood blessing could give. I didn't feel comfortable pronouncing one, so I called the mission president and asked him to send the elders. He asked what the problem was. I explained that I had lost my faith, and she took it hard. "Well, she can't possibly want to be with you now," he said. The elders came, and she was comforted by the familiar ritual. But I couldn't stop thinking about the president's words. Was the end of our marriage really inevitable?

I tried to contain the damage caused by my loss of faith by reassuring Lorey that I would maintain most LDS standards. Among these was the prohibition on alcohol. I felt no desire to drink and wanted to show Lorey that even as an unbeliever I could live a Mormon lifestyle, fully supporting her and our children in the church. I felt bad enough about breaking my church promises and responsible for all the misery that ensued. This was one promise I was sure I could keep.

Our tour in Mongolia ended a few months later. With the family back home, I continued to travel, returning home every few weeks. The following year, business took me to parts of Europe and back to Mongolia. I hadn't imagined how much pressure there would be to drink in professional and social settings outside Utah. My resolve weakened; eventually I broke my promise. I was honest with Lorey about my drinking and explained the reason for my decision, but she took it particularly hard. Lorey's father was an alcoholic. As a child, she watched alcohol destroy her parents' marriage. The last thing she wanted was for it to destroy ours.

Our constant arguing and my increasingly worldly lifestyle put our marriage under almost unbearable strain. We attended marriage therapy at LDS Family Services in Provo. This was only partly effective, as everything was viewed through the lens of Mormon doctrine. I felt that, given my irreconcilable differences with the church, no agreement was possible on those terms.

It would have been easy for me to give up then, to claim that our differences were irreconcilable and that each of us was better off without the other. Of course we both wanted to make our marriage work for the children. But that wasn't all. Our disagreements did not blind me to the fact that my wife was a beautiful, strong, amazing woman. By a stroke of astonishing good fortune, she had found me and decided to share her life with mine. I could not stop loving her. I vowed to do my best to regain her trust. During our second stay as a family in Mongolia, two years after the first, our marriage began to improve. In that environment we had only each other to rely on, and coming home each night removed me from the expat social scene and the pressure to drink. As we navigated the new waters of our changing relationship, they turned out not to be as treacherous as we feared.

Ironically, although the church was the point of contention threatening to end our marriage, in the end it may have helped save it. A kind bishop met with Lorey while I was overseas to hear her concerns and offer advice. She told him that she was finished and wished to end our marriage. I had changed too much. My criticisms of the church frequently sparked heated arguments, and my drinking and expat lifestyle were disrespectful to our marriage and invoked painful childhood memories of her father.

Our bishop heard all of this. Yet rather than condemn me as an apostate and advise Lorey to leave me for a worthy priesthood holder, as others might have done, he said, "Give him time. Eric has a good heart. Just keep loving him, and he'll find his way back eventually." It was this counsel, Lorey told me years later, that stopped her from filing for divorce.

More than a decade has passed since I lost my faith. Both of us are older, wiser. Our marriage weathered that storm and emerged intact. We've found a happiness and contentment that just a few years ago seemed impossible. In time, we adapted to our new landscape of belief. I became less sensitive toward the church's teachings. I now attend sacrament meeting with my family and support their church activities. She no longer feels threatened by my agnostic worldview and holds out hope that our marriage truly will be eternal. "You may be stubborn," she says, "but I can be stubborn too. Somehow I'll make sure you end up with me, believe it or not." I would love to find out, in the end, that she is right.

And thus we find ourselves, standing on either side of the threshold between faith and unbelief, holding hands and looking into each other's eyes as we did on our wedding day—before I threw open that door and ran into the world. From her side of that threshold, Lorey sees past me into the scientific world I inhabit, open, uncertain, and full of wonder; while looking into her world, I see the beauty, hope, and order that characterize her experience of Mormonism. We may have different worldviews, but we have no trouble separating them from the person who holds them. Our marriage is now defined not by shared beliefs but by us.

My One and Only

CLYDE KUNZ

My "coming out" was a slow, lengthy process and really began when I left the family home in Logan, Utah, following a two-year mission in Brazil. After several years trying to find my footing at Utah State University in Logan, dating women, and living at home with my parents, I finally moved to Salt Lake City to study at the University of Utah. There I began coming to terms with my sexuality and my growing attraction to other men. Even in the world of dating men and—more frequently than I'd like to admit—engaging in random anonymous sex, I was always searching for "my one and only."

My upbringing in a culture focused on eternal marriage taught me to believe at my very core that there was some *one* in the world destined to be my eternal partner. The fact that I'd learned to expect that person to be female notwithstanding, I entered the world of male relationships with that ideal ingrained in my psyche. I truly believed that somehow, somewhere, the perfect man for me was himself looking for his own special someone and that he would eventually find me. Two people being somehow "ordained" for each other was simply a given.

Confusion about my sexual orientation created a lot of confusion in other parts of my life; I found myself repeatedly changing majors, periodically dropping out of school for a semester, and working low-level jobs to support myself. I started drinking heavily and smoking, which—looking back now—was a fairly deliberate attempt to announce to the world that I was no longer Mormon. My lifestyle took a toll: I contracted a severe case of mononucleosis, which sent me back to the family home in Logan. My mother doted on me until my health was restored.

Through friends in Logan, some of whom were gay, I met a company of dancers performing at Utah State as part of the annual Festival of the American West. I became friendly with one of the dancers, who urged me to visit him and his partner in Los Angeles and offered to let me use their guest room. Having never spent time in a city bigger than Salt Lake, I jumped at the chance.

I arrived in LA on a Saturday. On Sunday my friend's partner, who owned a temporary agency in Hollywood, asked me if I could type. When I responded, "Over one hundred words a minute!" he suggested that I "make some money" the week I planned to be there and set me up with a typing job in a firm that specialized in research for the entertainment industry.

The job was hectic but gratifying; it was my first "real" job, and my skills were appreciated. By the end of the week, I'd been offered a full-time job at $22,000 a year. It was 1981, and that amount sounded like lottery winnings to me! Friday after work I drove to Utah, loaded my car with my life's possessions and my dog, and drove back to LA to start my new life. My parents were themselves traveling at the time, so I simply left a note to let them know that I'd "moved to LA."

Coincident to all of this, my friend in LA and his partner decided to part ways, so my friend needed a roommate. The guest room I was staying in became my room, and I became an official resident of Los Angeles.

In the early 1980s, the bar scene in LA was pretty raucous. AIDS had not yet surfaced, and gay sex seemed to be everywhere. I plunged in headfirst and partied even more than I had in Salt Lake. I was always looking for that "one," however. I continually analyzed everyone I dated (or even had casual sex with) as to whether he was the person I was destined to spend my eternity with.

I thought I'd found that person when I met Ted at a gay club in the San Fernando Valley. Ted was different from most of the party boys I'd been seeing. He was recently divorced from his wife of ten years and had two daughters. He, like me, had come from a religious household, though he'd been Baptist, not Mormon. He had actually read and studied the Bible! And although his relationship with his daughters and ex-wife was strained to the point of breaking, I thought, "Here's the one. Here's the one who has the same kind of religious roots and the same love of family that I have!"

I soon moved into a guesthouse Ted was renting. Ted was instrumental in helping me see the shortcomings of my job and encouraged me to take a position in the company he worked for, which did data processing for banks. I realize now that his objective (conscious or otherwise) was to put me physically in a place where he had control over me, or at least could know everything I was doing, and where I was throughout each day.

Within just a few months of our relationship, I became suspicious that Ted was having sexual encounters with other men. At first I tried to ignore and essentially forgave (or at least overlooked) those indiscretions. After all, he was "the one," wasn't he? *My* one. My DNA kept telling me that "it will all work out," that this was the relationship that was meant to be. My entire life I had been taught to expect a relationship that was "ordained by God." And although

I knew that my relationship with Ted, a homosexual relationship, was certainly *not* the relationship church leaders had in mind, I nonetheless convinced myself that I needed to remain committed to the relationship, no matter what. I kept telling myself that everything would be OK. In my fantasies I imagined that God, possibly even the church, would one day recognize this relationship, *my* relationship, as "ordained."

Over the next few years, Ted became more and more possessive, always wanting to know where I was going, who I would be with, what we were doing. It didn't occur to me that his paranoia that I was somehow being unfaithful to him was a reflection of his own infidelity. I discovered that he had opened a post office box where he could receive his mail in order to hide from me the pornographic photos and videotapes he ordered and received. He kept a small locking filing cabinet in a corner of our bedroom, refusing to let me know its contents. There were so many signs of problems that I'm embarrassed now that I stuck with the relationship at all.

Periodically, even in the beginning, Ted would belittle me for my looks. He was obsessed with having a perfect "gym body" and insisted I join his gym. At first that seemed to placate him. But soon he started telling me that I "wasn't working hard enough on my body," which eventually led to "I'm embarrassed to be seen with you!" I tried to hide the hurt I felt and would resolve to work harder at being as fit as he thought I should be.

Still I thought that stable, "eternal" relationships were like the one my parents enjoyed: raising children together, buying a home together, vacationing together, and all the rest. My expectations for my own relationship included all of that. When Ted suggested, since we shared an interest in skiing, that we purchase a cabin together at Big Bear, California, it seemed not only natural but important to me that we do so, despite the obvious signs that our relationship was in trouble.

I periodically became frustrated by my relationship with Ted and the infidelities that plagued it. But the idea of ending the relationship was anathema to me. Everything I'd learned growing up taught me that couples don't split up, that relationships should simply work, and that when they don't, well, the finger of blame was likely to be pointed directly back at me. I needed to make this "forever relationship" work!

I also imagined the criticism I might encounter if my family learned that I'd broken up with Ted. At that point, my Mormon family had never experienced a divorce. My parents' marriage, solemnized in the Logan Temple, had lasted more than forty years at that time and would surpass fifty years before my father's death. My five siblings were all married, all but one in temple marriages. If my relationship ended, I imagined my entire family self-righteously declaring, "You see! Immoral relationships between two men can't last!" I saw it as my duty to prove to them that my relationship was just as valid, just as sacred, just as permanent as theirs.

One evening, after learning that Ted had been involved in yet another sexual dalliance outside our relationship, I confronted him, demanding to know what made him think he had a right to be unfaithful to me.

"I make more money than you do, so I contribute the most to this household," he said icily. "Until you can contribute as much financially as I do, I have a right to see other men!" He looked me up and down, his lip curled in disdain, and added, almost as an afterthought, "If you would work harder on your body, I wouldn't have to be attracted to other men." There I sat, shamed on not one but two fronts!

I was stunned and very hurt, but unbelievable though it is to me now, I actually accepted his reasoning and continued the relationship another year. After all, he was "the one," the one I'd bought real estate with, the one I was destined to be with forever. Somehow I made myself overlook the obvious imbalance of power between us, his zealousness in monitoring my whereabouts, and the shaming behaviors. His cruelty to me didn't matter as much as the destiny I'd imagined and told myself I had to submit to.

We moved into yet another apartment, and his belittling of me escalated. He began coming home from work, parking his car in the apartment complex's underground parking lot, but not arriving at our apartment until sixty to ninety minutes later, claiming he "had to work late." One day I watched for his car to arrive, then saw him enter the apartment of a younger gay man in our complex. The confrontation that ensued when he finally arrived at our apartment resulted in his leaving and spending the night in the other apartment.

Caring friends urged me to end the relationship, and I finally saw that I had little choice. It was over. Ted moved out within a couple of weeks, taking most of the furniture we'd purchased together, claiming it was his. I kept the apartment.

I wish I could say that I grieved the end of that relationship, but I did not. Instead, I felt relief. But I was angry at myself for having wasted so many years with someone who clearly was not "the one." And I was embarrassed at the failure of what I had come to expect was my own "eternal marriage." I felt the shame of it whenever I talked with family members, even when nothing was said about it. But living in LA with most of my family two states away in Utah, I found it easy to avoid them and rarely communicated.

As mothers often do, my own mother came to my rescue a few months later when in a telephone call she told me she was sorry I was no longer with Ted. "I was glad you were with someone," she said. "I worry that you'll end up alone."

That was all she ever said to acknowledge my sexuality or the idea of my being in relationship with someone other than that married-in-the-temple wife she had always wished for me. But her simple acknowledgment that I deserved love, that I too deserved to be with someone forever, meant more to me than she will ever know. Although I was never "thrown out" by my family (as so many other gays and lesbians have been throughout the years), I nevertheless felt extraordinary rejection. Whether that feeling was self-imposed I really don't know. But that one comment from my mother allowed me to move psychologically a few steps back toward my family.

The year after splitting up with Ted saw me in regular sessions with a superb counselor who helped me understand the absurdity of searching for that "one and only." He helped me to examine myself and the neediness I felt about being in a permanent relationship and to analyze the qualities I should look for in a life companion. I started dating again, but really *dating*—not just settling for random sex. I began to get outside my own problems and started volunteering with an evening program at Fairfax High School, helping immigrants learn English. And as it was 1985 and the AIDS crisis was really heating up, I also volunteered at the AIDS Project Los Angeles.

One week my counselor gave me an assignment: "List all the qualities you're looking for in the person you'll have a long-term relationship with." I thought, "No problem!" and within a few days had compiled a list that took up two notebook pages, single-spaced.

The next session, when I tried to hand my counselor the list, he said, "I don't need to see it. But this week I want you to prioritize the list."

I struggled. And I struggled some more. But when I finally completed the assignment, I saw that the superficial qualities of body type, career trajectory, and all the rest came in far down the list. What were the top two characteristics?

1. Someone who reads books
2. Someone who has a good relationship with his family

In a support group for volunteers at the AIDS Project, I met Brian. During our first meeting, I learned that he was an avid reader and that he was very close not only to his two sons (then five and ten years old) but also to his former wife and her family. I thought, "Huh. The cosmos is trying to tell me something here."

Soon after, we began dating. Like Ted, Brian came from a religious background (although Roman Catholic, not Baptist). And like Ted, he had been in a ten-year marriage that produced two children. But unlike Ted, he enjoyed very healthy family ties. I was mightily impressed by the fact that he went to dinner regularly with his former wife so they could coparent their sons effectively. Clearly, she had been hurt by the breakup of their marriage, but Brian was somehow able to navigate things in a way that left them both friends and left his relationship with his children intact.

His mother and grandmother welcomed me into their homes and into their hearts when it became clear that Brian and I would continue as a couple, and

Brian's mother publicly introduced me as part of the family at a large gathering celebrating Brian's grandmother's ninetieth birthday a few months later. Since the beginning of our relationship, we've celebrated holidays and family birthdays with his extended family, including his former wife (who has become my very dear friend) and her mother. I credit Brian with the success of these continuing relationships—it is in part because of that success that I fell in love with him.

Brian and I have now been together more than three decades and married in California in 2014. Our wedding announcements boasted: "Following a whirlwind twenty-eight-year engagement, Clyde and Brian will finally be married." And the most gratifying part of the ceremony? Although my parents were deceased, my Mormon siblings, receiving my very tentative and multiply edited letter about our impending marriage, insisted on attending. Far from the finger-pointing I anticipated from them for so many years, they were most congratulatory and accept Brian as part of our family. It seems they always had.

My relationship with Brian has made me a parent, not in the way I would have been had I married a woman, but a parent nonetheless. Brian's sons from his first marriage are grown and married and have produced three amazing grandchildren for us. Brian and I fostered two adolescent children in Arizona, where we moved in 1991. And in 2003 we adopted a five-year-old boy, Michael, who has become a wonderful young man with a good heart. Our family—my family—continues to grow.

And Brian? Is he my "one and only"?

I no longer believe in a "one and only" for me or for anyone else. This is a good thing. Had I continued trying to convince myself that Ted was my "one and only," I could have wasted many more years and never met Brian or enjoyed the children and grandchildren now central to my life. I believe there are a lot of wonderful people in our world, many with whom I could potentially find myself in relationship. But Brian is the one I chose and continue to choose. We've built a life and a family together, and we've become stalwart Episcopalians, where we find acceptance as a couple and as a family. It is good.

That's not to say that my "Mormon DNA" doesn't surface from time to time. Trying to permanently alter it would be akin to trying to wash the Caucasian off my skin. But I'm now at least aware that it still lurks deep inside me and that I will likely never be rid of it. I'm at a place in my life that lets me recognize some of those "Mormon" values as a part of myself that I like; other times I recognize them and enjoy a good chuckle over them, allowing myself to move forward on a different path.

It is all good.

There's Something about Mary

KIM SIEVER

I'm not sure what first attracted me to Mary. Something stuck out to me the first day we met. I met a lot of people for the first time that day—it was my first Sunday in a singles branch since returning to British Columbia after my mission to Utah—but I've forgotten most of those first encounters. Hers persisted.

As she began inviting me to events and including me in her social group, I accepted. Impressions of her accumulated. I noticed her hazel eyes as she looked at me and her red lips as she smiled. I noticed her rich, dark hair contrasting against her smooth, porcelain skin. As time went on, my gaze lengthened and my heart yearned. I felt drawn to her in ways I'd never been drawn to others.

Our courtship was short. It was roughly three months between our first date and our wedding, five months from when we first met. People ridiculed us for it; a few even cautioned us. We heeded none of it—partly because of the independence and stubbornness of youth and partly because we knew there was something there, something knitting our hearts together.

Our marriage was tested early on. Infertility, miscarriage, relocating, poverty, disloyalty, joblessness, education, faith crisis. Grief, hurt, hunger, desire, hopelessness. Through it all, Mary stayed committed to our marriage. She always stayed committed to our marriage.

I'm flawed. I've been responsible for occurrences over the last twenty-five years that would've stressed, wrung, and broken other relationships. But ours has never broken. Mary looks past my flaws. She loves me despite them. She loves me.

Three years after our wedding, I uprooted our family and moved us to a new province with no job in place and hardly a cent to our name except for one more paycheck, all while Mary was four months pregnant. For over a year, we lived in poverty, with $5,000 in student loans to cover tuition and textbooks for an entire school year and semimonthly paychecks of under $500 each. We rolled pennies to afford a bag of fruit. We stood in the grocery store aisle debating whether to spend our last $20 on diapers or food. Wadding up toilet paper at the church to bring home and reroll onto empty tubes. Walking an hour downtown to cash a paycheck because we had no money for the bus and our bank had closed the branch by our house. One creditor taking us to court. A constant stream of bills in the mailbox that went unpaid.

If that wasn't enough stress, this was when my first faith crisis happened, partially fueled by the hopelessness of poverty. I was desperate for help and answers. I prayed multiple times per day. I fasted monthly, which then turned to weekly, which then turned to two-day fasts. I studied my scriptures daily. I went to the temple weekly as part of ward temple night. I did everything I was taught I must do to get help and find answers. For months. Neither help nor answers came.

As the silence waxed, my doubts grew. I doubted my own integrity, convinced in my evangelical outlook that I had somehow become unworthy of the help and answers I sought. That doubt in myself eventually grew into doubt in God; maybe I wasn't receiving help or answers not because of my own disobedience but because God didn't exist.

This doubt I shared with no one but Mary. Not my home teachers. Not my bishop. No one. Back then, image was important to me. It was critical that I provided for my family. It was crucial that I maintained a sure-footed testimony of the gospel. More important, that everyone saw me as the perfect provider and perfect priesthood leader.

Through it all, Mary never judged me. She never complained that I made her poor. She never complained that I caused her to go hungry when she was pregnant. She never complained when I doubted God. She never complained when I threatened the eternal nature of our marriage.

Mary is the epitome of unconditional love. I truly feel love from her that is unhindered by conditions or limits. When I have broken her heart, she still loved me. When I have tortured her soul, she still loved me. When I have threatened her eternity, she still loved me.

Let me be clear: I don't say this to put Mary on a pedestal. I'm not saying she's perfect or too good for me. I say this because her unconditional love has nurtured a similar love within me.

Long before we met, I had compiled a list of qualities I wanted in the person I married. It was largely superficial (I wanted a spouse with red hair) and occasionally ridiculous (I imagined I'd be happier with a spouse who hated olives). Unsurprisingly, it included no flaws. I had concocted in my mind, unknowingly, a flawless fantasy. That led to unrealistic expectations. Although Mary met nearly every item on my list (even disliking olives), as our honeymoon phase waned, I became aware of her flaws.

Her unconditional love encouraged me to open my mind and my heart to her, to overcome my tendency to expect my spouse to be perfect. Her unconditional love has taught me to love her for who she is. To love her not despite her flaws but because of her strengths.

Her dedication to hiding my flaws has encouraged me to hide hers. When other men complain about a spouse's annoying attributes, I keep my mouth closed. I perpetuate in their minds an image of my spouse as a woman of strength, just as she extols my strengths to others.

It wasn't always like that, though. I used to play into the temptation to discuss her annoying traits or habits with others. I guess it was a way to bond, to find commonalities. Eventually I realized how damaging it was to focus on your spouse's flaws. Well, not just focus but also ridicule. And if I, the spouse, shared and ridiculed Mary's flaws with others, it gave them license to see those flaws in her and judge her for them. I'd be inviting them into her life to choose which qualities are undesirable. Without her consent. That's just selfish and hurtful.

It's been years since that realization. And I haven't done any of that in such a long time. I stay quiet now, no matter how many around me are quite vocal. Maybe part of it has come as I've matured. I no longer have a desire to fit in, to be one of the boys. I think, however, a large part has been Mary's example. From the start, she has held my flaws close to her heart, never sharing them with others. I'm confident that this tendency has rubbed off on me.

Her steadfastness to keep my first faith crisis private (she was the only one I told) and to be my only source of support showed me how I must support her when she has craved it. How I needed to be selfless and understanding as occasion required. How essential it was for me to not judge when she struggled. How I had to just be there for her.

Her open-mindedness helped me evaluate my own values, change my opinions to match hers, be patient as her opinions evolve to match mine, and work together when our opinions evolve simultaneously.

When we started dating, we had a lot in common. We also differed in some things. I was pretty stubborn back then, so I dug my heels in deep when we disagreed. I was convinced, of course, that I was right on every issue. But as time advanced, and I educated myself, my beliefs and opinions on some issues changed. Sometimes, my opinions began matching Mary's. Sometimes, opinions I once shared with Mary diverged. Sometimes, my opinion remained the same, but her opinion changed to match mine.

Take marriage equality, for example. We both once opposed it, as faithful Mormons are wont to do. But my position started shifting in the early 2000s.

Mary's remained unchanged for quite some time. Today, however, we both embrace marriage equality.

Another area where our positions changed was home birthing. Mary was strongly supportive of it, and I was strongly opposed. By the time our oldest child was born, I had become supportive not only of home birthing in general but of unassisted childbirth, something that Mary was apprehensive toward. Eventually, she saw the virtues of unassisted childbirth, and our common appreciation for it helped create spiritual, intimate birth experiences when our six children were born.

My latest faith crisis is the most recent example of her desire to remain loyal to our marriage, to our relationship. In November 2015, the LDS Church announced two changes to policies related to its LGBTQ+ members. First, the church said that any member in a same-sex marriage was automatically considered apostate, a classification applied to only four other situations (publicly opposing church leaders, persistently teaching false doctrine, following the teachings of apostate sects, and joining another church). Second, the church said that children living in a home where the parents were the same sex and married could no longer participate in LDS ordinances (such as baptism and priesthood ordination) until they turned eighteen and disavowed their parents' marriage. As parents of LGBTQ+ children, Mary and I feel hurt by and disgusted with the church. But it affected me more strongly. I was on the verge of leaving the church; although Mary was deeply affected by the policy change, leaving the church wasn't something she considered, or at least not as long or as thoroughly as I had. To her, leaving the church means leaving the celestial kingdom. And even though I could tell that the threat to the eternal nature of our relationship was breaking Mary's heart and filling her soul with worry and despair, she never tried to influence my decision. Over two decades, I'd learned that Mary won't give up on me. Even if standing by me requires an infinite, eternal sacrifice.

Knowing that she'd stand by me no matter my choice gave me freedom, the freedom to pursue an authentic choice uninfluenced by wanting to save our marriage, something I've seen my LDS friends resort to. I didn't have to live a lie as a way to save the most valuable relationship in my life.

And I chose to stay. At least for now. My decision to stay was complex and one I don't consider finalized. Unlike my marriage, it's a commitment I remake frequently. One reason I chose to stay was that I consider myself Mormon; it's part of who I am. It's not just about going to church. As such, I find value in Mormon sacraments—another reason to stay. And not just as a recipient of them but also as a bestower of them in my role as priesthood holder, as a conduit between heaven and earth. Leaving meant I couldn't baptize our children or escort our eighteen-year-old, who recently left for a mission, through the temple.

My dad couldn't escort me when I received my endowments, and I didn't want our child to miss out on that, too.

A third reason I chose to stay is that there are good people in the church, people who truly try to mourn with the mourning. While I feel friendless at church, I know there are ward members who would show up if our house needed fixing, or we needed to move, or if I was out of work. I'm not ready to leave that. A fourth reason is the esoteric aspects of the church—angels, and symbols, and handshakes, and all that. Much of that has disappeared over the last two centuries, but the residue persists, and it appeals to me. Another reason is that if I leave, it means one more progressive voice is gone forever, and the church becomes that much more homogenous.

But even with this choice, I still feel pressure (some might call it promptings) to leave. The conflict between my choice to stay and the pull to leave is nearly constant. I reflect on it often. And I have come close to leaving multiple times since 2015.

In 2019, the church reversed aspects of its exclusionary policy. That changed nothing for me. No apology, and the wording used in the reversal never indicated that the church thought the previous decision was wrong or immoral. This wasn't a progressive move. The church is back where it was prior to the exclusion policy; it's not further ahead. It still opposes marriage equality both in principle and in the political sphere.

The constant friction I feel has not abated, particularly after I came out as queer myself in early 2020. So I don't consider my choice to stay finalized. Even so, I have full confidence that our marriage will survive if I change my mind. Mary knows I teeter on the edge, with one foot in eternity and one foot in tormented hell. But she doesn't stop loving me. And I can't stop loving her.

For Jess, after Eighteen Years of Marriage: Seven Fragments on Love; Or, Some Things I Carry

TYLER CHADWICK

The surety of your body beside me in bed, the rasp of breath—slowly in and out, in and out—through your hands cupped around mouth and nose to moisten the air, to ease chronically stuffed sinuses as you draw it in then press it out— slowly in and out, in and out—like Lord Vader, I've told you, only less ominous, you more at ease in your being, turned on your side, knees bent, feet pressed one over the other, ball to dorsum, toes folded over toes, the whisper of your breathing spooning into my restless soul—

Your name, familiar to me, almost, as my own, its sounds—their thrust and sibilance—settled into my ears and tongue, their imprint worn in my thoughts, in the neural folds of my being through years of repeated touch—

Your incredulity when I first confessed my love, when sitting by you on your parents' front steps I took your open hand in mine, bent your middle and ring fingers into your palm, and held the gesture as if holding my breath—*one one-thousand, two one-thousand*—until you pulled your hand free, pushed me by the shoulder, said, "No you don't!" while you leaned away—*one one-thousand, two one-thousand, three one-thousand*—then back to my side and wove your fingers through mine, scooting closer for warmth as dusk and a canyon breeze settled over our conversation—

You kneeling beside me in the dark silence of your parents' living room, the floral embroidery on their love-seat cushion coarse against my forearms, your hands woven into mine, mine into yours, your head turned and cocked toward my shoulder, cheek at rest on my upper arm, your breath hot against my shirt as I offered our deepening companionship to God, said we planned to marry, would he bless our union—then sudden fullness and peace, the warmth of tears parting my eyelids and lacing my cheeks, the warmth of your tears on my shirt: a mutual upwelling toward heaven opening and opening on our desire—

You sitting beside me at our wedding luncheon, your hand exploring my inner thigh, moved to greater boldness and appetite by our vows—

The way your upper arm yields to the needle's prick when I inject you with your arthritis meds, one hand pinching the flesh into a soft peak, the other sinking the needle—*one one-thousand, two one-thousand, jab*—although every time I'm afraid I'll balk, poke you twice, make you bleed, that I'll press the plunger too fast and send the drugs burning into your body—

Your name, still a strange country, still courting my interest, still fresh on my tongue, still piquing my nerves toward your presence and touch—

An Apology I've Been Working on for a While

JOEY FRANKLIN

On more than one occasion, I've placed a bra in the dryer. Sometimes I forget to refill the toilet paper, and just this morning I left the milk on the counter, again. On the other hand, I ask for directions on vacation, and I say "I love you," and I almost never leave hair on the soap. Which means, I suppose, I'm not entirely without hope.

Still, I wonder about the implication that most men are just that—hopeless. Hopeless slobs who can't remember to lift the toilet seat. Hopeless housekeepers who ruin laundry and load dishwashers incorrectly. Hopeless slaves to libido who exert their manhood through sexual conquest. And I wonder more about manhood in general, that infernal euphemism—asserted, displayed, defended, envied, cut off in vengeful rage.

I'm haunted by the myth and misogyny of "manhood." Phallic shadows of who I'm "supposed" to be lurk everywhere:

In a greeting card I once saw that showed on its front cover a large control panel of buttons and levers labeled "her" and on the inside a single red on-off switch labeled "him."

In the not-so-subtle frustration of the housewife, whoever she is, who first applied the name Better Than Sex to chocolate cake.

In the advice my wife, Melissa, received during our engagement: "The most important phrase you need to learn," someone told her, "is 'Not tonight, honey. I've got a headache.'"

What's more horrifying is the possibility that the stereotypes are the truest thing about me, that the haunting shadow is my own, that Lauryn Hill under-estimates the problem when she tells us *some* guys only care about "that thing."

Another euphemism: *that thing.* The track of one-track minds, the slime that fills the gutter, the be-all and end-all of Freudian masculinity—think frat parties and locker rooms—the proving grounds of male sexual aggression, *boys being boys.*

That's a phrase that keeps me up at night—not worrying but washing dishes. It's at least part of the reason I don't play video games, don't watch fights on pay-per-view, try not to turn my head when an attractive woman catches my eye. It also partly explains why I help our boys do their hair before church and (usually) insist they wear matching dark socks with their nice shoes and why I fold the towels in thirds the way Melissa wants them folded. On the weekends, it's at least part of the reason I leave the macaroni and cheese in the box and make chicken tikka masala, from-scratch naan, and cranberry-walnut salad. And it's definitely in the back of my mind each night at bedtime when I sing off-key lullabies to our boys in the dusky light of their bedroom.

And no, I'm not just trying to cut down on Melissa's headaches.

Though that's definitely part of it.

And perhaps that's why I feel guilty wanting a pat on the back. That and the fact that whatever I do around the house in the morning, after work, and on the weekends feels like little more than a shrug of the shoulders, a sheepish apology for all my man-privilege. I am the patriarch of my family after all—a father in The Church of Jesus Christ of Latter-day Saints born into a line of fathers stretching back to Joseph Smith's day—and my only real job is to win bread and keep the wolves at bay. Melissa is the one expected to be an inexhaustible fount of comfort, encouragement, and chocolate chip cookies. Or at least that's how it feels sometimes. Sure, within my culture there is no true "norm"—only the myth of normalcy. We have career mothers and stay-at-home dads and single parents; we have couples who can't have children, and we have couples who choose not to have children; we have entire congregations of single adults. Our birthrate is only a little higher than the national average, and our divorce rate about the same. For every family of ten driving off in their huge van to play miniature golf on a Monday night, there are plenty of Latter-day Saint families for whom such domestic romping would be anathema. And the pressure aligned with certain gender expectations can change from congregation to congregation.

Yet that pressure persists, even if it's largely a self-imposed pressure to live up to an imagined ideal—a pressure to check myself against how things maybe should or shouldn't be. Such pressure isn't unique to my religious community. The domestic balance of conventional TV families (think Ward and June Cleaver of *Leave It to Beaver* or Mike and Carol Brady of *The Brady Bunch*) is as persistent a myth in American culture as anything, but because such gendered ideas about nurturing and providing have been so thoroughly canonized in my culture, I think it's safe to suggest that this pressure is particularly poignant in Latter-day Saint circles. And here in Utah County, where we make up 90 percent of the population, the pressure's particularly strong. There's a lot of social capital attached to having that big van full of kids. Having a good recipe for chocolate chip cookies doesn't hurt either.

And so, whether by choice or by default, the domestic sphere often feels like Melissa's space, and I can't help but worry that my attempts to subvert traditional gender roles merely reaffirm them. After all, working outside the home gives me a ready-made excuse to leave housework undone. Sure, I usually load the dishwasher after breakfast, but only if I'm not running late. And that flexibility contributes to the false notion that housework is Melissa's responsibility. I end up "pitching in" around my own house, helping with "her" work, confirming my own damning dominance while incurring down-the-nose glances from women who find my efforts quaint, even calculating.

Melissa might be gone for an evening, and I'll hear a friend wonder what I'll eat. I've taken our boys to the grocery store and seen old women nod pleasantly and say patronizing things such as "Looks like you have your hands full without Mom" and "Aren't you a brave father?" I've baked something for a dinner party and watched women raise their eyebrows. "Wow, he cooks," they say, as if I've learned not only to roll over and shake but also to fetch the newspaper and play dead, too. At best I'm a permanent understudy, relief pitcher, babysitter to my own kids, sous-chef, second fiddle.

A woman at church hears me compliment Melissa and says, "When my husband talks like that, I know he wants something."

I don't.

Not exactly.

I mean, I do.

Of course I do.

But it's way more complicated than *that*. As a child, I saw enough of my own dad sitting around after dinner with a newspaper to know that I would wash dishes as a married man. I saw the way my mother folded her arms across her chest and looked at my father when he wasn't paying attention. How my mother must have fumed working twelve-hour days on top of managing a house full of five kids and a husband who seemed always sick and between jobs. To be a good husband, I concluded, one must start by not making extra work for one's wife.

But their situation has been so different from ours. If my mother hadn't worked, we would have starved. If she hadn't cooked, we would have eaten cold cereal. If she hadn't orchestrated weekly Saturday cleaning "parties" for us kids, the house wouldn't have gotten clean. If marriage is a partnership, my father has, more often than not, been a silent partner. Melissa and I, on the other hand, discuss everything, and during our early years, we cut the domestic duty pie just about every way you can cut it. When we were first married at age twenty-two, we both still had years of college to finish, so we took classes together, worked campus jobs, and split the cooking and cleaning at home. A few months later Melissa became pregnant and dangerously morning sick; she had to quit everything and focus on surviving. Much of the housework and all the breadwinning fell to me (with the help of a few student loans and federal grants). A year later, Melissa joined me back at school, and we passed our son back and forth between classes and got some help from her mom when our schedules overlapped. Dinner was up to whoever got home first. And during Melissa's final semester, I took a break from school so she could concentrate more fully on her classes while I stayed home with our son.

Through all this, we had a basic guiding principle: someone should be home with the kid. And while that idea can be chalked up, in part, to LDS doctrine, it had as much to do with our own experiences as children. Melissa appreciated her own stay-at-home mom, and I'd spent enough time as a latchkey kid to know I wanted something different for my own family. During college Melissa and I found a way for both of us to go to classes, but by the time we were ready for graduate school, we had two kids, and the prospect of doubling up on more student loans seemed financially untenable. On top of that, Melissa declared she was ready for a break from school—she wanted time at home with the boys. In the moment, we didn't think of this as an old-fashioned approach. It just seemed like the right thing to do, and we never seriously considered any other arrangement. The choice to embrace traditional gender stereotypes was ultimately an easy one, and it certainly didn't feel like a limiting option at the time.

* * *

Lately, however, I've begun to worry that our choice sells Melissa a bit short, and I'm afraid of making her feel exploited. No matter how much I do around the house or with our kids, I still get up in the morning and go to my office to write. I meet with students, teach classes, attend lectures, and go to lunches with visiting academics. I sit in my office and read with my feet on my desk, pick at a half-eaten chocolate bar beside me, and send some emails. Meanwhile, Melissa is at home cleaning macaroni and cheese out of the carpet, fending off telemarketers, sorting laundry, scrubbing the sink, and finishing one meal just in time to start cooking the next. In short, by taking on a sometimes literal laundry list of domestic responsibilities, Melissa allows me to pursue my career with a level of single-mindedness I couldn't afford otherwise. In the face of that reality, the guilt comes easy, but as with most privilege-born guilt, there's no obvious way to alleviate it.

* * *

One evening, sitting on the couch after the boys had fallen asleep, Melissa turned to me and said something like, "My sister sings. My mother sews. You write. But what do I do?" We sat for a moment looking at each other. She continued: "Sometimes I feel like I don't know who I am." And so this is it. The heart of the problem—Melissa's willingness to take on so much of the domestic load so early hasn't merely allowed me to focus on my career, it has kept her from discovering who she really is. I'm a father and writer. A father and a professor. But it took graduate school and professional experience to figure that out. When Melissa thinks about herself, she says, "I'm a mother and . . . what?" She carries around this blank waiting to be filled, and I can't help but wonder how she would have filled it if we'd prioritized her work and study as much as we did mine. Certainly our current situation leaves little time for her to figure that out.

And while this is our problem, I know it's a larger cultural problem as well. As steeped in traditional notions of gender as Latter-day Saint culture is, we've made a lot of room for men who are trying to redefine those expectations—conscientious fathers who play with their kids and wash laundry and run bedtime and braid hair. There's a premium on compassion and tenderness and grace for men, men who would never dream of dictating anything to their wives. Men like this (and I count myself among them) are helping reshape the image of masculinity in the restored gospel of Jesus Christ, but we also benefit from a cultural assumption that we men will "find ourselves" as we learn to balance our professional and personal lives.

But for the women around me, motherhood still persists as the presumed path to self-fulfillment, and there's little talk of balance. We've started to emphasize the importance of men being more nurturing, and that's a good thing, but we're not yet very good at encouraging women to find themselves on their own terms. And perhaps this is the reason I didn't know what to say when Melissa asked me that question on the couch. She and I don't have a good model for how to find balance in both our partnership and our personal aspirations. Sure, our kids won't be young forever, and even if we change nothing, time will grant Melissa space to find her own answer to that tough question of self-identity, but in the meantime, I know parts of her suffer from neglect. And I wonder what, if anything, we can do differently.

I could follow the example of my friend Matt.

Matt's wife, Linda, is a professor in the Midwest. Matt stays at home; does much of the cooking, the cleaning, and the grocery shopping; and homeschools their two boys while Linda teaches composition courses and works overload hours for her department. They both seem at ease with the situation: if Matt's Facebook feed is any indication, he relishes the time he gets with their boys, while Linda appears to enjoy the community and recognition academia can bestow. I know a half-dozen other couples doing this same thing—modern dads comfortable in their rejection of traditional gender roles and sensitive to millennia of sexism that have given them an unfair advantage over their wives, and liberated women free to explore and succeed in their chosen careers. At least that's what it looks like to me. I don't know if Matt pulls out his hair some mornings, wondering if the four walls of his home aren't closing in on his personality. And surely there are days when Linda would rather pitch her books out the window and head home to be with her children than stand in front of another class of bored composition students.

And it seems to me that their situation simply reverses our own—one spouse acquiescing to the other's ambitions. I'm restless for some kind of middle ground where every dish I wash and diaper I change doesn't turn into an apology for being male, where I can buy Melissa flowers and rub her feet without feeling as if I'm merely rebalancing the scales or, worse, buttering her up. I want a reality where we both can pursue our own interests and careers and the kids still get everything they need. Where developing my own sense of identity doesn't preclude Melissa from developing hers. I don't think Linda should feel guilty when she leaves in the morning, and neither should I. But the reality seems to be that if someone is to going to stay home with the children, there *is* no middle ground.

So what if we both worked? Passed our boys back and forth like we did when we were first married? Maybe hired some help?

During graduate school, my friend Liz once asked me what I do for childcare and then stopped herself. "Oh, I forgot about your wife," she said, not angry, but exasperated, not at me, but at her situation. She and her husband, Christopher, had a child while they were both still in graduate school and took the day-care route so they could finish their degrees. As a result, they were constantly juggling part-time work, classes, papers, reading lists, and the needs of their young daughter. On this day, Liz was trying to prepare for a class while arranging last-minute childcare over the phone and also thinking about what she and her family might cobble together for dinner that evening. Standing in the hall with an armful of books, bag over her shoulder, a note from her babysitter in hand, she furrowed her brow. "I want a wife," she said and sighed. "Where can I get a wife?" Then she shrugged and walked away, her bag swinging at her side.

A third option does exist, though it's a ship that has already sailed for Melissa and me. We could have waited to have kids, stayed in school together, and focused on our careers. This was my sister's plan. Misha and her husband, Chad, married in their late twenties after they'd both finished college and established their careers. They remodeled a duplex, adopted a pair of Maltese puppies, and even took night classes together to earn their MBAs. They eventually rented out that duplex, bought a house in the suburbs, and started gardening, throwing dinner parties, and hosting a monthly poker night. They were happy and working hard in tandem to pursue their own respective career goals. And that worked great, for a while.

But in their midthirties, Misha and Chad decided they were ready to have a child. After Zoe was born, they did what they figured two career professionals had to do to make room for a little person in the family. They each found a way to work from home one day a week and signed on to a good day-care center for the rest of the time. Their plan worked, but as my sister describes it, each morning they'd race to get ready so they could drop Zoe off at day care and then get off to work themselves, only to race home at the end of the day to pick up Zoe from day care, find something to eat, and then squeeze in a little family time before racing off to bed so they could get up early and do it all again the next morning. Misha felt she was giving all her best energy to work and had little left over for parenting. Ultimately, she decided she wanted to be home with her daughter, so she and Chad talked it out, sold the duplex, rearranged their budget, and hit the domestic reset button with Misha as a stay-at-home mom. And though Misha says this transition was like "climbing into a life raft from an icy ocean," it wasn't easy. They have less disposable income, and she's had to shift the center of her self-worth from the public kudos of professional success to the private victories of patient parenthood. The adjustment has taken a few years, but they've found a balance that feels right to them, at least for now.

In some ways, I think many parents suffer from the same ailment. Too many of us cling to the pipe dream of balance—a false hope that there might be a way for us to pursue our own careers and aspirations independently while still reaping the benefits of a traditionally managed home—clean bathrooms, home-cooked meals, a drop-of-the-hat shuttle service for the kids. That is, of course, absurd. Two parents cannot work full-time and still run a home like Ward and June Cleaver, any more than Ward and June Cleaver can carry on the way they do and expect June to avoid a mental breakdown. The traditional domestic paradigm is too often a zero-sum game, a one-size-fits-nobody ideal fraught with unattainable expectations.

So why do I still worry about it?

Because of my grandfather.

My mother rolled her eyes a lot about my father, but she spoke with reverence about her own. Oel Hess was a rough-skinned Idaho farm boy who worked in sheet metal and wood and could as easily sling a shovel all day as haul railroad ties or drive a plow through baked dirt. Up before the sun, out before breakfast, and home after dark, he was, to my mother, the ideal male, the type of man she'd always dreamed of marrying. In addition to working as a sheet-metal fabricator, tending a half-acre garden, and serving as bishop for the local congregation, Oel took the time to show my mother how to paint foundations, repair fences, dig ditches, train dogs, and run a chainsaw. Grandma Venna cooked and canned and sewed and brooded over the children and, the way my mother describes it, waited every night to embrace my grandfather when he came through the door. As she often retells it, the divisions of labor in her childhood home were simple, clear, and deep. There was no middle ground. There didn't need to be.

The notion of their precisely balanced relationship became our family's hallmark of a successful marriage, as if Grandma and Grandpa had arrived at some utopian patriarchal arrangement where they both worked tirelessly at their own tasks only to collapse blissfully into bed each night, the dishes done, animals fed, kids tucked in, and doors locked. Do it like Oel and Venna, Mom seemed to say. Do it right.

But the reality is that Oel worked his fingers raw and worried constantly about money. He took an administrative job with the union for a higher salary, but the stress of local politics caused a mental breakdown. He had to be released early from his service as bishop, and he became so mentally unstable that he admitted himself to a hospital in Ogden, Utah, where he received electroshock therapy for depression and anxiety. Venna had to enroll in nursing school so she could cover the bills. And while Oel eventually went back to work, he never fully regained his ability to support the family.

My mom knows this history, of course, but it's not how she chooses to remember it. In her mind, as in my own and maybe as in my friend Liz's, there persists a notion that such an ideal balance can be struck if we just reach a little harder for it. But while ideals may serve as commendable cultural targets, they risk morphing into cookie-cutter imperatives—the kind that landed my grandfather in the hospital. The reality is that Liz and Christopher, Linda and Matt, Misha and Chad, Melissa and I—we're all approaching the questions of marriage and division of labor differently, and that may be the end of it. Regardless of the specter of cultural expectation, they'll continue adjusting as their situations change, and we will too—though I'm not sure I'll ever stop feeling guilty.

But perhaps there's a way to mitigate some of that guilt. If I can quit worrying so much about how things "should" be and at the same time stop making excuses for how things are, then perhaps we can get down to the business of figuring out together what we want for ourselves; that is God's first commandment of marriage, after all—to cleave to one another and no one else. Even then, our only guarantees may be that searching for balance in marriage is messy, that cultural expectations will as often cloud our judgment as clarify it, and that what "works" in a given moment may no longer satisfy in a week or a month or a year. Still, I'll keep trying, and I'll keep washing dishes and sweeping floors and rubbing feet, and maybe I'll eventually get to the point where trying to be a good husband feels like something more than an apology.

Never Good Enough

MICHAEL CARPENTER

I'm not sure if it was being a middle child that made me a people pleaser. Maybe it was growing up in a family with high expectations. Maybe it was growing up in a religion that emphasizes perfection. Maybe it's just part of my DNA. One way or the other, I never felt like I was good enough.

One confusing thing is that I could see that others around me weren't so concerned about perfection and the rules. But I was serious about it all. Obedience is the first law of heaven, and I was trying to get to heaven.

An LDS mission is a study in rules. There are rules about what you wear. About when you get out of bed and go back to bed. Rules about everything you do in between. It was impossible to enforce rules about how many people missionaries should contact or teach every week, so instead there were rules requiring missionaries to set outrageously ambitious goals for how many people to meet, how many lessons to teach, and then to work your ass off to meet those goals.

I felt guilty every time I slept in ten minutes over the limit or got home ten minutes late. Other missionaries did whatever they wanted, seemingly without any guilt. We were repeatedly told that our success as missionaries was determined by our obedience to the rules. But some of the most successful missionaries broke all kinds of rules.

Home from my mission, I was told that the most important thing I could do was get married. I shouldn't wait; it was more important than my education. So within seven months, I was married. I didn't have the maturity to understand how that would affect my education or the rest of my life. My new wife and I didn't really know each other, but we had faith in the words of Prophet Spencer W. Kimball: "It is certain that almost any good man and any good woman can have happiness and a successful marriage if both are willing to pay the price."

Or maybe I just didn't understand what the price would be. President Kimball's talk "Oneness in Marriage" continues: "If two people love the Lord more than their own lives and then love each other more than their own lives, working together in total harmony with the gospel program as their basic structure, they are sure to have this great happiness." How do two people do that? How many people work together in total harmony with the gospel program as their basic structure? I doubt I even stopped to consider how unrealistic those expectations were. As a computer science student with only three semesters of college under my belt when I committed to share the rest of my life with someone, I had no idea how hard marriage would be. Our oldest child was born when I still had three semesters left before graduation. Once I graduated, it took every dollar we had to move to California, where my first job waited. We lived off credit cards for a few months until we finally got above water. Our second child was already on the way.

* * *

All my church training taught me that my main responsibility was to be a husband and father and the spiritual head of the family I provide for materially. Oh, plus give 10 percent of my income to the church. With that, I started my professional life. I soon learned that a salaried, competitive job will take everything you have and still demand more. As a people pleaser, I was often the one to come in early and stay late to solve a problem. Often, the reward for a job well done was more work. There were months I averaged sixty hours a week, sometimes working night shifts.

Anyone with more maturity than a twenty-four-year-old would know that this would cause problems at home. As a stay-at-home mom in a strange new city, my wife felt abandoned. When she took her frustration out on me, I felt trapped between trying to earn enough to pay the bills (and tithing) and spending more time at home. Most of my peers were single and childless. When the job needed us to stay late, no one called them, wondering when they would be home.

I quickly felt that I wasn't good enough as head of the household and also not good enough at work.

One thing many people like about the LDS Church is that you have an instant base of friends when you move somewhere. That's true, but you also have an instant side job. I found myself in the Elders Quorum presidency, a task that would grind me down so much that in about a year I would ask to be released from the calling—something I'd been taught we shouldn't do. So in addition to being not good enough at home or at work, I was also, apparently, not good enough at church.

Around this time, I found a book about Mark Hofmann and his crimes. A rare books dealer and forger, Hofmann used homemade pipe bombs to murder two people in Salt Lake City in 1985 to buy himself time when his schemes to sell forged historical documents began to fall apart. Among his most notorious forgeries was the so-called Salamander Letter. Purportedly from one of Joseph Smith's most enthusiastic supporters, it claimed that the being who led Joseph Smith to the golden plates from which the Book of Mormon was translated was not an angel but a white salamander. It was designed to embarrass the church, and it did, because they bought it—literally. The church paid Hofmann handsomely for the letter, and leaders worked hard to reconcile its ridiculous story with the church's official story of the Book of Mormon's origin. What bothered me most was that no spirit of discernment or prophecy helped the church's leaders protect themselves from this audacious fraud. They clearly believed that it and many of Hofmann's other forgeries were authentic. Instead, the first people to declare the Salamander Letter a forgery were outspoken critics of Joseph Smith and the church, even though they would have been vindicated in important ways had the letter been real.

The whole nasty business made me question the church for the first time in my life. I even feigned sickness to avoid church for a few weeks. But that caused such a conflict with my wife that I shelved my doubts and convinced myself that it wasn't the church; if I had concerns it was because I wasn't sufficiently obedient. It had to be my fault that I wasn't good enough.

One of my regrets about my time at BYU is that I was so focused on getting out of school and providing for my growing family that I didn't take a wide range of classes in my major—I just took what I needed to graduate ASAP. Once I was working full-time, I discovered gaps in my knowledge I wanted to fill, so I began a master's degree. Soon after, I was called to be in the bishopric. I drew out a schedule, and between work, school, and church, I had about six free hours per week. Six whole hours! Somehow, I thought that meant it was doable and would all be OK. But after a year, I realized it wouldn't work. The master's degree was the least pressing of the demands, so it had to go. Consequently, I wasn't good enough in my educational pursuits—and I felt I was competing at a disadvantage at work too.

I never felt I got answers to my prayers. I would wonder, "Why do other people get answers, but I don't?" Being in the bishopric was like seeing the sausage being made. I soon realized that there was no divine pipeline from God to the bishop to guide the ward. We were just a bunch of guys trying to do the best we could and getting it wrong as often as we got it right.

My parents divorced when I was six years old. My father wasn't part of my life after that; Scout leaders and other men in the ward were my surrogate fathers. My way of paying them back was to do the same for the boys I worked with in the Scouting program at church. For twenty-five years I did my best to help boys grow through Scouting activities.

Eventually, the hours I spent in church work and the doubts I accumulated started grinding me down. I remember a poorly attended Saturday afternoon stake priesthood leadership meeting; less than half the people who should have been there showed up. The stake president used the occasion to berate us for not doing enough, for not spending enough time in our callings. That's right: the people attending a 4:00 meeting on a Saturday afternoon were the ones not doing enough.

I went home in tears and told my wife. She said I had no reason to be upset, that I was doing enough and more than enough. That didn't stop me from feeling inadequate.

My struggle with not receiving answers to prayers or having the spiritual experiences that others reported kept returning. I would always reach a point where I would think, "It must be something wrong with me. I just need to pray harder and read the scriptures and go to the temple and be more obedient." I would double down and try harder, but with the same results. There's a saying that the definition of insanity is doing the same thing and expecting a different result. Despite my failures, it never occurred to me to give up the struggle or leave the church.

One day during the 2008 Republican presidential primary, I saw a link to a YouTube video of John McCain's mother saying terrible things about Mitt Romney, whom I'd met in Massachusetts during my mission; I served in Romney's Belmont ward and had dinner at his home a couple of times. I wanted to hear what McCain's mom had to say; it was standard bigotry against Mormons and not as sensational as the headline. But when the video finished, I noticed a suggestion on the side of the page: "Why People Leave the LDS Church," by John Dehlin.

When I finished watching Dehlin's screencast, my life had changed in some way. I don't know why I had never considered this before, but I realized I was not alone in my doubts. (I guess the church's constant message that people who leave are weak or sinners really worked on me.) I found others on the Internet who were struggling or had left, and I read the stories of their journeys. I began reading and studying intently. The day Richard Bushman's biography of Joseph Smith, *Rough Stone Rolling*, was delivered, I arrived home to find my wife reading it. That began a period when my wife was learning right along with me, although I knew it would be difficult for her to reach the same conclusions I was reaching.

One night, we were reading in bed. As I remember, she was reading a book on early church polygamy. She abruptly shut the book and said, "I'm done."

I knew she wasn't finished reading that particular book. "What do you mean?" I asked.

"I'm done reading things critical of the church, and I'm done thinking about it." She wanted to go back to being a believer. I, however, could not put that genie back in the bottle.

* * *

Attending meetings after my realization that the church isn't what it claims was terribly painful. Every Saturday night, I dreaded church. Every Sunday I left church wondering if I should kill myself rather than return the next Sunday. I wasn't even good at losing my faith! I finally decided that I needed time off to think about it, so I would take a one-year sabbatical from attending church. It was cold turkey. One Sunday I handed the bishop an envelope with my temple recommend and a short note explaining that next Sunday would be my last for at least one year. I was the Scoutmaster and a counselor in the Young Men's presidency. My note said that he needed to find someone else for that job.

During that year, Sundays were still difficult. To replace my "church family" (and there's no arguing with the fact that the church provides a community), I joined various Meetup groups. Most Sundays I would go hiking or out to lunch with one of these groups. When I came home, my wife would be upset that she had attended church by herself while I was out having fun. I also know that she felt a loss of status in having to sit alone in church, especially since our children were grown by that time, with the youngest away at college. She felt judged. Occasionally, I would convince her to go with me or spend Sunday just the two of us doing something fun. But skipping church with me Sunday morning or afternoon meant that she spent Sunday night feeling guilty that she had missed church. There was no winning; she was upset either way, and the only solution, in her mind, was for me to go back and pretend I believed.

After my one-year sabbatical, I resigned my church membership. Soon after that my wife told me that since we were no longer married in the temple, maybe we didn't need to be married at all. We were divorced within a few months. I won't say that the church caused our divorce, but the teachings about temple marriage being the all-important goal in life certainly played a part.

The first therapist I went to after leaving the church assigned me *Healing the Child Within: Discovery and Recovery for Adult Children of Dysfunctional Families,* by Charles Whitfield. I was hesitant and maybe a little offended at the implication that my family of origin was dysfunctional. I was and still am defensive of my mother, who raised five children by herself. There was no way I would let my crisis of faith turn me into a disloyal son! After reading the first few chapters, I drove to my appointment asking myself why I was reading this book.

I was in the car when it hit me: the church was my dysfunctional family. Before getting out of my car at the appointment, I opened the book to the checklist of signs of a dysfunctional family: control, fear, conflict, perfectionism (bingo!!), poor communication, lack of diversity. The therapist was not familiar with the LDS Church, so we walked through the signs. I explained some of the ways the church controls its members. Fear of loss is a major factor: the church promises so much, in this life and the next, and tells you that you can lose it all if you ask questions or don't conform. You would think that poor communication would not be a problem for a church that has satellite broadcasts of conferences twice a year and publishes three magazines a month, but it's the emphasis on control of information over clarity that creates the dysfunction. Bishops are often given handbook updates or other instructions that the members don't have access to. Many things fall under the "unwritten order of things" (in the words of Apostle Boyd K. Packer); it is assumed that you know these things, but they are rarely, if ever, discussed.

* * *

The book and the conversations it made possible turned another light on for me.

So at fifty-two years of age, I started over. I moved into a one-bedroom apartment and lived alone for the first time in my entire life. It was even the first time I'd had a bedroom to myself! In my parents' house, I always shared a room with my brother; since I lived at home while attending BYU, I never even lived with roommates, except on my mission. I realize that for a lot of people, getting married is the final stage in growing up. But if you've never had time to develop an adult self on your own, it just suspends you in a state of perpetual adolescence—which the church exacerbates. Don't be independent. Follow our plan; don't come up with your own.

I was a fifty-two-year-old adolescent who'd spent his whole life being not good enough. After years of therapy, I still feel not good enough.

I'm writing this almost five years after starting over. I moved from the Intermountain West to California. The church is much less in my face here. I don't drive past a temple under construction or past three meetinghouses every day on the way to work. One measure of my recovery is my reaction to Mormon things. When I get very angry, I realize that I'm not quite over them. I'm still processing the anger. When I can ignore them or have no emotional reaction to them, I feel like my recovery is progressing.

My inner voice still tells me that I'm not good enough, but I'm trying to turn the volume down on it. And I have to ask myself, "What does *good enough* even mean?" I don't have an answer, but I do know my life would be different if I hadn't spent it trying to live up to impossible standards that I questioned too late. The church does a good job of giving you a plan for your life—and afterlife—as long as you don't think too hard about it or question it. It's a way to keep you from thinking about what you really want. But now I'm without a premade plan and must try to figure it out for myself. And I'm hoping that someday, I'll feel good enough.

Mormon AF

NICHOLAS DON SMITH

I'm forty, single, and I've never been married. I haven't even dabbled with marriage's celebrated lesser cousin, engagement, the gas station donut to marriage's multitiered designer cake. It's not out of some undying hatred for the ancient tradition. It's not like my parents were mercilessly slain by a bloodthirsty wedding officiant. No stack of bridal magazines fell on me while I browsed the role-playing games section at my local Barnes & Noble so that I swore an oath never to walk down the aisle.

Nay, gentle readers, the actual circumstances are not so melodramatic and campy. It's primarily because my life has been chaos due to much tragedy and misfortune in my family that made me primary caregiver for my mother through the entirety of my twenties and most of my thirties. Not until the last few years, after my mother's death, have I been able to delicately, tentatively enter the world of dating.

It's just as well. I was raised Mormon and, as we will examine, had lots of deprogramming to do and self-examination and therapy and all those wonderful, fun things that come from gradually pulling yourself away from a peculiar religion with difficult ideas about relationships and marriage.

I grew up in a staunch Latter-day Saint household in the heart of Mormondom, Utah County, in a smallish town called American Fork, fourteen or so miles north of Provo. Hmm. Now that I take a moment to ponder, I think Provo is actually the heart of Mormondom, what with Brigham Young University right there and the Mission Training Center and Dry Bar Comedy (because everything is funnier when the audience is sober, amirite?). I guess that makes American Fork more akin to the liver of Mormondom. Granted, not as romantic as the heart, but pretty damn vital, according to five out of seven physicians who responded to my Twitter poll.

So yeah. I grew up Mormon AF, as the kids say (before President Russell M. Nelson announced in 2018 that God was fed up with members of his church calling themselves Mormons for one hundred and eighty-eight years and better stop it, *right that minute*). I grew up knowing that marriage was the zenith of LDS accomplishment, even above going on a mission or not murdering people. Everything hinged on getting hitched, because without it, you couldn't make and raise children in The Church where they could meet that special someone and get married and have kids of their own, perpetuating an endless cycle of procreational matrimony (Is that a thing? It is now! I'm trademarking it, folks!) to establish the Kingdom of Heaven according to God's divine plan.

I remember the authority figures around me vehemently emphasizing that if what you were aiming for wasn't TEMPLE marriage, you could fuck right off. Or fetch right off, as they say in Utah County.

In the LDS world, temple marriage is the industry standard, the benchmark by which all other types of matrimony are measured. It's like if you want that authentic Philly cheesesteak experience, you go to Geno's or Pat's. If you don't care what God thinks of your choices, you pick up something from Arby's, Jesus weeps, and once again the Eagles aren't making the Super Bowl. I hope you're happy!

During the temple wedding ceremony, you and your spouse make eternal covenants with The Lord Almighty, ensuring that you're bound to each other forever and ever, along with any and all offspring you bring into the world together. After you die, you get to live with all your worthy friends and family with Heavenly Father for eternity, eventually attaining Godhood and making worlds of your own and having tons of spirit children with your many wives! This is complicated and a touchy subject, and some people want to pretend we never believed this, but I and many awkward teenage boys were promised that in heaven, we would get additional wives because, get this, there will be more worthy women who make it to the highest kingdom than men, because women are more spiritually attuned, unlike their male counterparts, who fell and will continue to fall prey to temptation (mainly porn) in higher numbers but are still trusted with the most important spiritual authority, keys, and positions in the church.

It was repeatedly impressed upon me that if you were married and weren't bringing babies into this world ASAP, you were endangering the whole operation and the spiritual growth and salvation of your future children. How? Well, I'm glad you asked. This is how it was explained to me on several occasions:

Before we came down to live on this sad floating asylum we call Earth, we resided with God the Father in what is known colloquially as "the preexistence." During these millions—possibly even billions—of years, we contracted with select spirits to be their moms and dads here on Earth.

So let's say my future wife and I decided on raising seven children. But while chilling on the mortal plane, the wife and I get corrupted by real dark satanic shit like, I don't know, liberalism and rock music and decide to have just two kids. What happens to those other five? They end up born to other moms and dads, parents they were never supposed to be raised by. Like maybe sex workers or feminists, or they end up in a war-torn country far from any true teachings about Christ. They lead sad, miserable lives, destroying their chances of returning to God. Oh and because of our sin of utilizing birth control, the missus and I will have to face these children during the final judgment and account for our sins.

Seriously, someone told me that before I could grow a beard. I wasn't authorized to drive a motor vehicle, but I was already expected to shoulder the burden of planning for half a dozen kids just like me.

Trying not to freak out, I would ask, "How will I know how many kids to have?" and the Sunday school teacher would say, "Easy! You and your future wife will pray to Heavenly Father for inspiration to know if you should try for another. And you just keep on doing that until you eventually receive confirmation via the Holy Ghost that you've had enough or your wife's body literally crumbles into dust."

"Oh," I said, before collapsing under the weight of all that thick, prime-cut, locally sourced existential dread.

Another facet about marriage repeatedly hammered home was making sure I was worthy of my spouse, and that especially meant sexual purity. Seemed a simple enough task when I was getting ready for baptism at eight years of age. The challenge increased once I hit puberty and hormones got in the way of that goal. I heard a lot about Matthew 5:28, which read, "But I say unto you, That whosoever looks on a woman to lust after her has committed adultery with her already in his heart."

According to that scripture, by the time I was fourteen, I had committed adultery about ten thousand times. Small wonder I was spiraling into a vortex of guilt, shame, and self-loathing. I was touching myself every day, double that on Saturdays; what worthy young lady would want me? It got to the point that I could only fantasize within the context of marriage. That was my "work-around" with the Lord. "Look, God, I know I'm a real pile of garbage, but at least I'm not having premarital sex in my fantasies, right? That counts for something, yeah? God?" Adultery, we were told, was a sin so grievous it was akin to murder, so I worried sometimes that my self-abuse may have amounted to at least the equivalent of one homicide, probably more. Masturbation meant I was practically a serial killer. Yet another generous helping of existential despair.

And of course the other side of that was making sure you dated only young ladies who adhered to all the same gospel principles and maintained their purity.

They had to attend church regularly, pay tithing when applicable, not say curse words like "butt" and "frick," keep their clavicles and knees covered so as not to trigger impure thoughts in boys' hormone-addled brains, stay out of Girl Scouts where they might learn about careers and self-sufficiency and witchcraft, not defile their holy countenances with makeup before age fifteen, or disfigure themselves with ear piercings (again, before they were fifteen). And they most definitely couldn't be a feminist, because that would mean they were gay.

There was also this weird belief prevailing among some LDS boys, myself included, that lust just wasn't something girls had to contend with. The idea that they could become aroused, let alone achieve orgasm, was inconceivable. ("Women having orgasms?! Poppycock, Fitzgerald! I won't hear of such far-fetched nonsense during my morning Postum!") We just figured, I don't know, once you got married to your beloved, sexy stuff unlocked like some special feature in a video game.

Then we got older and more educated and discovered that both parties have the capacity to feel super fun-time sensations, but that's only for The Marrieds, and the point of sex varied drastically depending on which generation you were talking to. People my parents' and grandparents' age took the position that genitals were to be used strictly for the purpose of bringing life into this world, NO EYE CONTACT, PLEASE, THINK OF A HYMN, IT WILL BE OVER SOON, which sounded horrifying and sad. A handful of my older Gen X cousins maintained that sex was something fun and wonderful for the whimsy and delight of both parties involved, and it was no one's bloody business what the two of you got up to in the bedroom. The latter was definitely more my speed, and I adopted that view.

The ultimate failure was seeing your marriage end in divorce. The Adversary was always looking for new ways to destroy your celestial marriage, so we had to be mindful and diligent of the snares and pitfalls Satan would put in our way. Like staring at porn, which was equated to injecting black tar heroin into your veins. Allowing your wife to go back to work "once the children are old enough" was considered by some to be another great pitfall, putting career over family. "ENJOY HAVING PREGNANT TEENAGERS IN GAY SOCIALIST BIKER GANGS, STACEY! HOPE YOUR MBA WAS WORTH IT!"

Given all this, you might not be surprised to learn that *lots* of my self-worth was wrapped up in marriage and creating and nurturing a family of my own. So when I was unable to comply with one of the most basic and fundamental aspects of LDS doctrine, I felt like an abject failure, akin to a metal guitarist unable to play power chords or a bag of uncut cocaine without a wild Vegas after-party.

These feelings and societal pressures stuck with me even after my faith withered. But as I got older and matured, I reexamined my life and realized I don't have to tether myself to that specific path, I don't have to do something because it's custom and tradition, and if I was being honest, a part of me just wanted someone around to alleviate the loneliness and rescue me from my life—but that was selfish and bullshit and unhealthy, and whoever I ended up in a relationship with deserved a helluva lot better than that.

VOICE-OVER
So what's my life like now?

EXT—DAY—SNOW-COVERED MOUNTAINTOP

Nicholas, attired in sleek mountaineering gear, stands on a red snowboard fitted with rocket engines.

NICHOLAS
I eventually discovered my calling, which is yelling jokes at a sea of strange faces from stage. I started dating and got some therapy and stopped treating myself like garbage most of the time. Now that I've embraced atheism, I can smoke weed and drink booze. And kids, that's pretty cool.

Nicholas slams a Monster Energy drink, does a sick jump with his snowboard off the mountain, high fives a yeti, activates the rocket engines, and flies into the sunset.

MOTORHEAD's "Ace of Spades" plays.

FADE TO BLACK

Fin

Liken the Scriptures

ANDREW SPRIGGS

The Book of Mormon's first hero and prophet, Nephi, states in 1 Nephi 19:23 that readers of the book should "liken all scriptures unto us, that it might be for our profit and learning," meaning that we should see how sacred stories apply to our personal lives. As an active Mormon, I struggled to find characters and situations I identified with. However, since I've left the church, the passing of time has either fuzzed my knowledge of scriptural particularities or loosened the institutional church's grip on my interpretations of scripture, such that I feel more able to claim something about scriptures for me or at the very least to claim Mormonism for myself. And, given that, I must say: no matter how hard Mormons kick against the pricks in their fight against same-sex marriage, my marriage to my husband is the most Mormon thing I have done and will continue to do.

I understand a same-sex marriage may not seem very credibly Mormon at first glance. Several years ago, I took an online quiz called "Bob's Mormon Cred Scale 2.0" that aimed to quantify the taker's Mormon credibility "independent of [their] position toward the Mormon church today." Given how much of my self-identity was (and to some extent still is) wrapped up in being a cultural Mormon, I probably had a vested interest in thinking that my cultural Mormonism was at least somewhat credible. Mormons often view themselves as a "peculiar people" religiously, to quote 1 Peter 2:9, but this spills into many Mormons seeing a cultural peculiarity outside of and separate from any religious context, as signified by things like their collective love of squeaky-clean fun—church softball or scavenger hunts—and processed food like Jell-O or a potato casserole often served at funerals and hence called funeral potatoes.

So there I was, wanting to claim Mormonism as my culture, regardless of my belief or adherence. Reviewing the questions today, I imagine the sinking feeling, the knot of alienation that must have materialized in my gut as I moved from question to question back then. Questions about living in Utah or of attending BYU would probably have raised the knot to my chest as it combusted into plumes of smoky indignation: *How dare someone equate Utah upbringing with Mormon credibility?* Thanks to the standardization of Mormon institutional practice and teaching known colloquially as "correlation," I was confident that my Mormon upbringing as a military brat in places as mundane as Lawton, Oklahoma, and as exotic as Seoul, Korea, was theologically and institutionally comparable to any in Utah. After all, the point of correlation is that Mormon practices, theology, and vocabulary are standardized across geography much as the practices, rules, and vocabulary of American football are standardized across geography and team franchises by the NFL and the NCAA.

But the indignation would have cooled and condensed into something heavier when I reached questions about marrying in the temple or having children. I had no case arguing with any faithful, conservative Mormon in *any* location about the validity of these common Mormon rites of passage as signifiers of Mormon credibility. Even more, I knew that while it would merely be a lamentable tragedy if I were *accidentally* deprived of a temple marriage and children, my *intentional* choice to forgo these rites (and my inborn orientation against them) constituted absolute heresy.

Ultimately, I scored a measly 5 out of 100 points. I didn't even "feel entitled to 5 points of Mormon cred for reasons not covered" by the quiz to bump my score up to 10 points. I had to admit: if these were the criteria for Mormon credibility, I probably deserved my poor score. How had I fallen so far, Mormon-wise?

Things might have been different. Had you talked to fellow ward members who knew me growing up, there would be no question: I was one of "those righteous Spriggs boys." Maybe I should have likened myself to that Book of Mormon hero Nephi—born of goodly parents (albeit mine were converts to the church, so I got no Mormon cred from a multigenerational Mormon family), dutiful in familiarity and understanding of the scriptures, insightful and animated when exhorting others through talks and speeches, and, most relevantly, impeccable in adherence of the laws of God, including the law of chastity. When I was growing up, it was easy not to do anything inappropriate with the young women around me—it's awfully easy not to do something verboten when you have utterly no inclination to do so.

I can't remember today precisely how I would have processed others' perceptions of me, especially given my private desires and actions . . . but given that so much of my self-identity was (and to some extent still is) linked to the concept of competency, I probably would have had a vested interest in thinking that my lack of affection for women was a reflection of my personal righteousness. My teenage journals seem to be written by two selves who don't talk to one another.

There's the me who presents himself to everyone (and myself) as just gifted with a righteous asexuality but who publicly and privately hopes that some girl will come along and sweep him into a relationship when the time is right (without his needing to take any sort of active role). Then there's the much rarer me who writes explicit private passages fantasizing about men. How did I get away in interview after interview with church leaders mentioning absolutely nothing about masturbation—or the sex of the participants in the material I would view during such? Was it just my projected asexuality? No matter what, my journals betray no hint of guilt about either the masturbation or the lies of omission.

So I hate for others to infer that my fall from Mormonism happened *because* of my homosexuality, because I don't see it that way. I didn't "leave to sin"—apart from masturbation, nothing Mormons consider sexual sin was even part of my consciousness until years after I left. And yet, things *did* start falling apart because of matters best categorized as sexuality.

First, my hopes that I could passively acquiesce to a heteronormative relationship combusted into so much unrecognizable soot. In middle school, I became friends with the girl who sat next to me in band class: she played the tuba, and I substituted for the euphonium on baritone saxophone. I was interested in writing a sprawling self-insert fantasy novel, and so was she, so she and I would spend the hours we had to wait for our respective legal guardians (my parents, her grandma) to pick us up after school by comparing binders of worlds we had crafted to incubate characters (including ourselves) away from the more mundane reality of life in a midsize Oklahoma town. Her prose contained words like "redolent" that I didn't understand at the time (but that made such an impression on me that I still remember them when I don't remember what I ate yesterday), but she also extended me the grace of believing enough in my intelligence to always assume that I did.

This girl at some point *did* express an interest in me beyond comparing notebooks. I had no idea what all she was interested in doing, because my anxiety and distress over the unwanted attention was so visceral that I avoided any sort of physical or emotional involvement at all. To put it bluntly, I was the sort of jackass who severed contact with a friend because I was too immature to deal with a one-sided desire that the friendship become something more.

I decided against serving a mission, but not out of any anxiety over being in close proximity to other guys. I frankly didn't think the proximity would trouble me: it would be easy not to do anything inappropriate with the clean-shaven, barely adult men around me, because I wasn't attracted to them, any more than I'd been attracted to my classmates at school. It would be several years until I knew enough about myself or even gay subcultures to have words for my preference for hairier, stockier men. Mormons today like to talk about something called a "tender mercy of the Lord" (1 Nephi 1:20), and I suppose one for me was that because I was attracted mainly to adult men, I didn't have to worry about attraction until I was an adult.

In any case, the anxiety that drove me to forgo a mission—despite it being such a crucial task for maturing young men in Mormonism—was the far more immediate and persistent knot of anxiety regarding the prospect of teaching people to live their lives according to a narrative I did not believe myself.

As I've often said when sharing the story of my Mormon upbringing, I didn't have a faith crisis (as many former Mormons will describe) so much as a *lack of faith* crisis. This crisis forced me to confront my perception of myself and others' perception of me as a competent, righteous Mormon. I had to admit: though I could force myself to learn the right answers for Sunday school, I couldn't force myself to believe those answers were true. Scripturally, perhaps I was more of a Laman or a Lemuel, the wicked older brothers of Nephi—but even here, I didn't like how so many scriptures presented nonbelieving characters who neverthe-less had supernatural experiences. Where were the characters who experienced nothing out of the ordinary to trigger the iconic burning in the bosom that could serve as the basis of their testimony?

The only thing burning in my bosom was my frustration as I debated religion with my non-Mormon classmates, all of whom were far more passionate about the heretical status of Mormonism than I was about its veracity. I wavered emotionally between the weight of the stone sunk in my stomach from not believing the arguments I relayed to them and the rising airy heat spurring me to speak more passionately in defense of my tribe anyway. But the heated pas-sion of defending my tribe, though it could motivate me in a cafeteria or on the school bus, utterly failed to motivate me to spend two years of my life teaching strangers to change their entire life trajectories and convert to Mormonism.

So instead of going on a mission, I went on the next most acceptable alterna-tive: university. Perhaps I could channel the spirit of 2 Nephi 9:29, which advises that "to be learned is good" as long as one "hearken[s] unto the counsels of God"? Because of my lack of belief, I wasn't excited about hearkening unto any counsels of God (and therefore not excited to attend church), but I also had no strong feelings *against* going to church. As teenage me had felt regarding dating women, I thought that if a fellow Mormon invited me, I could passively acquiesce to attending church in college. Sure enough: upon finding out I was LDS, an LDS classmate invited me to attend church with him. But when I went to the singles ward, the service was based entirely upon preparing for missions for those who had yet to serve and matchmaking for everyone else. Within one Sunday, I confronted the stark and terrifying reality that the only thing (or perhaps just the primary thing?) Mormonism could offer me was the beatific vision of my life raising children in a heteronormative marriage. I didn't and don't oppose this vision for those it suits, but for me, these messages were not only thoroughly irrelevant but alienating. Mormonism had felt foundational to my identity because it was a private language I knew and could speak with Mormons anywhere we met, the same way any football aficionado could instantly find common ground speaking to any other fan about their favored teams and players. But the experience at the singles ward was like realizing that although you'd been infused in a football-crazed community (as my alma mater, Texas A&M, was), you simply didn't care for the sport. No matter how fluent you were in the lingo or how much you forced yourself to watch, there would be an unbridgeable gap between a fan and a spectator.

And so that Sunday in my first year of college, sometime in August or September of 2007, was the last time I would go to church.

Even after that, I maintained Mormon practices for several years. I didn't drink coffee, tea, or alcohol (they all tasted gross when I tried them), and I didn't date. I was more comfortable acknowledging that I was gay, not asexual. (Younger Andrew would never have deduced that when you're attracted to hairier, stockier dudes, then the sorts of changes many people fear and lament about aging instead just fill the world with increasingly more attractive people.) Yet I was also very comfortable not pursuing any relationships. (Older Andrew now understood in part the fear behind the stereotype of teenagers going to a school dance and then staying as far away as possible from their romantic crushes.) The one advantage over my middle school self was that I didn't imagine that I could "passively acquiesce" into a same-sex relationship while at conservative Texas A&M University.

I experienced no anxiety over being single. I was fine on my own. Bachelorhood might not be respected in Mormonism, but there's good New Testament justification for it. I could be like St. Paul, who declared in 1 Corinthians 7:1, "It is good for a man not to touch a woman." Paul acknowledged that not everyone had his "gift" for celibacy, and he grudgingly allowed that "it is better to marry than to burn" (1 Cor. 7:9) with passion. I didn't burn with passion, and so I thought it was good to stay unmarried, as I was.

I can't remember now precisely what motivated me to sign up for the dating site OKCupid. Perhaps I just got curious? No matter what, I return to my case for cultural Mormonism. Notwithstanding Paul's implication in 1 Corinthians 7 that unmarried life could be not only acceptable but desirable or spiritually sanctified, as a nonbelieving former Mormon, I would have had another scriptural verse on my mind, even if subconsciously. It was the same impulse that drove teenage me to publicly and privately hope to fall into a heteronormative relationship and the same impulse that drove college me to at least try going to church: the sense that in Mormonism, far more authoritative than 1 Corinthians 7 is the Genesis 2:18 declaration from the Lord God himself: it is not good that the man should be alone.

I don't mean to assert that being single is bad or wrong, only that my relationship with my now husband has been challenging and fulfilling in ways that I likely would not put myself in situations to experience if I were single—and these experiences feel to me to be the reason why the LDS Church prioritizes marriage so much.

My husband looks over as I write this and wonders if I'm writing a novel. I tell him it's an essay that includes him. He asks if it will include the fact that he corrupted me from being a good Mormon boy. After all, now I can no longer say I follow the Word of Wisdom or the law of chastity in any conventional Mormon sense.

I laugh at his joke. In that conventional Mormon sense, it's all accurate.

But no, I cannot write that (or only that), because that's not how I see him and our relationship. Instead of being corrupted, I see that I am uplifted.

I think of the way he listens to me talking about extremely complicated accounting and tax concepts and then asks insightful questions about them after having only known about them for minutes. I think about the way he offers to walk through problems at work that seem intractable to me, providing an outsider's perspective. I think about how he also does all of this with interpersonal issues. As I struggle against his very personality, I know why Mormons talk about the importance of *difference* in relationship. This difference between us in our relationship makes me want to be single so I don't have to engage, but my husband offers—insistently, albeit with patience for me to select the time I'm ready—to talk me through the emotional turmoil I experience in transitioning from independence to interdependence.

I think about my surprise at how opaque we are to one another. The single me naively believed that people in relationship simply osmose each other's feelings in a passive, telepathic way. But we have both learned that it is in fact very possible to completely miss the message of another's silent treatment. What seems to the silent one a deafening klaxon broadcasting on all wavelengths can be something the other is oblivious to, unless he consciously attunes himself to the right wavelength. Far more effective (but far more difficult) is to talk over what ails us.

I think about my surprise at how opaque we are to one another even through the positive aspects of our relationship. When we hug, I want to believe the additional surface area is additional substrate for a chemical reaction between us: that with more surface area, the rate of reaction can increase, and more energy can be transferred. But I realize that I'm no closer to feeling from his point of view; likewise, he cannot feel from my point of view the warmth of infatuation and appreciation. Instead, I must speak, must instantiate my feelings in words.

The single me believed that love is just something that happens and that the changes required to live with someone you love happen passively. Under this belief, at several points when we were dating, I tried to push him away when I realized that working through differences in personality doesn't come naturally or automatically. I told him that I was just the way I was, selfish, and he should run away. I knew that from any outside perspective, it would look bad on me—I was trying to run away and push away so I could be comfortable alone, because alone I didn't have to worry about even the slightest interpersonal demands being placed on me.

But despite the worst I threw at him, he stayed, and I learned that the reality is that I can act consciously rather than merely through instinct or passive acquiescence or the path of least resistance. I can do this even through the opacity. I can do this even though, as Paul discusses in 1 Corinthians 13:12, "we see through a glass, darkly."

And it strikes me that consciously choosing the challenges of my marriage is an extremely Mormon thing. The Book of Mormon prophet Alma exhorted his followers to "compare the word [of God] unto a seed" that could "be planted in your heart" simply by your desire to "give place for a portion of [the] words" (Alma 32:27-28). I don't know about the word of God, but I know that my marriage encourages me to give place for seeds of habits to be planted in my heart. It encourages me to practice a variety of life habits, to build a testimony of their goodness, by having enough trust to just try. Though I cannot see whether the seed of this practice or that will "swell within [my] breasts" (as Alma 32:28 continues) before I try it, marriage means committing to try—without a self-defeating skepticism.

Being in relationship therefore teaches me to practice. Being married gives me a commitment and pledge that I will continue to practice. Together, through this, we have come to the scriptures we most liken as an ideal for ourselves from 1 Corinthians 13:4–7, 13:

> Love is patient, love is kind. It does not envy, it does not boast, it is not proud. It does not dishonor others, it is not self-seeking, it is not easily angered, it keeps no records of wrongs. Love does not delight in evil but rejoices with the truth. It always protects, always trusts, always hopes, always perseveres.
>
> Love never fails.

Figure 3. Gabe and Andrew Spriggs, November 2018, Rome

Andrew writes, "My husband loves to travel, whereas I am much more of a homebody. If I had my way, I could easily see myself locked in my room indefinitely! So every photo of every trip we take is a reminder that marriage is a constant opportunity to practice (literally) stepping outside of my comfort zone, to experience more, and to grow and know more joy in the process."

The Care Package

KEVIN BARNWELL

One summer day in 2018, I arrived home from work to a house that felt strange: for the first time since our oldest child was born twenty-nine years earlier, my house was empty. Our three older children had graduated from college and were on their own, while our youngest was on a mission in Canada. My wife, Renay, had flown to Pennsylvania to be with our oldest son, whose wife had recently died. He was starting his third year of medical school and raising a two-year-old daughter. He needed Renay for six weeks to bridge two rotations and a move. We'd each spent a week or two helping him at various times, but not for this long.

Somehow I had convinced myself that my month and a half of solitude would be bliss. A meditative retreat of sorts, an extended staycation, a sabbatical from adulting. I could catch up on neglected reading before work or late into the evening. I could eat out every night if I chose or take a forbidden plate of chimichangas into the basement and watch a repeated ninth-inning collapse of a Diamondbacks game. I could take out the trash when convenient. I could do laundry how I wanted, conserving both time and water by mixing colors, whites, and darks together. I could even toss an entire Bounce sheet in the dryer instead of a measly half. Nirvana!

So I thought.

My second night alone, I had unconsciously memorized the start-up and shut-down cycles of the air conditioner: a sequencing of three clicks at one-second intervals, then a two-second pause (which was the relay to the compressor), then a transfer to the blower, where I could feel the draw of electricity, and finally the sound of frigid air surging through the aluminum duct system. It had scarcely registered before. Now it was inescapable.

I needed a distraction. I had to find something that made me feel less alone in my eerily silent, empty house. Before Renay left for Pennsylvania, we agreed to celebrate our anniversary when she returned. Busy helping our bereaved son and granddaughter, she would have no time to devote to me. But time I had—forty-two days. More pressing, my heart was telling me that this year I needed to reach deep and create something extra meaningful for her. I would put together a care package containing standard anniversary items: her favorite dark chocolate (60 percent Ghirardelli cacao), favorite flower (sunflower), sentimental trinkets like seashells collected from beaches we had strolled from Oregon to Mexico, sappy love poems from Elizabeth Barrett Browning and e e cummings, John Donne and Emily Dickinson. But I also wanted a personal touch that spoke to our private, bedrock connection, because we had weathered some intense storms in our marriage and still remained intensely committed to each other.

I decided the focus of the gift would be a photo album filled with pictures of just the two of us—because while we love our children, parents, siblings, cousins, and friends, Renay is uniquely precious to me. It took a week of sorting through thirty-two years of shared experience—friendship, courtship, marriage, graduations, the births and deaths of our firstborn twin girls, moves, travel, holidays, birthdays—to find the six dozen photos I wanted to use.

Having grown up in a family, having been the product of a marriage, having watched my parents dissolve their marriage and each embark on another, I assumed I knew quite a bit about marriage and family by the time I got married myself. Yet each passing year showed me that I knew very little. Until there I was, sitting alone at my kitchen table, surveying all those photos and reliving the experiences they documented. The images and memories were familiar and alien at the same time, like they'd happened to someone I knew, but not necessarily to me. Was this my life? If so, how did I get here? Had it really been thirty-two years since I met Renay, thirty-one since we married? Where did those years *go*?

The church brought us together: we met at BYU. But in retrospect, I saw that our faith journeys diverged early on. Attempting to make sense of the death of our firstborn girls after only a few days, we began to comprehend vast differences in how we framed aspects of mortality and of suffering. We also began to observe that how we each constructed meaning and found purpose was fundamentally different; how we viewed the nature and role of deity and of institutionalized religion also grew more disparate. Sometimes we framed it as a question of who was right and who was wrong, but at some point, it didn't matter. Despite these differences, we remained devoted to each other and to our marriage. And, notwithstanding my concerns with contemporary Mormonism, we agreed to raise our four children in the tradition and culture that brought us together, including supporting our kids on missions and in temple marriages.

In January 2014, I resigned my membership in The Church of Jesus Christ of Latter-day Saints, upending many personal relationships in devastating ways.

My ancestors had joined the church in 1836 and trekked across North America to reach the safety of Utah after Mormons became pariahs within the United States. I had always been taught to value their faith and sacrifice, so rejecting the life they bequeathed me, a life I loved in so many ways, was the most difficult, calculated, and still somehow unavoidable decision I ever made. It had been in process for decades. I was fatigued by my trepidation, procrastination, wavering. I could no longer pretend to compartmentalize the contradictions or reconcile the duplicity. For me, the retrenchment, authoritarianism, fundamentalism, and general failure of nerve proved more than I could countenance.

Yes, it was liberating to finally make a decision, to move on. But I did so alone, while my family watched, stricken and confused. Who enjoys hurting the people you love most? Would my marriage survive? Despite having been married to Renay for almost twenty-seven years at that point, I did not pretend to know how she would make sense of or reconcile this decision, any more than she could have predicted that I would one day leave the church.

Renay chose to put our marriage first. Despite my heresy, she chose me. She could have said, "This is not my loving husband" and vanished, and I suspect she got well-intentioned but fearful advice from family, friends, and ecclesiastical superiors to do just that. Instead, she chose to stay in the marriage. Why?

As the finishing touches on the photo album came together, I was struck by the story the seventy-plus photographs told. I arranged them in nonlinear sequences, creating a kaleidoscope effect. In each picture we were holding hands, or kissing, or holding the other closely. Our facial expressions and connection to each other were spontaneous and genuine. Regardless of location or circumstance, the pattern and texture woven into this story was that together, our lives were more—more meaningful, more fulfilling, more indispensable. That we not only needed each other but also unequivocally *wanted* each other. Yes, it was both fun and jarring to watch us transition through fashions, to see wrinkles appear and lines deepen, to observe our hair grow, get cut, turn gray—or, in my case, disappear. But more powerful than the obvious myriad changes was something that stayed the same: our profound love for each other. A love emergent and evolving.

For a moment, as if I'd taken a haymaker to the parietal lobe, I was emotionally broadsided. *How has this marriage survived?* The question wasn't a random musing but one of the greatest mysteries I would ever confront. For thirty-one years I have loved Renay, and she has loved me in return. Although so very different in temperament and personality, perception and belief, we have loved each other deeply enough, so far, to defy alarming odds. She sits alone at church. I sit alone outside the temple during weddings. Yet we seem to make it work.

The epiphany in assembling the surprise anniversary package was apprehending that the only thing real in my life—*really* real (metaphysics and epistemology aside)—was simply that I loved her, and that this ethereal connection was possibly the only tether grounding me all these years.

I mailed the package so it arrived before our anniversary. She called me immediately after opening it. I knew, the moment I heard her voice, that she understood what I was attempting to communicate with the contents: my astonishment, my gratitude, my joy that she loves me, and how lucky I am to be the person privileged to know her better than anyone else, even as she remains a wondrous mystery to me.

The paradox of the anniversary package for her was that the gift turned out to be mine. I would spend my anniversary alone, knowing I was never really alone.

Figure 4. Renay and Kevin Barnwell, July 2019, Silver Creek Falls, Oregon

Kevin writes, "Exploration and discovery are an integral part of our journey together. Whether we are hiking in a Sonoran Desert canyon at dusk, tide-pooling along the Pacific coastline, or watching a magical sunrise in our own backyard, finding beauty together and being a witness to each other in these moments sustain us."

PART II

Sex and Its Consequences

Figure 5. Theric and Lynsey Jepson, July 2000, Fitzgerald Marine Reserve, California

Theric writes, "Everyone's impressed by this photo, as it is very pretty. Weddings are supposed to be pretty. Which, as Lynsey points out, is to say: artificial.

"The Fitzgerald Marine Reserve is a short walk from the Half Moon Bay Ward Meetinghouse. In other words, some Sundays, when being the only girl in youth Sunday school with a bunch of obnoxious boys was too much, Lynsey would skip the last hour of meetings and come down here and commune with the wind and the waves, the sea anemones and the hermit crabs. And so, after our sealing in the Oakland Temple, we came here for photos. It's still her beach. But now, also, it's our beach."

Fertility

THERIC JEPSON

The post-op instructions tell me I should be able to go about my normal routines tomorrow. They also say I should be able to return to work in two days. And that more vigorous activity will be possible in a week. Sex is allowed in five days if I feel up to it. The five-inch-thick layer of gauze can come off in two days. I should be able to lift a bag of groceries in three or four. Exercise in a week or two. The full range of human possibility, save one, should return in a couple weeks. If not, call my doctor.

So to return to that first sentence, the post-op instructions presuppose that my normal routine is lying in bed with a bag of frozen peas on my crotch. It would be more accurate to call that my *aspirational* routine.

Having one's genitals dyed orange with iodine and then swathed in blue towels and clamped with metal clamps for maximum visibility and access is one of those things that, when the time arrives, you find you can do. The enormous, burly woman who preps me is generous, dousing my nethers with a gallon or so of stain. We have much to chat about, as I am a high school English teacher and she loved her high school English classes, reading all of *Romeo and Juliet* the night the first scene was assigned, buying her own copy of *To Kill a Mockingbird*. The doctor, in his turn, loved *Gatsby*. He started buying and reading Fitzgerald and had exhausted the complete works before leaving high school.

This is good because the only topics I can think to chat about are a bit too literal. I do learn new words like *lumen* (not the flashlight word but the inside-anatomical-tubes word) and *intra-abdominal* (not the kind of surgery I'm doing today—mine's merely intrascrotal), but sometimes the thrill of new vocabulary ain't enough.

In a way, it's a lot like visiting the dentist. My wife, Lynsey, and I find dentistry relaxing. Lie back, eyes closed, chatting optional, a professional scraping away.

Sure, sometimes it's uncomfortable, but grabbing my pants legs or clenching my toes suffices to get me through. I'm not sure how Lynsey copes. Maybe she falls back onto hypnobirthing—it worked during labor, after all. In *this* room, however (which is much like a hygienist's nook), I have no pants, and my arms are crossed on my chest. If things get uncomfortable, all I can do is put my feet under their rests and push up.

When it comes to vasectomizing, Dr. Li prefers all three methods of closure. After snipping out a quarter-inch length of each vas, he electrocutes their insides (lumen!) to cauterize (which I could feel just fine, lidocaine or no lidocaine, my body jerking on the table like a B-movie actor being brought back to life), clasps them shut with titanium clips, then folds them over upon themselves, stitching each half to itself.

Then everything gets shoved back in the tiny hole, and I get a giant stack of gauze to pad my codpiece for two days. I'm left alone in the room to wipe off some of the orange and get dressed. I've never worn a jock strap in my life, and the tighty-whiteys I bought for some unremembered purpose are unfindable, so I put on the tightest-fitting pair of garments I own—a style I haven't purchased since my mission (my no-longer-virginal genitals no longer requiring such close supervision)—pull them ALLLLL the way up, roll down the waistband, pull on my pajamas, and take baby steps into my no-more-babies future.

Because I myself am a big baby, it's only seven hours later that Lynsey feels the need to tell me, for the record, that pushing four humans out of her own tiny hole was still worse. This is nothing I deny. In fact, it's part of the reason I went under the knife today. But! She did have one advantage: I was there, feeding her ice chips and whispering koans about her motherly strength and pushing a tennis ball into the small of her back. Me, I was alone with Dr. Li. And sure, he loves Fitzgerald, but still . . .

I missed her.

And sure, I know breasts are for feeding the baby in the waiting room, but one to hold might have endorphined some of the unpleasantness away. Or a hand—I also would have accepted her hand.

We were done having babies a long time ago, Lynsey and I, the youngest of our three boys now seven. We started early so we could have a nice long empty-nest period. We filled our tiny house quickly, but since we only had boys, they fit in the one available room, stacked on top of each other. Done.

And, consciously, we *were* done. Subconsciously, however, maybe not. Prioritizing penetration over prophylactic delay is hardly the way to stop at three, after all, but if Lynsey secretly (even to herself) wanted another, who was I . . .

Holding my beloved as she wept, night after night, mourning the existence of this new thing growing inside her, I finally understood abortion. Because although she dreaded leaving our home, she was also ready to do something with her hours besides care for the children. And this thing inside her just stole those dreams away. Or at least delayed them, maybe a decade.

Not that abortion was ever on the table for us. It wasn't. And even though Lynsey lurched about motion-sick for eight months, now that Colleen's here, even though there's nowhere to put her, we are so glad.

My current stance on abortion strikes me as exceedingly Mormon, though perhaps a *Deseret News* poll would disagree. But if we can agree that certain circumstances make abortion morally sound (and the *General Handbook*, the church's official position on all things worth having an official position on, says yea), then abortion should be legal and available, full stop. Take rape: unless abortion is readily accessible, forget about rape as justification for abortion. The courts move slower than a developing fetus.

Choice may be the most sacred principle in my faith's theology. If something can ever be allowed, how dare you choose for another whether they can or cannot do it? But this isn't an essay about hot-button political topics, my fluctuating opinions on which no one cares about.

Lynsey and I were married when I was barely still twenty-three and she was barely twenty-one. This is what our parents hoped BYU would do for us, and, amazingly, it worked. I had no capacity to flirt or date and thus was doomed to live in small, dark rooms scribbling books; Lynsey had no desire to get married whatsoever, and would instead move to Manhattan and wear black and be dangerous. It took some divine intervention to get us inside the Oakland Temple and sealed, but that's another story with another angle on choice. (She's still a bit peeved at God, if you ask her about it. And who can blame her? Have you *met* me?)

If we'd met and stayed in Oakland instead of merely wedding there, likely we would have arranged a different time frame—one more in keeping with our Bay Area peers'—but being in Provo, we decided three years without kids was our longest morally defensible option. Therefore, after three years, we would start having kids and get them raised and gone before we were old. Three years five months later, Oliver was born. To look at photos, egad were we young.

We moved home to California and decided to have another baby. Our apartment complex in Lancaster was adjacent to the site of a fatal shooting the weekend before we moved in. The desert was colorless and smelled bad. We had no neighbors who were neighborly. Lynsey felt like she was in prison, while the school I worked at was designed by a builder of prisons—and looked it. Our life felt as barren as we seemed to be.

When the way opened for us to move to the Bay, we snatched at it, and Lynsey had only one period in El Cerrito before Samuel was conceived.

Fertility is a confused sign of God's favor. Mary was so favored she got knocked up sex-free. Sarah was so favored she was infertile for almost a century. In both cases: magic baby. God loves you.

* * *

Samuel's arrival wasn't the disastrous, caesarian-interrupted labor of our first go-round, but labor is intense regardless, and Lynsey still wanted an experience to match her mental image. And, happily enough, twenty-six months later Alvin's birth came only a half hour after we arrived at the hospital—a clean, simple sliding-out awash in joy and motherly success. So while pregnancy number four was miserable, Lynsey craved the high of giving birth to another child. "You are strong, you are strong," I said as the contractions hit. "You are a mother."

"I am a mother."

"Your body is doing what it was built to do."

"I am strong. I've done this before."

"You've done this before."

I knew that babies' genitals are swollen from months in the stew and that foolish fathers often misidentify girls as boys, but I still made that error in the quarter second I saw our baby before she was taken away so they could double-check her color. Less than a minute later, Lynsey held her on her chest, high on motherdom. It was ten minutes before anyone discovered we thought she was a boy.

A girl. Us? After three boys? Is such a thing even possible?

We wept.

This secondary miracle making the moment even more joyous.

We were told when Samuel was born not to let older siblings first see their fresh sibling held by their shared mother. Let Mom hold the older child as Dad introduces baby. It seemed to help. But when the boys arrived from Grandma's four days later, it hardly seemed to matter which of us held Colleen. They said hi to Mom as I brought Colleen in from the back room and—it doesn't matter. Her much older brothers aren't interested in competing with her for Mom's love and affection. They're interested in providing their own love and affection.

We now have an oldest child, a middle child, a youngest child, and an only child—one of each. And by the time she is the age of the youngest, he'll be her only brother left at home.

As we stopped for lunch on the way home from the hospital today and I was telling Lynsey about having my balls electrocuted, she was generously filled with remorse for not taking prevention upon herself. But that's nonsense, of course. Snip-snip (correction: snip-snip-snip-snip) (hypercorrection: stab-stab-slice-snip-snip-snip-snip-bzz-bzz-clamp-clamp-doublestitch) might take—*gasp*—

two weeks to recover from, but my body has not yet accepted (nor ever will) equal consequences for our reproduction—and it would have been grotesquely unfair to postpartumly douse my beloved in hormones we wouldn't accept in a cheeseburger or to thrust a strange device into a womb that deserves ennobling retirement after building the four children we now have, one two three and one.

So. Farewell, seed without number. I've no doubt we would have loved you. But our house is finite, and another pregnancy might kill us, since we would never kill you.

Opposites

ROBERT RALEIGH

They say that opposites attract, and that trite wisdom was certainly true in the case of my connection to Juanita. I met her at "B-Y-Woo," where marriage was sort of always in the air and where an unmarried returned missionary was an offense to all that was right and true. Juanita was in my Biology 100 class, one of those giant gen ed classes in a huge lecture hall. I spotted her the first day and was instantly attracted to her, but I couldn't imagine actually meeting her—I was much too shy for that. I proceeded to admire her. From afar, which was my MO when it came to romance.

A few weeks into the semester, the professor assigned a reading held on reserve in the library. When I went to do the reading, I found, to my pleasure and consternation, that the dark-eyed beauty from class was there in the library. I picked up the reading at the reserve desk and, summoning all my courage, sat across from her at a table. It was a perfect opportunity to speak to her—but I didn't say a word. I found her astonishingly gregarious, enthusiastically greeting friends and acquaintances, despite the fact that libraries are supposed to be quiet. I finished the reading and left without speaking to her.

Not long afterward, shortly before biology class was supposed to start, I spotted her in the bookstore chatting with someone. By some miracle (which I afterward attributed to the influence of the Holy Ghost), I somehow mustered enough courage to speak to her. I don't remember what I said, but it was something about biology. She was infectiously bright and cheerful and friendly. I was still in shock at having actually spoken to a pretty girl, so I summoned more courage and walked with her to class. We exchanged names—hers was Juanita—and minor information about each other. I followed her into the classroom and sat down beside her. She looked at me with surprise. "What are you doing?" she asked.

"Class," I said. "I'm in this class."

She burst out laughing. "Oh! I thought you were just telling me that you had biology, not that you were in my biology class."

We had a good laugh. Afterward, having paid little attention to the lecture but emboldened by how well things had gone after I spoke to the prettiest girl in the class, I did something wildly uncharacteristic: I asked for her phone number. Actually, according to her, I didn't ask: I *told her* to give me her number. She always teased me about this. She liked to joke that I gave her no choice in the matter, so she had to comply. Shortly afterward I called her, and we began dating.

Juanita, I soon learned, came from circumstances very different from mine. I grew up in a fairly typical middle-class Mormon family, with a dad who worked a 9-to-5 job and a stay-at-home mom. I led a tame, stable life, going to church, going to school, watching *Gilligan's Island*, playing Dungeons and Dragons, getting good grades. In my house, contention was of the devil.

Juanita grew up in Mexico, the oldest child of five, with four brothers. Her mother left when Juanita was only eight. Consequently, her father, Henry, moved the family to Los Angeles so they could stay with one of his sisters. Henry was a janitor at the University of California, Los Angeles, so the family lived on very little, even though they lived near UCLA in a nice part of town. Juanita was expected to take on many of the responsibilities abandoned by her mother, cooking and cleaning and doing laundry for her father and brothers. Her brothers were constantly in trouble; eventually the older three joined a West Los Angeles gang, Sotel 13. By the time I met Juanita, one of her brothers, Marcelino, was in prison for attempted murder. The oldest boy, Henry Jr., had also done time in one of California's maximum-security prisons.

Juanita, for her part, found stability in two things: the Mormon Church, which she joined when she was fourteen, and her friend and lifelong mentor, Marilyn, a do-gooder in the finest sense of the term. Though Marilyn never had any children of her own, she helped mentor many children over the years, taking them camping and to museums, helping them stay out of trouble, and eventually helping many of them get to college. With Marilyn's help, Juanita attended Ricks College (now BYU-Idaho). Partway through, she went on a mission, where she told people she was part of Jesus Christ's gang, and she would flash a J and a C as gang signs. Since Ricks was then only a two-year school, she eventually transferred to BYU to finish her degree in Spanish education.

Juanita was a whirlwind of enthusiasm and energy. She knew many people on campus, and if she saw one of them, she would shout out a greeting, no matter how far away they were. Eventually she became the first president of the BYU Mexican American Students Club. In contrast, I was serious and much more solitary. It's not that I didn't have friends, but I favored having only a few very close friends who were, like me, deeply curious, intense, and voracious readers, absorbing information and using it to question everything, including our most fundamental beliefs. We spent many hours discussing human nature, philosophy, critical theory, feminism, history, science, politics, psychology, sociology, anthropology, and, of course, religion. To me, it was a rich, intense, wonderful experience. While Juanita appreciated our interest and enthusiasm, she found our discussions dry and pedantic. She preferred to joke and laugh and dance with her friends.

While dating, we broke up, or nearly broke up, repeatedly. One thing that didn't waver, though, was our physical attraction. We loved making out and did so frequently. We were hopelessly attracted and unable to stay broken up for long. The solution? Get married, of course.

When it came to marriage, I was of (at least) two minds. On the one hand, I believed in something like soul mates. At fourteen, I'd been in a production of *Saturday's Warrior*, a Mormon musical performed frequently for LDS communities throughout the West in the 1970s. Its storyline about people who love each other in the preexistence and then finally cross paths on Earth penetrated deep into my psyche.

Always running contrary to the idea of the foreordained love of my life so cherished in Mormon popular culture was the advice I heard repeatedly from the prophet, at that time Spencer W. Kimball: the very idea of soul mates is a fallacy. Any two people doing their best to live the gospel can find a happy life together.

The question I've asked myself many times in the intervening years is: Why did I marry Juanita? At the time, I believed I was doing the right thing. (President Kimball also spoke frequently about the evils of delaying marriage.) However unlikely Juanita and I seemed as a couple, surely the prophet must be right, and we would find happiness if we just did our best to live according to the precepts of the gospel. I greatly admired Juanita for her astonishing courage and persistence. Getting into college at all, for someone from her background, was no small feat. Gutting it out, night after night, through years of studying that were such torture spoke well of her character. Wasn't admiration at the very least fertile ground for love? Also, I persuaded myself that we complemented one another. She could learn from my studious, serious ways, and I could learn from her extroverted enthusiasm. We had so much to teach each other!

In hindsight, I realize that our choice to get married was mostly about sex. When you're doing your best to be a faithful Mormon, dating has two possible outcomes: breaking up or getting married. Only one of these outcomes leads to sex (at least if you intend to abide by the commandments). At the time, despite our many differences, it felt as though we were on a raft being carried on Lust River to the brink of a waterfall, Sex Falls, and were powerless to stop. Going over the falls would be a complete disaster. So I decided to ask Juanita to marry me before disaster could strike.

I realized right away that I had a big problem: my religious beliefs had morphed into a kind of Mormon version of Catholic Revolution Theology, which meant that, among other things, I was deeply antimaterialistic. There was one aspect of Mormon marriage culture I despised: the diamond engagement ring. In what way did a ridiculously expensive shiny rock signify love, and how could this idea possibly square with the teachings of the Bible and the Book of Mormon as I understood them? One of our mutual friends, though, was aghast at my plan to propose without giving Juanita a diamond. The friend told me she had been wooed by a rich older man who had given her a diamond ring and that she had rejected the man but kept the ring. She convinced me to take that ring and give it to Juanita. I was dubious, but she insisted, and eventually I gave in. Juanita enthusiastically agreed when I proposed. We barely managed to avoid crossing whatever lines would have forced us to postpone the temple marriage, though with the greatest difficulty.

We were married in the Manti Temple. I remember feeling dazed the day of the wedding, as if the experience were happening to someone else and I were merely a bystander. In the fine tradition of Mormons without means, we had our reception in the cultural hall of a Mormon church. Juanita arranged for the decorations, but I was in charge of the music. I created a slideshow of our history together set to Louis Armstrong and Ella Fitzgerald singing about the pronunciation of potatoes and tomatoes. Someone asked, "Why would you use a song called 'Let's Call the Whole Thing Off' for your wedding reception?" I patiently explained: if you listen to the whole song, at the end they decide that what they better call off was the idea of ending their relationship. It was a song about people unsuited for each other who stay together because they can't bear to break up, and it probably describes a lot of couples.

We moved into a rickety fifty-foot trailer in Springville, just south of Provo. This trailer had, the previous year, been the home of the experiment in communitarian living my friends and I had undertaken. Faced with finding housing, we had asked ourselves: Why not move in together and pool our funds, in the style of the United Order, a communitarian principle expounded by Joseph Smith? There were three men and a woman, and it was against the rules, of course, for single people of the opposite sex to live together while attending BYU, but we viewed such rules as pharisaical. We even all slept in the same room, though none of us was sexually active. These were my serious, bookish, counterculture friends, the same people with whom I had started a small literary journal to publish essays on subjects like feminism and anarcho-syndicalism. These are the same people with whom I would later start a leftist/feminist/literary bookstore and coffee shop in Orem.

These were the same people who would pose one of the biggest obstacles to my new marriage. Not because any of them actively interfered. They initially found my choice of marriage partners dubious, and they told me as much, but once I made my choice, they were all supportive. It was Juanita who struggled with their presence in my life. Why did I spend so much time talking to them instead of to her? Why didn't I talk to her about whatever it was I was always talking to them about? Why did I need these people in my life in the first place? Shouldn't she be enough?

What I didn't realize then but understand better now is that we come to most experiences with numerous expectations, many of which are hidden, even from ourselves. We like to believe that we come to new experiences willing to learn and adapt, and though this may be true in theory, we've likely accumulated a lifetime's worth of expectations. Marriage, of all the social institutions, is probably one of the strongest examples of this tendency. We may think we come to marriage with open hearts and a desire to compromise. In fact, we've spent a lifetime, however short to that point, watching our parents, watching our relatives and friends' parents, watching movies and TV shows and reading books, listening to talks in church, and talking to friends, all of which have filled our heads with notions about marriage, what it means, how it functions. How could it be otherwise? Maybe some people are more aware of their own expectations, but unfortunately I was not, and I believe that Juanita was no more aware than I of the emotional landscape we were navigating, so much of it submerged beneath the surface of our consciousness.

Juanita imagined us as an indivisible couple joined for all purposes and at all times when we weren't separated by responsibilities, not just physically but mentally and spiritually as well. I figured getting married wouldn't change my life that much, except that I'd live with a woman and we'd get to have sex. She would be one of my circle of friends, but by no means did I intend to give up my burgeoning intellectual life, in which my friends played key roles.

In response to her complaints about not sharing that side of myself with her, I made a game effort to bring her up to speed. Before you can have certain discussions about Nietzsche, you must understand a long and meandering thread of philosophical thought beginning with Plato, progressing through Aquinas and Descartes and Hume and Kant, among others. I tried to talk to Juanita about the basics of philosophy, the groundwork of intellectual history that I found so stimulating. She sincerely tried, but like most people, she found philosophy insufferably tedious, the very definition of pedantry, bearing no relation to everyday life.

She also did her best to educate me: she wanted me to stop being such a stick-in-the mud, to relax and enjoy life and our new relationship. Why did I refuse to hold her hand or kiss her in public? Why was I embarrassed by her loud voice and her shouts across campus to her friends? Why, when we were at a party with her Latino friends, was I so shy about meeting people or dancing or having a good time? How had I lived so long and never learned to enjoy myself? I admit that at the time, I was not a very good pupil.

Perhaps strangest of all, to me anyway, was that despite the throes of passion we couldn't escape when we were dating, it turned out that we had a pretty miserable sex life. Somehow we weren't able to connect in ways satisfying to either of us. Our failure was probably a product of our ignorance. At the time I believed that sex is just something you do—not something you learn. My experience to that point had been one of nearly unceasing libido, a constant companion, the *other* still small voice, from which there was no surcease. Shouldn't it follow, then, that sex would simply happen, that at the exact moment that the difficult and awkward barrier of chastity was removed, and sex became not just acceptable but ordained by God, the force of desire would simply overtake us both, leading to unremitting, yet holy, delight?

Through our first few years of marriage, I think we both honestly tried to look past our differences, to muddle through our problems as best we could. We hadn't yet learned to understand what caused the not infrequent explosions between us, but we were also both willing, after each stressful fight, to forgive. Again with the benefit of hindsight, I think that despite my willingness to forgive, I wasn't as good as she was at forgetting. I could forgive, and I was a patient person, but the fights wore me down. I think this was related to our different temperaments. She was someone of extreme moods, very happy when she was happy, very angry when she was angry. It wasn't uncommon when she was angry for things to get thrown and possibly broken. But for her, just as fast as the storm rolled in and the lightning flashed, once she had unburdened herself of whatever internal pressures had been building, she became a sunny day and forgot all about the tempest we'd just undergone. I was someone who prided myself in staying steadfast, moderating the extremes. Juanita would sometimes chide me for my forbearance. Why couldn't I just yell a little and get my resentments out of my system rather than holding them inside me, where they would eat at me like poison? Part of me saw the wisdom of her approach, but part of me held back and resented that her peace was earned at my expense. It felt sometimes as though we were negotiating a trade treaty but using different currencies and without any idea, or with very different ideas, of the exchange rate.

Though I had tried for years to adapt my view of Mormonism, to make it more flexible and less literal, it was increasingly obvious that I just couldn't square my own views of right and wrong with both the doctrines and culture of Mormonism. I couldn't accept that God would have excluded Blacks from having the priesthood and would continue to exclude women. I hated the soft Calvinism that Mormons believed, equating righteousness with financial success. The questions multiplied, but answers did not.

After Juanita and I had been together about four years, I awoke one Sunday morning and realized that my attempts to stay in the Mormon Church, despite my many misgivings, had reached their end. The thought of going to church that morning made me physically ill. I'd known people who'd given up their belief but kept dragging themselves to meetings every Sunday, who pretended something they didn't feel and hid themselves from relatives, friends, and sometimes even spouses. I was determined not to go down that road. I told Juanita that I was done. Though she knew about my many doubts and problems with both LDS doctrine and culture, I think she always expected that I would pull through, because rejecting one's fundamental belief system is difficult to even contemplate.

Though my choice to stop attending or participating in the Mormon Church hurt our relationship, we did our best to adapt. She kept going to church. She said it was very hard, being there without me. She felt that people pitied her, and she couldn't stand this thought. She had also known people whose spouses left the church, and sometimes it caused them to stop going or even lose their testimonies. As much as I didn't want to be the person who keeps going and fakes it, she didn't want to be the person who lets her spouse drag her away from what she strongly believed to be right.

For obvious reasons, she was hurt and confused. I, on the other hand, felt ebullient, as though I'd been given a great gift. In addition to getting a significant amount of time and energy—not to mention 10 percent of my income—back to do with as I pleased, what made me the happiest was that I could stop experiencing such intense cognitive dissonance. I didn't have to keep the peace between warring parts of my brain. For the first time in several years, I experienced the most fundamental meaning of the word *integrity*: the state of being whole and undivided. I felt at peace. Or at least I did for a while.

I soon realized, far more than when I simply had doubts and questions, that everything that had previously been the foundation of my thinking, my most basic notions of right and wrong, was now up in the air. What did I really believe? What really mattered to me? It was an exhilarating thought, but also frightening.

I no longer accepted, or at least I seriously doubted, the existence of any kind of divinity or even any force or power that might order the universe. It made sense to me, however, that respect for one's fellow beings, for life itself, allowed the multitude of living things on our planet to coexist with the greatest chance of mutual happiness. Something like the Golden Rule seemed crucial to me to any ordered system of morality. Just as I didn't want to suffer, why should I not wish for maximal happiness and minimal sufferings for my fellow travelers?

One key item of my previous belief system, however, began to crumble, and it set off alarm bells for Juanita: I was no longer sure I wanted to have kids, not just in the short term, but possibly ever. It seemed presumptuous to me to bring children into the world. For starters, we live in a world fast running out of resources, quite possibly headed toward any variety of human-caused catastrophes: environmental crisis; famine on a scale never experienced before, due to our poor inability to distribute resources equitably in a world with ever greater numbers of people; or even the unthinkable: nuclear war. In other words, I had become one of the people mocked in *Saturday's Warrior*, blocking spirits from getting to Earth to fulfill God's plan. Furthermore, I was prone to depression and other health problems, and I hated the idea of inflicting these problems on hypothetical children, who never asked to be born. Juanita was six years older than I and already thirty when we got married. She worried about how much longer she would be able to have children and was unmoved by my compassion for the planet and my hypothetical children. She wanted kids more than anything else she had ever wanted in her life.

The question of whether to have kids was not the only issue that came between us, but it was the biggest, the one we couldn't talk our way through or around, no matter how hard we tried. Even with that chasm between us, we didn't give up but kept trying to find a place of compassion and compromise. Eventually, though, it became too much, and these new differences, combined with the many we had already faced, caused us both to stop believing we could make each other happy. While we were on a vacation to California (staying with her friend and mentor, Marilyn), the huge and growing cognitive dissonance I was experiencing finally boiled over. As we went to bed that night, I suggested that maybe we had made a mistake and that we would be happier apart.

She was devastated. Even though we'd had plenty of fights, I think that up to that point, she had assumed they were just storms that would pass like the weather, with sunnier days ahead. "How could you do this to me?" she asked.

"I'm not saying it definitely needs to happen, but I think we should seriously consider whether we'd be happier apart," I replied. "We have such different goals." We kept up a brooding and ever more depressing conversation all the way home, including when we stopped briefly at Yosemite. After a particularly dark conversation, she left to be by herself, and she threw the diamond ring I had given her into the Yosemite River.

No matter how amicable, divorce is deeply painful. One builds one's life and identity around the choice to get married. Even though we both agreed it was for the best, it was impossible, for me at least, to avoid feeling like a failure. Whatever our differences, it felt like tearing away part of myself. Because we had no assets and no children, we didn't get attorneys. We agreed that I would help her financially until she got on her feet. The divorce became final not long after her graduation, and she got a teaching job right away in Price, a couple of hours south of Provo. We talked regularly, seeing each other sometimes. We managed to do that rarest of things among divorced couples: we stayed friends—not just nominally but actually. We kept talking, we kept visiting.

Within a year, Juanita began dating a man named Kimball, though his friends called him Kim. Their relationship progressed quickly, and they soon married. I was thrilled for Juanita. However, I was surprised to find out that Kim, though he had been raised LDS, wasn't active. Juanita, for reasons she never tried to explain to me, also stopped going to church. Kim did possess the one thing that I had lacked, though: he wanted to have kids as soon as possible. Not long after they married, Juanita and Kim had a son, Mason.

Our friendship changed after that. It never went away, but we talked only three or four times a year and then, as the years passed, maybe a couple of times a year. I visited her a few times in her new house and met both Kim and Mason, and she also visited me from time to time.

After several years had passed, around Thanksgiving, Juanita called to say that she and Kim had decided to get active in the church again. Mason was eight, and they'd recently baptized him. They also wanted to get married in the temple and be sealed as a family. "The bishop said that for us to get married in the temple, I have to get permission from you for a temple divorce," she told me.

"You're kidding," I said.

"Nope."

It seemed ridiculous that she needed my permission, but I didn't want to interfere with her happiness. On the other hand, I also didn't want to go to the trouble of writing a letter, printing it, signing it, and mailing it. "Could I send an email?" I asked. It was still a newish technology.

"Um, I can ask," she said.

Her bishop didn't like the idea of my giving my consent by email but eventually relented. I sent a brief email granting my permission to nullify the marriage that ended years before. Juanita told me that she and Kim planned to be sealed as soon as the permissions came through and that they were excited to have Mason sealed to them. I wished her well.

About three weeks later, shortly before Christmas, I got a call from one of her brothers. Apparently Juanita, Kim, and Mason had gone to hear the Mormon Tabernacle Choir on Temple Square. On the way home, Kim lost control of their SUV and crashed head-on into another vehicle, after which their SUV went up in flames. I don't know whether they died in the collision or in the fire, but none of them was alive by the time rescue workers reached them. The most likely explanation for the crash is that Kim fell asleep at the wheel. After a long day visiting Salt Lake, probably they were all sleepy.

What does it mean to lose to death someone you've already lost to divorce? My grief was difficult to articulate and impossible to quantify. Divorce is supposed to be a kind of final separation, a severing of all that once tied two people together. Of course, it's never anything so simple. Despite our separation, I had never stopped loving Juanita or valuing whatever role she was willing to play in my life. Her death changed nothing about my day-to-day life, but the world felt different without her in it. I was happy for her that she had found happiness with Kim and Mason. I wanted nothing more than for her to find the fulfillment that she and I had been unable to bring to each other, so it broke my heart that all this had been lost.

Because it was an entire family and, I suppose, because they had recently become active again and intended to marry in the temple soon, a high church official was invited to speak and preside at their funeral. According to the *General Handbook*, which contains the rules that govern how local Mormon congregations should be run, funerals are to be considered, first and foremost, "an important opportunity to teach the gospel and testify of the plan of salvation" and, only secondarily, "an opportunity to pay tribute to the deceased." Consequently, the usual order of things at Mormon funerals is to start with people who knew the deceased well and then move up the chain of authority, saving the person with the greatest authority but who typically knows the least about the deceased to give the final message. This funeral followed that pattern. The first speaker was a little girl, Mason's best friend, who talked about the things she and Mason loved to do. As I remember, one of Kim's relatives spoke next. The final speaker, the general authority, who had never met Juanita, Kim, or Mason, spoke in general terms about the Plan of Salvation, the Mormon blueprint for getting into the highest degree of glory in the celestial kingdom. At the gravesite, where the graves were sealed, Juanita's brothers waved me up to stand with the family, a kindness that exemplified her brothers and spoke well of her role as their substitute mother.

I no longer believe in God or the celestial kingdom. I don't believe that the righteous are rewarded or the wicked punished in this life or the next. I don't believe there's an afterlife, that some immaterial part of us, a spirit, survives our deaths. I'm not arrogant enough, however, to believe that I have anything approaching certain knowledge about such mysteries. I would love for there to be an afterlife, and if there is an afterlife, I sincerely hope that Juanita and Kim and Mason are together somewhere, happy, living out the lives stolen from them in this world by such cruel and random misfortune.

Eternity in an Hour

BOYD JAY PETERSEN

"Before the trip, I want to come out to Boyd." I read the words again and again. Inadvertently, my wife, Zina, had left the email addressed to her psychologist open on the family computer. "Classic Freud," I said to no one. "Zina's unconscious desires winning out over her rational efforts to keep this information secreted away." But as the words on the computer screen sank in, something repressed in *my* life was coming to light. I felt disoriented and disconnected, like I was watching myself from across the room. Was I angry? Was I sad? Nothing registered. I didn't know what to feel. My marriage's history played out before me, so much making sense for the first time: All the girl crushes Zina had poured herself into, leaving me feeling jealous and alone. The wall I felt between us. The increasingly infrequent sex. My pent-up and occasionally explosive anger from feeling neglected and lonely. How had I not seen this sooner? How blind could I have been? How could she have hidden it from me? How long had she hidden it from herself?

I finally understood why she had just quit her tenured position at BYU, a financially suicidal move, since she was in her early fifties. I knew she was unhappy teaching there—especially since the church's November 2015 policy declaring gay couples apostates and barring their children from baptism—but I knew many other professors who were also unhappy with the policy, and they weren't resigning their jobs. Now I realized just how impossible it must have been for her to teach at a school where gay people must remain invisible.

I also understood why she had been less than enthusiastic about our upcoming two-week trip to England and Scotland, a trip to celebrate our thirty-three-year marriage and to visit literary sites we both taught about in our college English courses. I understood why she'd given me a lame excuse when I'd found her crying a few nights back. The email described her sadness after a woman she had loved dumped her. My wife was suffering from a broken heart.

My heartbreak was just beginning.

* * *

My mind buzzed. What should I do next? Confront Zina? Wait for her to say something? Could I hide my new knowledge from her? And what about our marriage? Our future? Our children's future? I needed to talk to someone, and I knew that my friend and colleague Dave would be up for lunch. Minutes after I discovered that life-changing email, we talked over fish tacos.

"It's sort of funny, Dave," I said. "I used to joke about all my midlife crises— buying the guitar, the boat, the truck. I would joke about how they were cheaper than having an affair or deciding I'm gay, like some friends had done. I had no idea that those words would come back on me with such a vengeance."

"Yeah, the gods love to mess with you when you say shit like that," Dave agreed.

"The weird thing is that I'm not angry. If she'd been having an affair with a man, I'd be furious, and the marriage would be over instantly, but this is different. I don't know whether it's because it's who she *is* and not what she's *done* or what. Maybe I'm just in denial."

"Probably denial," Dave said matter-of-factly.

"Yeah, probably. I just don't know why this didn't come out sooner. How could she not have known?"

"Well, this is typical midlife crisis stuff," said Dave. "You wake up and find your life half over and realize you want something you haven't got."

"Yeah, but it's not exactly the same." I paused, trying to put my finger on what *was* different. "In my midlife crises, I confronted the fact that my career didn't go the way it was supposed to and that I didn't have the life I thought I'd have. She woke up and accepted who she really is, what she has always been." I picked up a taco, then set it down without taking a bite. "The good news is that I'm waking up and realizing that our rocky relationship wasn't my fault, that it wasn't because I've been a shitty husband."

"Hey, now, her being gay doesn't mean you weren't a shitty husband. They aren't mutually exclusive," Dave joked.

"Well, thanks, buddy."

"What are friends for?" he asked, grinning.

"I just can't believe I didn't see this coming. Looking back, it all seems so obvious. How did I not *see* this?"

"You can't blame yourself. We're all blind to what we don't want to see. But I can't say *I'm* really surprised."

I stared at Dave a moment, nonplussed at his comment. How had he known something I was so blind to? "What do you mean, you're not surprised?"

Dave shrugged and looked pensively at me. "Well, I just got this vibe." Then his tone shifted back to sarcasm. "She does fit the stereotype, though—short hair, intellectual, feminist. And she has horrible taste in men." Dave laughed.

"Yeah, right, asshole," I said with mock indignation. It was comforting to engage in our usual friendly banter of insults and put-downs even during this crisis. It gave me something constant to hold on to. "I do wish you'd said something, though."

"What would I have said? 'Boyd, your wife looks and acts like a lesbian'? I'm sure that would have gone over well."

"Yeah, OK. So what do I do now?" I asked. "I can't unlearn this. And I don't think I can act like I don't know it when I'm around her. But I just don't know whether I'm ready to have this conversation with her."

"You've *got* to tell her that you saw that email. You just have to. And you have to do it before you leave," said David.

"She'll be pissed that I was snooping."

"Look, that's the least of your troubles. You just don't want to have a big breakup in England. That could get ugly. Just get it over with. You can always cancel the trip, but you don't want to get over there and have this huge fight. That could be a disaster. Just do it."

* * *

That night, as Zina climbed into bed, I pulled her close beside me. I had tried to talk with her earlier that day, but we never had a moment alone, and I didn't want my teenage sons around when I did, so I postponed until bedtime.

"So you don't seem all that excited to go to England," I began. "We don't have to go, you know. We could cancel, and they'd refund most of our money, if you want to stay home."

"No, I really want to go," Zina said. "I've just been distracted."

I'd hoped that the possibility of canceling might prompt her to speak up, like she said she wanted to in her email. But when she didn't say anything more, I took a deep breath and said, "You left your email open on the computer downstairs. I saw the message to your shrink."

Zina began crying softly. I held her close to reassure her.

"Look, I'm not mad, I'm not angry, I'm not going anywhere. Let's just go on this trip and have a good time, and we can decide about the marriage after we get back." This prompted full-throated sobs.

"I'm so sorry," Zina said. "I'm so so so sorry." Her voice trembled. "I'm so so so so sorry."

"No, look, I'm just sorry that you've had to keep this secret for all these years. This isn't something you've done; it's who you are. And it explains so much about our marriage."

My wife's tears soaked my shoulder. "I'm so terribly sorry," she said again and again.

* * *

I stood by the door to Canterbury Cathedral's cloister near where St. Thomas Becket met his grisly death in 1170. Thomas had been appointed archbishop of Canterbury by his best friend, Henry II, who wanted his lackey running the church. However, Thomas shocked Henry by taking the religious appointment seriously. Enraged by Thomas's commitment to his own spiritual vows and his refusal to simply accede to political directives, Henry had allegedly demanded, "Will no one rid me of this turbulent priest?" So a few knights obligingly hacked off Thomas's head. The king later paid penance for the murder, insisting he had never wanted his friend assassinated, and Thomas became a saint. But Thomas was dead nonetheless. The site of Thomas's martyrdom is marked by a haunting sculpture depicting the knights' swords, with reddened tips, hovering menacingly over an isolated altar. I remembered the altar in the Salt Lake Temple where Zina and I had kneeled, joined hands, and made our marriage covenant. That ceremony's words and those of the fateful email that would cleave my marriage apart swirled in my head and bore down on me: "for time and all eternity," "come out to Boyd."

I hoped we could somehow save our marriage, but the possibility was slipping away. It was agonizing. But even as the emotional pain of that awareness became excruciating, my relationship with Zina was, surprisingly, better than ever. The trip gave us uninterrupted time to talk, and we found emotional tenderness in each other's pain. Over time, a wall had emerged between us, separated by a secret too painful to admit. For years, Zina fought to ignore her sexuality even as she grew more frustrated by the lack of emotional intimacy in our marriage. For years, I felt she resented me and hated sex, which frustrated me. I kept trying to give her what she wanted, but I couldn't. She kept trying to give herself to me, but she couldn't. In the end, we lived isolated, lonely lives, more like roommates than husband and wife.

But as Mormons we had committed to giving ourselves to each other "for time and all eternity." Anyone can be married for time, the church tells us, but only by living righteous lives and being sealed in the Lord's house can we be married forever and have our children born in a sacred covenant of eternal togetherness. Zina and I had committed to this; we would be steadfast and unswerving. Forever. As the years wore on, I no longer focused on a happy present, but I was doggedly determined to have a happy future. We would stay together despite our unfulfilled desires. We would sacrifice present happiness for future joy. And now I saw that future falling away. A sword was falling on my turbulent eternal marriage.

* * *

We walked on Dover's pebbled beach, the famed castle, safeguarding England from invaders since the eleventh century, perched atop the white cliffs above us. On a clear day, France is visible from these beaches. Zina began reciting Matthew Arnold's famous poem: "The sea is calm tonight. / The tide is full, the moon lies fair / Upon the straits."

"How long have you known?" I asked Zina.

"I think I always knew. But it just didn't fit the Mormon paradigm. There was no place for it. It wasn't a secret in the sense that I knew it but couldn't speak it; it was a secret I knew but didn't allow myself to *know*." Her words trailed off to silence.

"So it was unconscious?" I asked.

"Not exactly." Her eyebrows furrowed. "I was aware of the desires and images in my head. I was just revolted by them. In high school I made out fiercely with boys in an effort to squash them down."

"And you made out fiercely with me," I said. I smiled, remembering how our younger selves had repeatedly pushed the boundaries of Mormon virtue. Our make-out sessions were often followed by guilt and resolve to do better, though eventually we always succumbed again. We made it to our temple wedding as virgins only in the technical sense of the word. I felt guilt about these "sins" for years, but from my fifties looking back, they seemed so sweet, so normal. Now I wondered if there were signs of Zina's sexuality that I missed even then. True, there was passion in those early years, but I did have a vexing sense that something was *off*.

"I thought marriage to you might fix me," Zina said as if reading my mind. "But I could never be there for you. I've never been there with you when having sex."

"Yeah, I see that now. I always thought it was my fault. That I wasn't good enough or handsome enough or kind enough."

We both spoke calmly, kindly, without anger or resentment, while trying to make sense of our marriage.

"Well, I did blame you," Zina said softly. "I blamed you but couldn't allow myself to finish the thought—for not being a woman."

The calm ocean waves filled the silence as Zina's words registered. We were at a turning point in our lives—thirty-three years of denial and pain and frustration were turning to wreckage on the shore of this new reality. What could we salvage from them?

"Why now? Why did you recognize it now? Why so suddenly . . . ?"

"It wasn't sudden. It's been growing since my sex drive changed with menopause. Menopause just forced me to see how thoroughly I had compartmentalized my desires."

"And this is the reason you left BYU . . ."

"I had to leave BYU," Zina admitted with resignation and bitterness. "I will never be able to do and be what they want. I want to come out of the closet. I don't want to have to hide who I am any longer."

"I get it now," I said. "But I sure as hell didn't when you told me. I thought it was nuts to quit your job in your fifties."

"I really thought for a long time that I could navigate BYU. I thought I could be a refuge for gay students. I came out to a few. I admitted that I was queer or bisexual. I thought they could look up to me as someone who accepted who I am and was still in a faithful temple marriage. But I just can't be Mormon anymore. They don't want me."

I sat down on a rock while Zina continued walking, examining pebbles strewn along the shore. I thought of Matthew Arnold walking this beach during his 1851 honeymoon. I remembered my own honeymoon. It should have been a sign to me: our car broke down five hours outside of town, and my parents had to rescue us. I also realized that the soundtrack to our engagement was breakup albums: we were constantly playing Billy Joel's *Innocent Man*, composed following his first divorce, or Paul Simon's *Hearts and Bones*, his homage to his failed relationship with Carrie Fisher. Arnold's plea to his wife rent me with agony:

> Ah, love, let us be true
> To one another! for the world, which seems
> To lie before us like a land of dreams,
> So various, so beautiful, so new,
> Hath really neither joy, nor love, nor light,
> Nor certitude, nor peace, nor help for pain.

* * *

The train to Whitby ambled along the lush Esk Valley toward the seaside town in North Yorkshire. A fine English mist engulfed us. The passing farms and woods were quintessential British countryside. Despite its association with *Dracula*, Whitby is a charming town, with boats in the harbor and quaint cottages clustered along the hills surrounding the bay. On the eastern cliffs is an abbey. Established in the seventh century, it was destroyed in 1540 during the Dissolution of the Monasteries after Henry VIII broke with the Roman Church.

There's a romantic beauty to the ruins and the lush green lawns. I wandered around the abbey's crumbling walls taking photographs—the mist creating an eerie fog—but was quickly drawn to the nearby graveyard of the Church of St. Mary. With no new burials for over a century, the tombstones are weathered and neglected. On the far side of the church stands a large stone Celtic cross erected to the memory of the mid-sixth-century poet St. Cædmon, known today as "the father of English sacred song." His famous hymn about God's creation of the world is inscribed on the monument.

Creation and destruction, life and death, beauty and dread, seduction and horror all began to merge in my mind, just as they do in *Dracula*. With Dracula's bite on the neck, he offers eternal life—or rather waking death. You don't need Freud to recognize Dracula as an erotic character. Dracula merges seduction and annihilation.

I know the seduction of death. Since childhood, I've suffered from depression and have periodically thought of suicide. But suicidal thoughts are not only about the desire to retreat from life's miseries; they're also about the desire—an erotically charged desire—*for* death. Only once before, after a particularly bad time in my life—the death of my father and collapse of my career expectations—have suicidal thoughts become serious enough that I planned out my death. Antidepressants usually help, but during that time none were sufficient.

Now my situation was worse. Foolishly, a few months prior to our trip, I had discontinued my meds altogether. It was a beautiful spring, I had a trip to look forward to, and life was good, so I slowly tapered off the medications to give myself a break—that way they would work better when I needed them. Unfortunately, I hadn't thought about needing them on this trip. I began to sink into a deep depression, and by morning I was contemplating—no, longing for—suicide.

After Whitby, we boarded a high-speed train for Scotland. The train was packed, so we were forced to stand by the door. I slowly began to inch down a window near where I was leaning. I couldn't climb all the way out the window, but I could easily get my head out and into the path of an oncoming train. It would feel so good to die. I wanted to be free of the pain, and death was inviting me, wooing me. Just then, I felt my phone buzz in my pocket. A glance revealed an instant message from a stranger. It turned out to be Mike, a man from an online (mostly Mormon) straight spouses support group I'd joined just before I left the States. For some reason, Mike reached out to me at that moment. His life paralleled mine in many ways; he was in a similar situation with his wife but further along in the process. We chatted for the remainder of the train ride, about an hour and a half. Grace, pure and simple.

* * *

Edinburgh was an essential stop on our literary tour through Britain primarily because of my interest in Robert Louis Stevenson, author of *The Strange Case of Dr. Jekyll and Mr. Hyde*. The novel was inspired by Deacon Brodie, a respectable citizen, cabinetmaker, locksmith, and town councilman by day. By night, however, he burglarized the houses of the wealthy people for whom he made locks during the day, then spent the money gambling, drinking, and bedding two mistresses—neither of whom knew of the other—with whom he fathered five children. His dual identities eventually caught up with him, and he was hanged in 1788.

What interests me about *Jekyll and Hyde* is how it thematizes human duality. All of us have a shadow, something we try to keep hidden from the world. My shadow was rage. As a lesbian married to a man, Zina couldn't possibly love me fully, couldn't be passionate about our relationship, couldn't be fully present during sex, and couldn't bond in any deeply romantic way. In my twenties through forties, I grew more and more resentful the longer we went without sex. But when we finally had sex, I often felt she was just taking care of my needs rather than making love—I felt I was being "serviced." So I felt guilt and shame for wanting sex. I hated myself for needing sex. I resented Zina for not needing sex. And this would lead to more guilt and shame and self-loathing, which would often erupt into bursts of anger that scared my wife and my children and made me feel even worse.

However, it wasn't the infrequency of sex that made our marriage difficult. It was the lack of attachment. Zina could not look deep into my eyes, touch my face, be with me in a romantic way. And this made me feel inadequate and unlovable and alone. I weathered three decades in the dark about the source of my rage. I always assumed the problem was me. Feeling so isolated and disconnected, I closed myself off—ignoring Zina, not listening to her, acting indifferent to her needs. This made her feel alone and unloved and resentful. As we got older, we settled in. My sex drive dropped as I reached my fifties, and I invested my energy in my career. Our lives became a smoother road of lowered expectations and disappointment.

* * *

The next stop on our tour was Liverpool. A lifelong Beatles fan, I had to do the pilgrimage to their hometown. As Zina and I wandered around town, my dreary mood contrasted sharply with the beautiful weather and cheery sights.

"So what does this change about us?" I asked Zina. I wanted to keep the intimacy we had so recently discovered, but I knew nothing could ever be the same. "I mean, we've lived together for thirty-three years. Can't we make it work for the remaining . . . what? . . . twenty or thirty?"

"Why *should* this change anything?" Zina replied with a sharpness that surprised me. "Because I want to be gay and not Mormon. And I want you to be straight and Mormon. I want to find a woman to love before I die. I want you to date; I want you to marry and give your love to a woman who is not a guilt-soaked lesbian." The anger in her voice trailed off into resignation.

"So you don't love me? Have you ever loved me?"

"I *do* love you. You've shaped my life. And we have children together. We're a family. But we aren't a marriage, not now—and we never really were."

"You want a divorce?"

"Look, let's not talk about divorce. Let's call it a 'release.' I want to release you from the 'calling' of being married to a gay person—with a sustaining vote of thanks," she said, employing the language Mormon leaders use when publicly releasing a church member from their teaching or leadership duties. "I regret that some good things are over, but I'm also relieved that some weird and deeply sad things are over too."

"So what *do* you want?"

"I want to wait for the boys to get launched—to finish high school and get settled—and then I want to get out of Utah. Then we can go our separate ways. But in the meantime, I want you to date. I want you to get what you can't get from me somewhere else."

I thought about what she was saying. Our youngest children were sixteen and fourteen and would be living with us for at least another three or four years. More likely seven or eight. And I knew Zina didn't want to wait to start her new life, to find a replacement for the woman who dumped her. I also knew that I couldn't do an open marriage, not emotionally, not practically, and not spiritually. I couldn't live with the jealousy. I couldn't endure the pain of seeing her with someone else. And I couldn't possibly start a relationship with someone else until our marriage was over.

"I can't date until I'm divorced. Remember, you want me to stay Mormon."

Zina remained silent.

"Can you simply keep the possibility of us staying together an option? Is there any way we can make it work?"

"I think you're asking too much from me," Zina said.

"Asking too much from *her*?" I thought angrily. "What's she asking of *me*? What's she asking of our *children*?" This was the moment. Then and there, I knew that divorce was inevitable, that it would be sooner rather than later.

My stomach seized up. My head hurt. My chest tightened. I felt more alone than ever. Dr. Jekyll sought a potion to release his shadow and maintain his respectability. I was in no mood to be respectable. I simply wanted release. I wanted a potion that would numb the pain. Fast. Instantly. That night in Liverpool I downed an entire bottle of wine and three mini-bottles of whiskey. Mormons don't drink, and I had little experience with alcohol, so I shouldn't have been surprised that I spent the night in the bathroom intermittently heaving over the toilet and moaning on the cold tile floor. It was a hard lesson. But it did keep my mind off the emotional pain.

* * *

We returned to London the next day. I had one final pilgrimage to make: to the grave of poet, printmaker, and visionary William Blake, whom I had studied in grad school. Blake created his own mythology, adapting tropes from other myths and synthesizing them into something that expressed his unique theology. Blake's mythic narrative has been described as gnostic. For example, he saw the Garden of Eden's serpent as humanity's benefactor, urging Adam and Eve toward knowledge, whereas the creator god who tried to hold them back Blake considered the true demonic force. He summed up his differences with orthodox Christianity: "Both read the Bible day and night, / But thou read'st black where I read white."

Mormons likewise read the creation narrative in gnostic ways, positing a fortunate fall: God intended that Adam and Eve eat the fruit so they could understand joy and pain. Tragically, they could only appreciate the bounty and beauty of Eden after they had been kicked out. I felt this same tragic irony about my marriage. During the trip, Zina and I were able to talk honestly and openly for the first time. All the defenses and resentment vanished with the knowledge of their ultimate cause. After thirty-three years, we found emotional intimacy as we realized we were breaking up. We could only look back at Eden and mourn its loss.

Blake was buried in Bunhill Fields, a cemetery primarily for those who didn't conform to the Church of England's teachings and practices. Blake did not fit in. Neither do gay people in the Mormon Church. Church leaders once urged gays to marry straight spouses and spoke of homosexuality as an ugly and repugnant sin. In the 1970s, BYU psychologists used aversion therapy, attempting to shock gay people straight. Today the church insists that "same-sex attraction" is not a sin, but any sex outside of heterosexual marriage is a sin "next to murder." Church leaders contend that the same standards apply to both homosexuals and heterosexuals. However, a heterosexual individual can anticipate or hope for marriage, even if their chances are limited. Homosexual individuals who want to remain in the church must live a lonely life of celibacy or enter a risky heterosexual marriage, where a straight spouse and children often become collateral damage. Mormon children rarely grow up imagining any paradigm for their lives besides the heterosexual nuclear family model; instead, they typically squash feelings that don't conform. Many queer kids eventually crack. Some attempt suicide. Utah has one of the highest suicide rates in the nation. It's the eighth-leading cause of death in Utah overall and the leading cause of death for kids age ten to seventeen. Many queer people grow weary of living a lie or living alone and end up leaving the church and often their families.

* * *

When we returned from England, my children could tell that something was up, but I felt it was Zina's right to tell them. It was awkward around friends and family too. Attending church alone became the most painful thing I did all week. Church members knew something was up but were afraid to ask, and I couldn't have told them if they had. I had moved into the closet with Zina. Eventually, she began to come out, first to close friends and then to family. Neighbors and people we went to church with would find out through the grapevine. I filed for divorce a month after we returned. We each began dating.

After the divorce, my now ex-wife and I wanted to let our friends know that they didn't need to take sides, that this was truly an amicable divorce. So we planned a party to celebrate a new era, our third act. We decided to have a ritual, a reversal of a wedding ceremony, to honor our lives together—and our new lives apart. We each brought a girlfriend to the party. A mutual friend, Jerilyn, officiated the ritual. She began by asking us to release the other as spouse and to "promise to honor and respect the love, tenderness, hard work, and kindness" we had enjoyed throughout our marriage. Then Jerilyn asked us to make vows to the friends gathered with us. We dutifully said: "We promise to never ask any of you to choose sides. We promise to not make things awkward when we're all in the same place. We promise to not talk shit about each other." The audience laughed, and several attendees shouted, "Amen!" Jerilyn then asked everyone to vow that they would "honor and respect our diverging paths and not talk shit about us."

"I've been thinking a lot about eternal marriage lately," I began when it was my turn to make individual vows, "because that's what I signed up for. By the standards of my church, this would be a failed marriage. But this has *not* been a failed marriage. It was a hard marriage," I said, choking back tears. "But it was an incredibly productive marriage. Zina and I have accomplished many great things together, raising four amazing children and surviving four graduate degrees. We also created many great things. Zina was my editor and proofreader. She was my color consultant, since I'm color-blind, and she only messed with my color blindness a few times. She was my go-to source for medieval history, as well as my travel companion to Europe. Plus I am who I am today because of her. We married when we were youngsters. I was twenty two and Zina was only nineteen. We grew up together. We shaped each other's lives. So as I've thought about eternal marriage, I remembered that Joseph Smith once redefined the concept of 'eternal punishment' as 'God's punishment' (D&C 19:11), since 'eternal' is one of God's names. I like to think of my marriage as eternal in that sense: it taught and nurtured us in Godlike ways.

"So here's what you can expect and hold me to as we part ways," I said, transitioning to my "antivows": "I promise to teach my boys fifth-grade humor, to belch loud and proud. I promise to take them fishing and lie about how many we released, to spend too much money at Christmas, to be Zina's coparent and friend as we continue to raise our wonderful children into wonderful adults."

Zina read her vows. "Boyd, I promise to slip and refer to you as 'honey' in front of your girlfriend, fiancée, and eventually wife, because thirty-three years don't wear off easily. But I promise to catch myself and try to make it look ironic or super gay. I promise to swear under my breath about the patriarchy and the November policy that made me an apostate, and you won't have to run damage control, because I'm no longer your wife." Zina choked up as she continued. "I promise to allow you to have your life and relationships as fully and blissfully as you possibly can. I promise to share what you invite me to share, and no more. And I promise to allow you to share in my new life but not to burden you with old griefs and sorrows. For to paraphrase Joseph Smith, 'Come, dear husband, since our marriage is past, for friends at first, are friends again at last.'" The audience held a respectful silence as Zina and I amicably shook hands.

Jerilyn asked us to face each other and raise our right hands. We repeated after her: "As you have given yourself to me for thirty-three years, I release you. While our journey together is over, my love for you continues this day and forever more."

"Now slap those hands together in a high five," Jerilyn said. "Zina and Boyd, inasmuch as you have decided to peace the heck out of matrimony, have promised your love and respect for each other's paths by exchanging these vows and these high fives, I now declare you divorced with all the benefits and privileges the law allows.

"Ladies and gentlemen, I present to you the uncoupled, Zina and Boyd," Jerilyn concluded. The audience erupted in cheers.

* * *

William Blake challenged us "To see a World in a Grain of Sand / And a Heaven in a Wild Flower / Hold Infinity in the palm of your hand / And Eternity in an hour." The idea of capturing the infinite—of finding an eternity in an hour—seems impossible. But the truth is that we do experience eternity with each passing hour. Within each hour there are sixty minutes, and within each minute there are sixty seconds, and within each second there are a thousand milliseconds. Within each of these milliseconds there are microseconds, which can be divided into nanoseconds, and so on. Scientists recently discovered the zeptosecond, or a trillionth of a billionth of a second. Eternity *does* exist in a single hour. By putting my emphasis on a future happiness and ignoring the present, I squandered many eternities. Now I'm trying to live in the present, an eternal present, and not letting some future promise get in the way of experiencing an eternity of joy.

Pie Month

SCOTT RUSSELL MORRIS

Pesto Chicken and Artichoke

Because we love pie, Kirsten and I always celebrate Pi Day: March 14 (3/14, or 3.14). But because 3/14 could also designate all of March 2014, and because Pi or Pie Month happens only once every hundred years, I decided we should have pie every day that month. Once Kirsten sort of agreed, I added that I didn't mean leftovers. "We can't do this halfway. Only once in a century!" I said. We stood in front of the fridge, where so many such conversations happen. "We have to have a new pie every day."

So on the first of March 2014, while Kirsten and I were visiting Seattle, she searched Pike Place Market for fish, as any self-respecting foodie would, and I looked for pie. She returned with sushi, and I came back with a pesto chicken and artichoke pasty from a bagel stand—a fancy bagel stand, because this was Pike Place.

Key Lime and Peach-Raspberry

When God served up punishment after Adam and Eve partook of the forbidden fruit, there was a clear indication of the relationship Adam would have with the world. He would toil for food. He would till the ground 'til returning to it. By the sweat of his face he would eat his bread. "Thorns and thistles," the Lord said. "In sorrow shalt thou eat." Of course, it's hard to think of sorrow when eating pie, though we did consider the increase in butter we would need for the experiment, a direct ding to an already thin budget and our increasing waistlines.

There was sorrow elsewhere, if you backtracked far enough. Most of our butter-buying income came from Kirsten, an eighth-grade history teacher. It was a job she'd started a few months prior, mid–school year, because the previous teacher had walked out, literally, leaving her things behind. Kirsten's students were that bad and proud of it. This followed a year of teaching in Kazakhstan, where Kirsten's responsibilities had reduced her to tears several times, and prior to that—our first year of marriage—she'd also hated her teaching job in Utah.

I always felt a little guilty because I loved my job, even in Kazakhstan, where we worked for the same school and where I managed to stay low-key, low-responsibility while administrators seemed to gang up on Kirsten. But I did feel the pressure of Adam's call to work. "By divine design," states the Proclamation on the Family, "fathers are . . . to provide the necessities of life." I was not yet a father—we'd been trying since we returned from Kazakhstan, but to no avail. My job was currently just a part-time grad-student gig at Texas Tech in Lubbock. Feeling I could do more, I looked elsewhere for work and started teaching online for another university so I could provide a few more necessities. Like, say, more pie.

Sausage, Tomato, and Cheese

In Kazakhstan, we learned a Russian adage: "You never ruin the porridge with butter." This is also true of savory pies and cheese.

I thought of this as I rummaged through our kitchen the third night of Pie Month. We'd returned to Lubbock from Seattle the night before. Kirsten had the car, and I needed to leave for class when she returned. There had to be pie on the table; I had to use what was on hand. Luckily, making up recipes on the spot is my forte, an ancestral trait perhaps, as my mother had a name for it: leftover surprise. I pulled things out of the fridge and got to mixing. Cheddar, mozzarella, feta whipped with egg, poured into red ramekins with spicy sausage and sun-dried tomatoes.

When she returned home, tired and hungry, Kirsten was surprised to find I'd made a dinner that smelled so nice, perhaps because I had a lot of work to do after a weekend away. But cooking, like most arts, is best done while procrastinating. Another aphorism, this one James Richardson: "All work is the avoidance of harder work." Or perhaps Kirsten was surprised because the pies looked quite nice, the red ramekins highlighting the warm tones of the cheese and tomatoes, browned and crusty.

Kirsten said it was the best pie she'd ever had. Unfortunately, by the time Pie Month ended, Kirsten still said this was the best she'd ever had.

Apple Walnut

We'd just bought our first house, an Eden we didn't know how to tend.

Our fathers provided examples of handymanness, especially her father, Brad, an architect. We were always hearing about new projects, each more luxurious than the last. For example, Brad had recently built a covered deck in his back-yard. It was perfect, each detail something you'd see in *Sunset* magazine, the company my father worked for most of my childhood, which meant that our house was filled with glossy images of domestic style, models of perfect homes and gardens. However, like my mother, I was more concerned with *Sunset's* cookbooks than with our house's design or upkeep.

My father-in-law had volunteered to knock out our dining room wall to install a sliding door into the backyard. It wouldn't be trouble, he said, because he already needed to deliver the shelf he'd designed for the antique player-piano rolls Kirsten inherited from her mother.

Kirsten and I discussed her parents' upcoming trip as we shared the day's slice: store-bought, shelled in molded plastic, too small, too sweet. We were hoping for good news to share when her parents visited, to have ultrasound pictures to hang on the fridge, something more than what she normally told them over the phone: "We're still trying."

But even if she was a few weeks along in the summer, odds were Kirsten would be out helping her dad or grilling the steaks while I'd be in the kitchen, chopping greens for the Caesar salad. But as we sat in the grocery store café, sharing pie, there was no indication that her "condition" would be an issue.

Mac 'n' Cheese Pie

I was taught to believe in a historical Eden. Though my father didn't doubt the story's allegorical or symbolic nature, there was no doubt in his telling that Adam and Eve actually lived, actually fell, went from premortal to mortal. The science of the issue is muddy, especially for a church that doesn't shun evolution. In introductory biology and science classes at BYU, professors distribute pack-ets—fuzzy from generations of photocopying—of quotes from church leaders discussing and disagreeing on issues around evolutionary science, including theories of pre-Adamites. The main emphasis of the packet: you can be an evolutionist, but Adam was real, even if we don't know when, exactly, the Fall happened in the fossil record.

We cannot forget Adam and Eve, because their story is the key to Mormon culture. It's their story we see in the temple ceremonies, the highest form of worship. During that presentation, we're told to "consider yourselves as if you were respectively Adam and Eve."

Their basic story—disobedience, punishment, struggle, repentance, and then redemption—is easy enough to see in myself. Were there not two characters but one, were the punishments for Adam and Eve exactly the same, were the changes of culture over time clearly shown in the telling, I would have no trouble considering myself Adam and Eve. It's the *respectively* that vexes me.

Eve takes the brunt of the rub, and as feminists who want to believe but aren't sure of the story's full significance, Kirsten and I take issue.

Cauliflower Pie with Potato Crust

If we are to believe the Lord's grammar—with so many murky years of translation—then Adam's sin was not just that he ate of the fruit but that he did so after hearkening unto Eve. Which is to say, you can read his punishment coming because he followed the woman. Which exacerbates the story's misogyny. Adam will sweat, will work, work, die. His pain is all of the body. But for Eve, sorrow. Sorrow multiplied in labor and conception. It isn't just the different bodily punishments here, which are clearly the most mythological, but the stating of order. Adam must follow the Lord, but Eve must follow Adam. Why? We don't know, but we reread Genesis that month, asking ourselves why. Because Adam follows the rules when the snake tempts him, because Adam is being reminded that he is in charge, because men wrote the story?

And so her husband will rule over her. And, to make things worse, will, on occasion, feed her potato crust that tastes like dictionary pages and fill it with vegetable mash too salty to be truly desirable. The only saving grace will be the cheese, plentifully applied.

Four-Berry Ice Cream Pie

A few weeks previous, our furnace gave out on the second coldest night of winter, which was followed by the coldest night, 13°F, cold enough to freeze the kitchen pipes. We thought it was just the pilot light, an easy fix, though Kirsten looked up instructions online before we attempted it because no one wants to accidentally blow up a house—especially a new house. But it wouldn't light, and we were 90 percent sure we did it right. She called her brother for advice. I called a repair company, who said they could come the following Monday. By then, we envisioned, all our pipes would have burst, and we would be bundled in arctic gear, cuddling under the covers to prevent hypothermia.

I sent an email to the men's group at church asking to borrow space heaters. A man we didn't know volunteered to take a look. Turned out he once owned a heating and air conditioning company and kept saying, "This is fun."

Ten dollars for a broken part and an hour later, the heat was back on, leaving me with the song "Come On Baby, Light My Fire" stuck in my head, which was particularly ironic and disturbing because the week the fire gave out was the same week Kirsten recommended we up our chances for conception by using an app that tracked her ovulation, telling us the optimal time for sex, a schedule so precise that I had been unable to perform all week, despite suggestions it was the best time.

And the problem lingered.

Mormon Mocha Mousse

Because Kirsten was away visiting her sister in Colorado, I took the day off from writing, grading, and reading to bake pies. I purchased vanilla wafers for crumb crusts and eggs, cream, and chocolate for custards and mousses. I knew we would eventually have work we couldn't avoid, days with no time for messes in the kitchen, so I stocked the freezer with ready-to-go pastries. I pressed butter and crushed wafers into miniature disposable tins. I rolled out traditional pie dough, not much more than flour, salt, and shortening. Then, in a chaos of bowls, I mixed the fillings. Salted caramel banana, turkey potpies, curried apple and mushroom, mango float, apple cheddar. All would wait for Kirsten.

On the phone that night, Kirsten assured me she'd kept the pact; she'd eaten pizza for lunch. I told her about the pies, and she made me promise to save her a bite of the Mormon mocha—chocolate flavored with Pero, a roasted barley powder, instead of espresso. This is one of her favorite pies; I should have waited to serve it. But it was the one I wanted. I also wanted her to appreciate my versatility. On some level, I knew Pie Month was about showing how clever I was coming up with all these new pies, which meant I needed to save these other pies for nights when she could be suitably impressed.

But I didn't feel clever at all as I spooned the mocha mousse straight from the tin, my not-thin belly resting against the faux-wood countertop, alone in the house, selfishly feeling a little betrayed that she'd go anywhere during Pie Month. Then I wiped the cookie crumbs into my palms, washed my hands, and went to bed.

Mango Float

Kirsten was convinced my impotence was only temporary. "I never should have told you about the schedule app," she said.

Just because I'm a man doesn't mean I'm oblivious to the ovarian cycle. I know when her period is, know that the fertile window comes two weeks later. I didn't need the app to point out the calendar. Still, somehow talking about the ideal time made the whole thing seem insurmountable. Though I don't consider myself a stressed person, it seemed my to-do list for school and work, the deadlines, and this new deadline were all just too much for the little guy. I didn't want to believe that potential fatherhood was stressful. I felt completely fine with the idea. If I had doubts, they hadn't registered. A baby was the next step in our life together.

So, more worried than I let on to Kirsten, I went to the Internet, which said that though erectile dysfunction is associated with emotional stress, it's much more commonly a physical malady. It could be diabetes, WebMD said, cautioning me to worry if I felt excessively thirsty or had to pee often, which I then did every time I had to pee or needed water. I've always been one to drink a lot of water, though. Maybe that meant I'd had diabetes a long time and never realized it? And then, when we tried to make love and I had the smallest inclination to pee first, I worried again.

Burrito Pie

Traditional Christian rhetoric paints Eve as the great sinner, the enticer, the one who lost us Paradise forever.

But as we reread Genesis during Pie Month, we had questions, mostly Kirsten, who posited them to me from the couch with the Bible in her lap while I layered tortillas with beans and cheese: "How could she sin if she didn't yet know the difference between good and evil?"

She asked again while I served burrito pie on our blue-and-white plates, which she'd been collecting since before we were married: "The serpent, always dealing in halves and pieces, spoke the truth when he said they would become like the gods, knowing good and evil. So was Eve tricked or did she see the truth for what it was and seek to know light from darkness, pleasure from pain, transgression followed by the joy of redemption?"

As we picked at leftover mango float: "What I really don't understand is what that means for us. Eve was told to follow Adam, but 'they twain shall be one flesh.' 'Neither is the man without the woman, neither the woman without the man.' Am I supposed to follow you? Because that doesn't feel right either."

"I don't know that I want to lead, or to be the one in charge," I said as we cleaned up. "Do you feel like we're unequal?"

"No, and thank you for that."

Oatmeal Creme Pie

Kirsten texted me at lunchtime to say she'd bought an oatmeal creme pie for a snack and would prefer a light dinner.

I had already bought oatmeal creme pies, knowing they're Kirsten's favorite junk snack and knowing they would be fun on a day we didn't have time to cook. I'd hidden them on the top shelf of the pantry, behind the herbal teas, too high for Kirsten to see.

I took down the little packages and ate mine alone, standing at the counter, having never considered before that one could be miserable while eating childhood treats.

How now to spend the afternoon I'd scheduled for pie? "Perhaps I'll actually write that book review," I thought, "or grade a few more papers."

I really just wanted to make pie.

Curried Apple and Mushroom

Why did I want to make pie? Because I wanted to be productive. Pie was a *product*—tangible, sensory—of my creativity, something to show for my effort. I also thought I might write an essay, but that takes months, years. Pie can be done in a few hours. I could grade papers, but there's no satisfaction there. I wanted something to mold with my hands.

Writing, grading, cooking: these are the things I think to do when bored. Things not on that list: making the bed, putting in another load of laundry, mopping the floor, mowing the lawn. All things Kirsten would rather I did than make pie. I suppose in this way, I'm guilty of being that man who supports women in the workplace but still expects them to do the chores. So many conversations start with Kirsten saying, "I know you cleaned the kitchen, and I'm grateful, but there's more to the house than that." Then she worries about filling that horrible stereotype of the nag, and I feel guilty for needing the reminder, ever the absentminded and slovenly husband. We're uncomfortable with these roles but keep playing them out, the weakness of one edging up against the insecurity of the other.

When we started Pie Month, we worried that we would grow bored with pie, that we would fill up on desserts, or that hurried crusts with lame fillings would be our norm. When I say *we*, I really mean Kirsten, who was understandably wary of the experiment from the beginning. I, ever enthusiastic, was confident I could make something gourmet every time.

So I felt I'd failed when Kirsten lost interest.

As I write this, Kirsten worries that this essay makes her appear unsupportive, the killjoy to my boundless enthusiasm. But I worry that I'm passionate about things that don't matter, that my silly whims are forced on her. That I should put my energy into something lasting, or at least helpful.

Maple Pumpkin with Walnuts

Doubt about my enthusiasm isn't new; we almost broke up over it.

We sat in the dark on the concrete steps of my duplex. Kirsten explained where she felt our relationship wasn't enough. There were many small things, but they all came down to her feeling like I cared too much, just not for her. She asked why I couldn't be as enthusiastic for her as I was about my other interests: squirrels, essays, obscure holidays. She asked why all I ever did was invite her over for meals.

I told her: "You're the only one I ever cook for. Maybe I'll get better at it, but this is how I say I care for you."

Our worries continue: I keep cooking. She enjoys it, and I enjoy it, but we both know it isn't everything.

Caramel Apple

One of our running jokes, from when we were dating, is that Kirsten and I will tell each other, "I love you like _____." The first expression was "I love you like pizza" because, for reasons I don't quite remember, I yelled this out the window as a pizza delivery man drove by. But because of our love for pastries, this morphed into "I love you like butter." When we lived in Kazakhstan, far from the ocean, we said *sushi*. When Kirsten makes her caramel apple pie, I say *pie*.

"The pie makes you love me?" she asked. "Does it make you want to make love to me?"

"Yes," I replied, "but before we eat it; afterward, I'll be too full."

Salted Caramel Banana Freezer Pie

The most difficult part of foreplay became not knowing where it would lead. After kissing, caressing, moving our hands over each other, I'd feel aroused, have all the same sensations I had when I'd been healthy, but there would be no physical manifestation. I imagine it may have been something like the experience of amputees with phantom limbs.

Those tender preludes to sex, always pleasurable whether coy or brash, were now fraught, uncertain, unproductive. Whether I or Kirsten pulled away first, embarrassed for having tried, I felt ashamed for not living up to the task. If she reassured me that it was fine, I knew she was feeling generous; if she silently rolled over and tucked herself deeper into the covers, I knew she thought it was her, as though she'd done something wrong. Some nights I would press my body against hers by way of apology; some nights I turned too, and we slept back-to-back.

Pie Shakes

Pie was an important part of our courtship. We frequented Sammy's for pie shakes, a milkshake with a slice of pie dumped in. Also, the first Pi Day after we met, Kirsten told me she was going to make a pie for the pie party I was hosting. I didn't have high expectations for her pie. Not that I thought she was a bad cook, but she seemed skeptical of the pie party idea and only announced that she'd decided to make a pie at the last minute. Plus her sister was visiting, so I figured they had other ways to occupy themselves.

She appeared with a raspberry and cream pie with a large Π baked across the top. It was easily the most beautiful pie at the event and one of the most delicious.

I had made an asparagus potpie that oozed green roux and sat uneaten.

This was not the first time Kirsten surprised me with her baking skills. Our first date was to an art exhibit and lecture about bees. After the lecture, eager to prolong the evening, I suggested we get a dessert with honey in it.

"I can make baklava," she said.

So we drove to the store, and she picked out the phyllo dough, nuts, and honey. At my place, she showed me how to lay out the dough a few sheets at a time, brushing on the butter and then the nut-sugar mixture, layer after layer, pouring the honey glaze after it had all been assembled. It would be months before she realized how sexy that was, but that night we stayed up way too late, chatting on the concrete steps outside my duplex, the porch light shining down on us.

Shepherd's Pie

Concerned about my manhood, I begin taking precautions, all pulled from websites or common sense developed from no experience whatsoever. I already walked two miles to work, but I walked faster to increase my circulation. I stopped crossing my legs when sitting. I drank more water. I snacked on nuts and dark chocolate. I researched herbal remedies and bought a mix called Male Power, which was guaranteed to get my libido up and which I thought of as the "sex pills," the same joking name I had for Kirsten's birth control, though she hadn't taken that since we returned from Kazakhstan. When my pills arrived, I kept them hidden in my desk. But after only a few days, I was more ashamed of hiding them than what they meant, so I put them in the same place she kept her prenatal vitamins.

Bean and Cheese Empanadas

The night of the empanadas, I told a coworker about Pie Month. It was a chat-room meeting for my online job, so I couldn't read her facial expressions, but she seemed impressed.

"How fun," she wrote. "Your wife must really be taking care of you."

If the message hadn't been typed, the silence would have been awkward.

I explained that I was the one making the pies. The woman seemed surprised to learn that a man could cook. Or maybe she was amazed that a man *would* cook. Maybe it's unfair, but when a woman expresses surprise about my cooking, I assume her husband is unhelpful around the house, just sits on the couch watching sports while the babies cry. Really, I fear this about myself, that all I do is clean up my own kitchen messes.

A few days later, Kirsten posted a picture on Facebook of the fish tacos I made for dinner, and a friend said, "I'm jealous. Of your dinner. Not your husband. Unless he cooked it alone."

Perhaps it's conceited of me to say so, but the "alone" is comical. I didn't grow up to expect a man not to cook. I learned as much about the kitchen from my father as from my mother, and my brothers and sisters are equally capable with a skillet. My little brother baked more than ten cakes for our wedding reception, most of them from Julia Child's *Mastering the Art of French Cooking*.

I often prided myself when people made such comments. But then again—though I was teaching at two universities, trying to write more, trying to keep up with grading, doing most of the reading for my classes, occasionally taking out the trash without being asked, and never feeling keen about the lines society draws for household duties—when people expressed surprise about finding me in the kitchen, I was just as likely to think they were really saying, "Shouldn't you be doing something else right now?"

Lemon Meringue

We wanted chickens. Ostensibly, they were for the humanely sourced eggs, but there was some nostalgia there, too. Kirsten had hens as a child, and I, having successfully cultivated zucchini in ages past, considered myself something of an urban homesteader.

During Pie Month, we were still in the planning stages:

Kirsten researched how to build a coop.

I investigated which breeds lay colorful eggs.

Frito Pie

When we moved to West Texas, we visited the gynecologist together. It was almost seven months since Kirsten's emergency surgery in Kazakhstan, where doctors who did not speak our language removed a fist-sized tumor from her uterus. One nurse told Kirsten she would never have children. Countless others told her to stop crying. Our surgeon told us in accented English that she had "golden hands," waving them like a witch's incantation over Kirsten's sewn-up belly, and said everything would be fine. Six months and we'd be good to go.

The American gynecologist didn't even ask to look at the scar, but Kirsten insisted. The doctor poked it and smiled approvingly. She asked a few questions about how Kirsten was feeling—fine, no more pain. So the doctor said we were free to start trying for children. As we left, she said, "Have fun."

Little Debbie Snack Pies

We decided we wanted children on I-70, just east of the Colorado border, where the hills are green in late summer and the Rockies' full height purples the horizon. We were driving to visit her parents, our engagement still recent. We talked about waiting a few years, but not too many. We talked numbers: just two or three children, even though both of us come from typically large Mormon families. We knew we'd feel pressure to have more.

"We'll take them one at a time," I said.

We didn't talk about why we wanted kids. For both of us, it was a natural desire. But even then, before we knew there would be issues, before we knew about the surgery, about my impotence, Kirsten was practical enough to ask: "What if we can't have kids?"

We talked about that again as the difficulties arose, with childlessness becoming a foreseeable future. But the condition was so recent, adoption bureaucracy so thick, our time in Texas so impermanent.

"It'll pass," she assured me.

Mushroom Quiche

After a lazy Sunday afternoon nap, I woke to the smell of sautéing onions and mushrooms. Buttery crust.

"It was really easy," Kirsten said. "I'd make this again." She told me she even improvised, something I don't see her do much. "We didn't have dry mustard, so I used turmeric."

Six carefully placed spinach leaves broiled on the top. She hadn't mentioned the conception app in over a week.

Apple Cheddar

The Internet ads were the worst part. Because of my searches and the "sex pill" purchase, the sidebars pictured men in striped boxers sitting on the edges of beds, faces buried in hands, women in white negligees looking rejected or sympathetically sad behind them. I saw myself over and over in the clickbait: always wounded or wounding Kirsten.

"I know," I wanted to say. "Don't show me the problem. Offer solutions."

Pear and Pesto Pizza

One chilly morning, we built a garden bed. We measured and marked an outline with string and sticks, then built a gray brick bed in the spindly grass. We did the math together, calculating the cubic feet of dirt we'd need to fill the bed.

I learned to build gardens when I was young, one of the few handy skills I picked up from my father. As the seventh child, I came into the world when my parents were already established, when they'd already become suburban. We moved a few times, always into newer houses. The bare yards needed landscaping. With my father's guidance, I made dirt lots into something you'd want to look at. While I'm clueless with wires, screws, or hammers, I can, with some confidence, stack landscape bricks. I can lay sod and build paths through it. I can make the tomatoes fruit and the mint spread.

Even so, despite double-checking, we underestimated by more than half the amount of soil we needed. I made three trips to the store to haul enough dirt.

Angel Pie with Custard and Mixed Fruit

Besides not eating from the fruit of the tree in the garden, the only other commandment Adam and Eve had was to multiply and replenish the earth. Tend the garden. Make babies. Be fruitful. Don't eat that fruit.

Many traditions teach that had they not fallen, we'd be walking in the garden with God, not toiling for bread.

But Mormons don't see it that way. If Eve hadn't eaten the fruit, if Adam hadn't followed her, the two of them, ignorant of pain and progress, would be childless. The two commandments were contradictory: either stay, innocent and naive, or leave and populate the world. Eve chose, breaking one rule to follow a higher. Adam followed, knowing Eve couldn't do it alone. The temple presentation also teaches that the Fall necessitated Christ's condescension, making it something to celebrate.

"But why give contradictory commandments, then?" Kirsten asked, as has anyone who's thought about the story for more than a few minutes.

There are lots of Sunday school answers but no satisfying ones. I do know this: God let Eve make her own choices, even when she didn't know anything.

The Veggiepotamus Artisanal Pizza

Maybe a more relevant question was what the contradiction meant for us. What were we to choose? What do we choose when having children seemed not to be a choice?

Eve chose wisdom.

Adam chose Eve.

Pecan Pie with Cinnamon Swirl Crust

This one we made together. Kirsten rolled out the crust, sprinkled cinnamon, pressed the pinwheels to the plate, carefully arranged every twist. When we're cooking together, Kirsten does the technically difficult detail work. I made the filling, going heavy on pecans and spices. Kirsten placed each nut individually in a spiral on the top.

Everyone Liked this pie on Facebook. People were impressed by the crust. People asked for the recipe. But it wasn't worth the hype. We've made better. But those aren't the parts you share on Facebook; you just pass the links around and pretend everything is how you want it.

Fresh Berries with Cream and Custard

Kirsten's book club asked if she was getting tired of pie. She said yes and told me so later, as we stood before the freezer door, too sugar-sick to eat a whole slice, just taking a spoonful each to say we'd done it.

With a bit of guilt in her voice, she said, "Pie used to be a treat."

Welsh Pasties

My grandma Morris—a southern belle—learned to make pasties from her Welsh mother-in-law. They're peasant food: ground beef, potatoes, onions, salt, a pat of butter in a simple crust. My great-great-grandfathers took pasties with them into the quarries. As a child, I helped my grandma fill the pasties after she prepared the dough. Grandma served each pasty with a cabbage relish she called "corn pickle," a recipe I've improved on, adding garlic and bell peppers to the corn, cabbage, and onions.

Someday, I hope, I will have children and grandchildren to teach this recipe to. We'll eat pasties for family gatherings, for birthdays and wedding lunches, for graduations and extended visits. And when they ask me how to make the crust I will say what my grandma told me: "It's just like pie crust, but you add less shortening."

Sweet Potato Hand Pies

Sometimes, Kirsten asked, "What do you think is wrong?" and sometimes she just said, "Don't worry." Though I did worry, about everything: being a father and husband, writing papers, planning lessons, putting pie on the table. Would Kirsten think my lackluster performance meant I wasn't attracted to her? She told me she worried about that, too, that with her work making her more stressed, being a little depressed, her weight going up—all that pie—she wouldn't be surprised if I didn't like her anymore.

"Lots of men have these sorts of problems," I said, mostly to reassure her that it was just physical. I knew attraction wasn't the issue. But not knowing what the real issue was, I doubted my own conviction even there.

"I know," she said, snuggling close, the sheets pulled up to hide our nakedness. "It's just a little speed bump."

She meant it in all seriousness, to reassure me. But I started laughing at the word *little* and couldn't stop.

Rocky Road Mousse

The last day of Pie Month, and neither of us wanted pie. Purely to say we did it, we each took a bite, obligatorily nibbling the chocolate, marshmallows, and pecans.

Though we felt glutted from too much dessert, we looked at Pie Month and called it good. We had conquered it together.

Still, it was hard to feel entirely pleased with ourselves as we stood in our kitchen, the windows out to the garden black. Kirsten's job was busier and harder; she wanted to quit. She came home crying most nights. She wanted to be the one to make dinner but didn't want to take that away from me. My semester was winding up, getting busier and busier, as it always did. We hungered for good news to share. But, more full than satisfied, we returned the remains of the pie to the freezer and went to bed.

The Highest

T. KAY BROWNING

"I have something for you," my mission president said in his soft Spanish. He reached into his desk and withdrew a small manila envelope, the smallest there is, just big enough for a matchbox or some business cards. He passed it across the table and indicated that I should open it.

Inside was a hard piece of plastic folded along a hinge into a credit-card-sized rectangle. One side bore a scripture, the other an image of the Buenos Aires Temple, which I had visited just once, on my first day in Argentina, before a long bus ride to Mendoza, on the other side of the country. I recognized the bit of plastic immediately: it was a sleeve for a temple recommend.

The temple recommend is a small piece of paper stating your name and a few other points of information. Signed by your bishop and stake president or, in this case, your mission president, the recommend represents the most significant badge of honor a Mormon can possess. We'd just finished a worthiness interview, with questions about my chastity and my willingness to pay a tithing on my (very hypothetical) future income and a commitment to following the Word of Wisdom's dietary restrictions. This slip of paper, which the president had just filled out, was handed to me to slide into the clear sleeve of the holder's bottom half.

He recited Doctrine and Covenants 131:1-2 from memory, a translation of the original English: "In the celestial glory there are three heavens or degrees; And in order to obtain the highest, a man must enter into this order of the priesthood, [meaning the new and everlasting covenant of marriage]." "Alcanzando el más alto," with its sense of "striving to reach the highest" rather than the more mundane "to obtain" of the original English, was plastered over mission materials and sung in mission meetings. I'm certain that some of the other missionaries figured out where the motto had come from, but it was different enough from the English that I was pleasantly surprised to realize the motto's hidden meaning pointing to missionaries' next stage in life.

I ended my mission on a spiritual high, convinced I'd succeeded at this two-year coming-of-age process and would return home to Utah a fully realized adult. And this adult would have one primary goal: a marriage that would truly be the foundational step in "obtaining the highest" (which, lacking the aspirational sense that "alcanzando" imparts in Spanish, does, I admit, sound more like an investment firm motto than an ultimate spiritual goal).

As a BYU freshman that fall after my mission, I began working toward this highest goal, even as I enjoyed classes and the freedom that "adulthood" entailed. Because I hadn't attended college before my mission, it was the first time that I was responsible for choosing when I got up, what I would eat, and what I would do each day. And while getting married was not an immediate priority, dating certainly was.

Being in a singles ward, where everyone in the congregation is single except for its three highest male leaders, made the parameters of that goal immediately apparent. I spent an absurd amount of time prioritizing with my roommates who I should ask out next. Their enthusiasm over my options helped encourage me along to my first relationship, with a music major who sang in the BYU choir and who was, like me, one of the most active attendees of ward activities. She ended our relationship after a few months, afraid it was heading toward a proposal much sooner than she was comfortable with. Thereafter I quickly became infatuated and pursued a successful friendship with a woman who lived in the house across the street from our apartments. Although a member of our ward, she was far less active and soon introduced me to the large community of BYU students fighting to retain the inexpensive tuition reserved for faithful Latter-day Saints even after they had lost their testimonies. Tuition is doubled for non-Mormons who want to attend BYU; moreover, Latter-day Saints who stop attending church while enrolled at BYU can be expelled. Consequently, BYU has a large underground community of skeptics trying to keep one foot in the church even as the other foot moves further and further from it, and navigating the challenges they face makes many of them thoughtful, interesting people. The yoga teacher who merrily posed for BYU's seminude portrait class made it clear that she did not return my romantic interest, but she did introduce me to the woman who would become my wife.

Cait lived in the same redbrick house as the yoga teacher, home to several women in a similar one-foot-in-one-foot-out position. At the time I was happily teaching the Sunday school class for our ward, and while I had met her before, I really noticed Cait when she caught what I considered a carefully planned twist in one of my lessons long before I wanted it caught.

After church I saw her on a bench outside of the chemistry building that served as our meeting house, reading a library copy of *The Time Traveler's Wife* by Audrey Niffenegger. The book had been rebound as a solid green hardcover with only the title and author's name embossed on the spine, which made it look like an obscure doctoral dissertation or little-known translation of a French novel instead of the mainstream literary novel that it was. Being a serious reader was the second-most solid aspect of my identity besides my Mormonism, so finding someone who also appeared to be a serious reader intrigued me further. Then and there I moved Cait to the top of my long list of women I wanted to date, which is exactly as unromantic as it sounds.

I don't think Cait was particularly interested in dating her Sunday school teacher, but she agreed to go out with me when she saw the book *I* was read-ing: *Living History*, Hillary Clinton's first autobiography. Our first date was on a Sunday, and I had a strict "no spending money on Sundays" policy; luckily, the improvised mini–golf course that I set up in my apartment and the burritos that were the mainstay of my newly discovered (and often abandoned) vegetarian lifestyle were novel enough to ensure subsequent dates.

I've always been attracted to strong-willed, intellectual, argumentative women, I think in part because they could fill holes in my more reserved, nonconfrontational personality. And while I found much I liked in Cait, to be honest, I think what I liked more was that I seemed a very good fit for her, at least at that time. Caitlin was on her way back to a more Mormon lifestyle after moving strongly away from it early in her time at BYU, almost getting expelled in the process. She'd found a mentor in her political science classes in Dr. Valerie Hudson, whose work "The Two Trees" helped many a woman at BYU declare, as Cait did on her blog, that she was not a Mormon *in spite* of her feminism but *because* of it.

Mormon teens are often asked to make lists of the traits they want in a spouse. On Cait's blog, I found her updated, feminist version of that list. While some of the qualities she wanted in a husband, such as "supports me in my career" and "liberal," gave me pause as I reoriented my politics and marital expecta-tions, "intelligent," "fit but not buff," "hard working," "good sense of humor," and "well read" were among the traits I was proudest of in myself. Fitting so well into Cait's profile of a perfect man, or at least an adequate man, was a major selling point for any relationship with her. The narrative I set up for myself, of the open-minded but unshakeable Mormon boyfriend to a questioning but flexible feminist girlfriend, was very appealing to me and a great alternative to what I saw as more "boring" conventionally faithful marriages.

While I was in no particular hurry to get married, when we began discuss-ing marriage just a few months into our relationship, it became clear that Cait wanted to get married sooner rather than later for complicated family reasons. Having no compelling reason to refuse, I agreed to marry someone less than three months after we first met.

Trying to have it both ways, being fully faithful while fully accommodating of my wife's less orthodox outlook, would, of course, prove impossible. Temple attendance soon became a major focus of tension. The temple was central to my spiritual life from the moment I returned from my mission. Beyond the regular temple attendance suggested by church leaders, I also volunteered weekly to help facilitate the rituals that occurred there. I expected Cait to start volunteering alongside me as other couples did, seeing each other briefly between sessions of ritual, carrying on quiet, slightly mischievous conversations. I figured this would go on until she had children, at which point women were required to stop volunteering. But when I shared my plan, she laughed and refused.

Cait saw the temple as the ultimate symbol of the patriarchy enshrined in Mormon doctrine, where, not out of cultural tradition but commanded by strict ordinance, women veiled their faces and promised to obey their husbands as their husbands obey God. I understood enough of Mormon feminism to know that the temple is sometimes considered a sign of equality to come, because women administer rituals in the temple in ways they cannot do outside of it. For example, my world religions professor, after praising the equality of men and women in Sikhism, admitted reluctantly that he didn't believe men and women were treated equally in Mormon culture but that he saw in the rituals of the temple a clear promise of future equality. Cait, however, held the much more common position in Mormon feminism that the temple caused far more harm than hope, and, though I resisted, I could, grudgingly, see her point.

Still, I had some of my most important personal revelations in the temple. In 2008, as the church worked to support passage of California's Proposition 8 banning gay marriage, I received firm assurance that I was not sinning in refusing to support the exclusion of gay couples from the civic institution of marriage. This was a huge turning point for my spirituality, establishing a conflict between personal revelation and institutional revelation in a way I had never experienced before.

Given Cait's dislike of the temple, you might wonder why she agreed to get married there. One selling point for the ever-frugal Cait: marrying in the temple is free. More importantly, I almost certainly would have refused to marry Cait had she refused to get married in the temple. For better or worse, or perhaps just for worse, Mormon marriages that take place outside the temple are stigmatized as inferior. In my view then, as well as the views of most Mormons, a home without wedding photos with a couple embracing outside a temple lacked something essential about what it meant to be in a Mormon marriage and a Mormon family.

And so, while Cait did concede to a temple marriage—after almost cancelling it the night before—that didn't mean that tension around this central symbol of orthodoxy was going anywhere, especially since temple attendance was supposed to be the ultimate bonding activity (well, besides sex, I suppose) between a Mormon couple. I remember one particular evening several months into our marriage, after a session in the temple organized by our ward that I had insisted we attended. "Don't you see how much the temple heals me, teaches me?" I said (OK, shouted). We were driving through the hills of Provo to a get-together at the home of our bishop after the temple session.

"Can't you see how it hurts me and tears me down?" she replied (OK, shouted).

And thus began the push and pull of choosing the person my marriage asked me to be versus choosing the person my faith asked me to be.

My temple recommend, enshrined in that folded piece of plastic from my mission, was one of the final mementos of Mormonism I discarded, six years later, when we moved from graduate school for my wife in Wisconsin to graduate school for me in Texas. Our two years in Wisconsin—my first residence, besides my mission, outside the Mountain West—had seen the complete collapse of my Mormon faith and a tentative feeling of call toward ministry in our newfound faith of Unitarian Universalism.

When we moved to Texas for my master of divinity degree with two kids and only what would fit in our midsize Mazda, each item had to be inspected carefully. My temple recommend had expired a year earlier, and since I was no longer active, I couldn't get a new one. "Discard what has no meaning, keep what does" was my minimalist motto, and the recommend holder, bearing a picture of the building I could no longer enter, backed by a scripture I no longer believed, containing a badge of honor that had expired, had to go. Easy as it would have been to pack this one meaningful plastic flap, it nonetheless found its way to a landfill for a destiny of incredibly slow degradation. Or maybe I was ambitious and recycled it, I cannot recall. I somehow doubt the church had recyclability in mind when they designed the object.

I didn't choose my marriage over Mormonism, as I think it might be easy to believe from the outside. I chose the man my marriage revealed I had the potential to become, over the man my faith had said I was destined to be. That might be an unimportant distinction to some, but for me, recognizing it made all the difference. Coming to this conclusion was not a simple process. By that time in my life, I could see much more clearly my strong inclination toward conformity. Where others tried to feel unique by bucking against systems, I tried to feel unique by throwing myself deeper and deeper into the system so that I had few peers in strict adherence. This was true at school, at church, and, I realized, in my marriage. We spent the early parts of our marriage dangerously codependent, although we were certainly not alone in this in Utah Valley.

I never stopped trying to reach the highest in my marriage, but I soon realized that this meant finding out who I wanted to be, apart from who my faith had told me to be or from who my partner wanted me to be. In fact, finding the difference between what my marriage seemed to push me to be versus what it needed me to be was perhaps the key moment of personal discovery. My desire to conform often made it easier to be passive, complacent, and withdrawn in the presence of a larger, louder personality. What I learned was that much more often my marriage needed me to be as assertive, engaged, and, most of all, present as I could be, even as I kept in mind the societal gender norms that influence all marriages, no matter what personalities they include. This ongoing personal and interpersonal discovery gave me the confidence to move forward with my marriage but without its Mormon foundation.

We're a very fortunate post-Mormon couple in that our decision to leave the church was made together when we moved from Utah to Wisconsin. On our way to our new Midwest home, we had taken a significant detour to South Carolina to spend the summer with Cait's family, which meant attending Cait's childhood ward. Aside from my mission, it was my first experience with a Mormon congregation outside the "Book of Mormon Belt" of the Mountain West. It coincided with the increased public scrutiny of Mormonism accompanying Mitt Romney's 2012 run for president of the United States. These factors gave me the space to see my faith more objectively. My undergraduate degree in Middle Eastern studies and Arabic, with its strong emphasis on understanding the beauty and meaning of Islam, also gave me tools to evaluate my religion and my role in it more carefully.

Our sojourn in that ward culminated with the blessing of our daughter Tallulah, who had been born a few weeks before we left Utah. Forming a circle with other priesthood holders, laying my hands on Tallulah's head while the men in the circle held and supported her, and blessing her with a name and a hypothetical Mormon future, would be the last time I used the Melchizedek priesthood, a position I had entered, as was standard for Mormon men, just before my mission. It would also be our last official act in the church until we submitted our resignation letters less than a year later.

The night before we left South Carolina for Wisconsin, Cait and I lay in her childhood bed, in the room over the garage. After I was quiet for a long time, she asked what I was feeling. "I think I'm ready to be done," I replied.

Cait began to cry with what I imagine was a mixture of existential dread and relief, and we agreed that when we moved to Wisconsin we would explore alternative spiritual and religious options.

When Cait first visited the University of Wisconsin to evaluate it as a potential location to pursue her doctorate, the school's recruiting office had connected her with several other BYU grads and Mormons, and she made some good friends. So at first in Wisconsin we split our time between the very liberal (for Mormonism) university ward a mile from our home and the very liberal (for anyone) Unitarian Universalist church just down the street from our apartment.

For a time this more-or-less fifty-fifty split worked, as we enjoyed participating in the December 2012 "women wear pants to church" protest (because, believe it or not, that was still something Mormon women were socially expected to avoid in 2012) and other movements that grew out of the liberal Mormon online forums we were both active in. But gradually the free coffee, the shared values, and, most especially, the nearness of the Unitarian Universalist church won out. We attended the LDS church one last time during our first spring in Wisconsin to see if there was anything left for us in that familiar, nostalgic setting. When a local leader dedicated his entire talk to the importance of keeping your kids quiet during meetings, we packed up our boisterous children, and never returned.

We were very grateful to have found a new church to go to, two atheist/agnostics looking for a community of spiritually striving comrades. In a fortune of fate, we landed in what some have called the "REI church" of Unitarian Universalism, where believing in God isn't all that important, but if you haven't spent a day in a national or state park in the last month or started a neighborhood recycling program, people look at you funny.

But leaving Mormonism doesn't just mean attending a different church on Sunday, or at least it didn't for us. Mormonism was the foundation upon which our family was built, largely the reason we had trusted each other enough to rush into marriage and parenthood. And although our marriage had been pretty smooth as far as marriages go between people of often very different temperaments, we were both very different from the people we had been five years earlier when we married.

It felt, for both of us, very important to choose each other again in this new context. For us, one way of making that choice without abandoning our marriage altogether was to become, at least for a time, nonmonogamous. And so we made the mutual decision to make our marriage an "open marriage."

For Cait, part of the process of leaving the church had been to embrace her bisexuality, a part of her sexuality I could never fulfill. After a few rash and rushed attempts early on, we discovered that OKCupid has an open format and an active polyamorous community that made it much easier to be clear about our intentions up front and find others in similarly open situations. While I dated several different women, Cait settled into a longer-term "romantic friendship" with a woman.

This might strike many as an odd way of "striving to reach the highest" in our marriage. But for us it felt like an essential process, freeing us of the monogamous commitment we'd made in our early twenties as Mormons while still holding on to the meaningful relationship and commitment we worked so hard to form.

However, predictably enough, as someone who, despite my mental commitment to feminism, still had a deep-seated masculine sense of sexual entitlement, I did not handle all my relationships in a moral way. I don't necessarily blame Mormonism for this sense of entitlement present in so many non-Mormon parts of society, but, as a religion, it did little to equip me to address it adequately. I was, for the couple of years that we opened our marriage, a much more active dater, consistently pushing the limits of what Cait was comfortable with, at the same time that I was the more consistently jealous partner, pushing Cait to reconsider the motives of her dates and her actions in those relationships.

I was also unfair in my other relationships. Guilt about the imbalance of our dating lives often caused me to terminate relationships with little notice. And although I was educated about the lines of consent, I was often quite selfish in my pushing up to and around those lines. While I would at times deactivate my account and take a break, I would not stick to those commitments and would soon return to dating.

It was the #MeToo movement that opened my eyes to how wrong I had been in those relationships. I began to see how deeply hurtful my me-oriented position in my relationships was. The 2018 article by Katie Way about her coercive date with actor Aziz Ansari impacted me strongly. Although he was much more aggressive than I had ever been, I still saw in his actions a reflection of my own willing dismissal of any consideration of "what would be best for this other person?" as opposed to "how can I convince this person to do what I want?" This pattern was particularly harmful when I attempted to turn several friendships into intimate relationships, permanently damaging relationships that I greatly valued.

The #MeToo movement, a secular movement that has asked for morality much more firmly than any religious movement I've experienced, has shown me that there really is something higher to strive toward. Of course, I knew that compassionate consideration of the needs of others was a hallmark of being a good person, but in my eagerness to "rediscover" myself post-Mormonism, I was willfully ignorant of how urgently that compassionate action is needed not only in society in general but also in my life particularly.

I sometimes wish, quite frequently actually, that I could return to the days when I knew for certain that I was one of the "good guys," standing, in my own way, against the forces of evil that would make me into something lesser, something mundane. What feminism and #MeToo particularly have taught me is that there is a structure set up to constantly reassure me that I'm one of the special good guys, entitled to unquestioned self-confidence and a moral compass that needs no outside correction, and that this structure is itself the problem.

So much of my identity post-Mormonism has resided in a sense of liberal moral superiority, leaving behind old, worn-out ideas of male/female, insider/ outsider, right/wrong. Realizing that I've fallen short of these new standards feels eerily similar to how I fell short of the old standards. The main difference, in fact, is that the path to redemption from those shortcomings, especially on a personal, private level but also on the level of repairing broken relationships, seems at times so unclear. At every turn, I must figure out the right response to the individual I'm interacting with, not rely on ready-made instructions about what good men always do.

For now, I'm taking an extended break from seeking partners outside our marriage. We decided to have another baby, and I'm home with our kids while Cait works on her PhD in sociology, studying sexual violence. It's a challenge I'm grateful for as I take time to consider where I want to go from here and who I want to be. Primarily, I'm trying to release false images of who I am and what I'm entitled to and learn to accept where I am now and employ self-compassion and inner trust to move away from harmful patterns.

I'm learning an unexpected gratitude. Rumi says that "this being human is a guest house," and all sorts of different emotions, good and bad, will visit our house, often as an "unexpected visitor." Even if these are the kind of guests who "violently sweep your house empty of its furniture," we are still to invite them in, because they have something to teach us, "clearing [us] out for some new delight" waiting to be discovered. I try to let in lots of guests I previously turned away. I was raised to believe that guilt, remorse, and sadness were signs that you'd fallen from God's presence and that in a righteous life such feelings had no place. Now I know that these feelings have something profound to teach, something about being in a human family, something about being human. I try to welcome them in with something like a smile each day as I sit in meditation and attempt to learn from them.

At the same time, I know that wallowing in my guilt will accomplish nothing. Self-motivated, earnest action is required, with no expectation of external award or acclaim. If I am to raise myself up to the nurturance culture that, as Nora Samaran put it, must replace the misogynist rape culture now governing male-female relations, I will receive no small paper badge of honor that I can carry in my pocket, flashing quickly to get into hallowed halls where I can don the robes of "the good guys." The only thing I can and want to expect is a return to discovering the man that my marriage showed me I could be. I believe he's still in there, and I believe the world will be a better place with him in it.

Figure 6. T. Kay Browning and Caitlin P. Carroll, October 2020, Stockholm, Sweden

T. Kay writes, "Our marriage has been through many versions so far, and, honestly, I'm surprised it's proven both so adaptable and so resilient. We were told recently that our marriage was admirable because we 'really seem like friends.' While we are all too often combatants and temporary strangers to each other, I do believe that our friendship, our willingness to assume the best and forgive the worst in each other, has not only preserved our marriage these dozen years now but also gotten both of us through some of our toughest moments.

"When I was growing up, marriage always seemed like the most predictable feature of adult life. I'm happy to say that it has proven to be most wonderfully unpredictable, and I am a much better man for it."

Being Jane

JOHN DOE

As a Mormon, I've found sexuality involves a mixed bag of emotions: shame, guilt, frustration, resentment, depression, humiliation, anxiety—and, OK, curiosity, excitement, and even some pleasure. I doubt I'm alone in this. I've heard often enough that the church doesn't enter the bedroom of couples married in the temple, but I was never sure what that meant for me and my spouse. At church in my youth, I was told repeatedly that sex is bad, but that once you get married in the temple, sex becomes sacred. However, as a bisexual cross-dresser, I feel sex is anything but sacred, regardless of my temple marriage. The church may stay out of the bedroom in theory, but the emotions resulting from how Mormonism has shaped our view of sexuality cannot be neatly shut off or corralled.

My wife, Claire, knew about my cross-dressing before we got married, but as Mormon virgins, neither of us understood what that meant for our marriage. We were childhood sweethearts who married young. I always knew a mission wasn't for me, so we were barely out of our teens when we married in the Timpanogos Temple. Claire was raised in an LDS home, but her parents were very progressive, atypical Mormons. While I had a very conservative upbringing, Claire was raised to be freethinking and open-minded. I valued these qualities in Claire very highly—they were some of the main traits I loved about her.

Open-minded as she was, Claire still wasn't interested in including cross-dressing in our marriage. Her opposition wasn't because she thought it was wrong or bad—she simply wasn't interested in pursuing it with me.

Consequently, it wasn't long after our wedding that difficulties appeared: I wanted to bring Jane, my alter ego, into the sexual aspects of our relationship. Claire, being heterosexual, was understandably not interested in sex with Jane. This is where shame, resentment, frustration, and humiliation entered the bedroom in full force. The sacred act of sex between a husband and a wife was corrupted by my cross-dressing, making us both miserable.

I was as delighted as any new father with the birth of my son, but eventually, contemplating the responsibilities of fatherhood made me so hopeless that death seemed preferable to life. I felt I would never be a good father to a son. Was I masculine enough? Was I a good example of a righteous priesthood holder? I feared the answer was an obvious no. These negative thoughts consumed me; I felt worthless and afraid.

A few months later, I tried to end my life with an overdose of Valium. I was on the floor—not very lucid—and I remember my wife trying to talk to me. I wasn't speaking in full sentences, but fortunately she realized soon enough that I had overdosed on medication. She immediately called poison control, who instructed us that as long as I could stay conscious and awake for the next twelve hours, I would be OK. If I started to lose consciousness, I would have to go to the hospital immediately. Those hours passed in a haze, but I was able to regain lucidity as the strength of the medication waned.

The next morning, my wife took me to see my doctor, who was shocked at what I had done. He started me on new antianxiety medication and put me under a contract to find a therapist. I never told him what had driven me to the point of suicide; I was too embarrassed to explain how I felt. Even after I found a therapist, it was difficult to open up about the challenges I faced. In fact, it took three visits with my therapist before I was willing to mention the cross-dressing.

An act as drastic as attempting suicide changes your life even if it doesn't end it. When I finally began to pull out of the depression, I faced the reality of what I had done, which produced further negative emotions. It took years, but eventually I learned to control those negative emotions through the process of accepting myself. My therapist and I discussed extensively my ideas of what made someone a "good" or "bad" person; examining this construct allowed me to realize that I was a strong, compassionate, and caring human being.

Although Claire didn't come to my therapy sessions with me, she was interested and engaged in the process. She was very supportive and reassuring, helping me recognize the many traits that made me a good person. Along the way, Claire and I found a balance of letting Jane exist without overrunning the intimacy we shared together. When I first introduced Claire to what cross-dressing meant, I would simply put on an item or two of women's clothing, such as a skirt and nylons. Claire would agree to kiss me while I wore this clothing, and sometimes she would help me to masturbate while dressed up, but this was rare.

However, after therapy, I was able to communicate my desires to Claire without feeling so much shame and guilt, and she began to understand how important being Jane was to me. Even still, I was surprised that she was receptive to my desire to explore cross-dressing further. Instead of just putting on an article or two of women's clothing, I added padding underneath my clothing, used fake breast inserts, shaved my legs and arms, put on makeup and a wig so that I was dressed completely as a woman. I looked like I could be a "Jane"!

It was very satisfying and fulfilling to look at my reflection in the mirror and acknowledge that I looked like a woman. The experience was not just sexually gratifying but relaxing; it let me shed both mundane concerns and ongoing existential worries and instead experience a completely new persona. Being "Jane" meant that I didn't have to think about work, church, my marriage, or whether I was a good enough father. Additionally, Claire helped me relax by affirming that she cared about my alternate persona as well, helping me by using sex toys as we explored Jane's sexuality.

When I stopped fixating on the shame of cross-dressing and instead developed my persona as Jane, things changed. Fully embracing my cross-dressing made me realize I had feelings for men, particularly when dressed as Jane. Since then, I've had crushes on a couple of men, which engendered a lot of confusion and shame. Not only was I ashamed of my homosexual feelings, I believed that these feelings tainted my heterosexual relationship with Claire. I felt that my sexual attention was consumed by my cross-dressing and bisexuality, taking away from the time, energy, emotion, and focus that Claire deserved. Having so much attention focused on my own needs or desires felt greedy and selfish. Even when I felt sexually attracted to my beautiful blonde wife, I felt I was betraying her because I still wanted more than being her straight male companion for all eternity. This made me feel like a failure and a disappointment as a man and as a Latter-day Saint. How could I ever enjoy an eternal marriage when part of my sexuality focused on men? Once again, I began to feel that the only escape was to end my life.

Over the years, I've improved the look of my alter ego to a point I would dare say she is pretty; I was actually hit on by a guy while I was out and about one day dressed as Jane. Another day I got a wolf whistle from a guy on the street. At first I was insulted by the whistle because I was being sexually objectified, but after a moment I realized I was sexually aroused by the whistle because it meant that another man found me sexually attractive.

Enter shame.

Urges to be with a man started to consume me, and I made many decisions at that point. First, I would not let this experience lead me to suicidal thoughts again. Second, I was committed to my marriage to Claire. We'd been married over a decade and had four children. Claire was my best friend in all the world; above all, I did not want to lose my life with her. Third, I wanted the only emotions in the bedroom to be happiness, fulfillment, pleasure. Finally, I would go back to therapy. However, I wasn't restarting therapy to get rid of my desires or change who I was. I went back to therapy to learn how to talk to my wife about these urges and how to approach a discussion about solutions we could seek together to help me with my sexuality.

My therapist had me write a list of things I wanted in my sexual relationship with Claire. The list would be given to Claire, who would then decide what she was OK with. I was to respect her decision, and I knew beforehand that this would produce a lot of shame on my part, because I felt I was corrupting the sacred gift of sexuality. In fact, handing her that list felt like the most shameful thing I could ever ask of Claire, even though she never gave me reason to feel that way. Shame was so ingrained in me at that point that when Claire agreed to do something on the list, such as buy a dildo for Jane so I could experience anal sex, using it the first time aroused only negative emotions. I was so ashamed that I fought the sexual pleasure. But instead of explaining that I was hurt and disturbed by my own shame as opposed to anything Claire had done wrong, I said nothing. I just didn't pursue another attempt for a while. Because I could take no pleasure in using the dildo, Claire was left thinking she had done something wrong, while I felt worthless because I didn't know how to articulate my feelings to her.

The therapist suggested we start more slowly the next time, such as simply role playing to have Claire compliment me on my feminine characteristics. Taking things one step at a time helped us explore this new terrain slowly.

Additionally, the therapist also was clear that I needed to communicate with Claire about helping me overcome shameful emotions. For instance, even a simple reassurance that Claire didn't think I was worthless or less of a man because of my homosexual feelings helped immensely. At this point, Claire was so used to my oddities that she was shocked to learn I felt shame and was glad to offer encouragement and reassurance that she still valued me—as her best friend, the father of her children, and yes, even her sexual partner. This was a relief to me, and we started exploring my list again, more slowly this time. After we'd become acclimated through simple things such as role play, we moved back into using toys to help me explore my homosexual feelings within the bounds of my heterosexual marriage.

I wish I could say the negative emotions are gone as I enjoy both Claire and Jane. They're not. They might not enter the bedroom as often, but they're still lurking in the hallway. I sometimes get new ideas of things I want Jane to try that Claire can do with me, and the emotions bang on the bedroom door, wanting back in. I have to brace the door sometimes, and often the emotions break through. Claire doesn't always understand the emotions, but she stands by me, and together we try to find the sacred in the shameful.

Soul Mates

SCOTT BLANDING

I always knew that "good Mormon boys" did three things: they went on missions, graduated from BYU, and married in the temple. Though my father wasn't Mormon, my brother was a hellion, and I was secretly gay, I wanted to be a good Mormon boy, so I became the epitome—annoyingly so. I attended church with my mother every week. Coca-Cola never touched my lips. I wouldn't see a movie on the Sabbath. I became an Eagle Scout. And I dated a variety of girls from my high school. It didn't matter that I also had a boyfriend, Joe, who attended the other high school in town.

What did it mean to be Mormon and gay in the 1950s and '60s? Let's start by stating the obvious: times were different. I grew up in a culture of postwar male nudity. At public swimming pools, guys showered together before they changed into their swimsuits in one open room. Boy Scout camp included group showers, and some guys even swam nude in the lake. In high school, we swam nude—everyone did, no excuses. No one gave it a second thought. There was never any discussion of homosexuality, there was no gay pride or gay rights, and our only sexual imagery was the omnipresent soft-core *Playboy* magazine and the nude photo of Marilyn Monroe hanging in my father's office.

The annual sex talk at church went like this: *Never have sex with a girl, because that's immoral and you must protect her virginity. Although masturbation isn't a sin, you should keep it under control, especially when you get older, because it trains you to ejaculate prematurely.* And that was that. Everyone see the loophole? Nothing about sex with guys. And since all these developing teenage boys had no Internet porn to compare themselves to, a major topic of conversation was "Am I normal?" The only way to answer that was to check each other out. As a teen I learned early on that almost any friend would compare penises, and once they were in view, most boys would masturbate with you. Every once in a while, a guy would be interested in a little fellatio. No one seemed to care.

The way I met Joe demonstrates this nonchalance. Soon after he joined our Scout troop, a couple of guys told me, "You should get to know Joe; you like the same kinds of things." Joe and I hit it off and were in a relationship that lasted from age fourteen to nineteen. We had a variety of sex, but it was all right because neither of us was female. I knew society in general frowned on homosexuality, but as long as I kept it to myself, having a boyfriend didn't seem forbidden. Joe and I even double-dated to our high school prom, each with a girl on his arm.

But when I left for BYU, something made me realize I should stop sleeping with guys. A year later, when I left for my mission, I'd been celibate for a year, excepting one minor incident in the dorm. In the Salt Lake Mission Home, after I'd been through the temple and before my departure to northern Europe, it was explained that not merely sex with women was forbidden. "Be assured," we were told, "homosexuality is a vile sin, and you are under condemnation if you have sex with men." I never felt guilty about being gay, but as an upright Mormon boy, I figured it was good that I'd largely stopped having sex.

I loved my mission. I learned to receive promptings from the Spirit. I loved the people and the culture. I baptized more than twice the average in our mission. I came home determined to serve the church every way I could.

I was home only a few days before I returned to BYU. A theater major, I wanted to audition for an upcoming production of a Shakespearean tragedy, so I stopped by the office of the professor who would direct it. Already in his office was a young woman named Kris, asking similar questions. Something about her caught my attention. Her smile? Her blonde hair? Though this was unusual for me, I gave it little thought. The next day at tryouts, I saw her again. Drawn to her, I suggested we audition together. We spent an enjoyable hour working on *Richard III*, act 1, scene 2, where Richard woos Lady Anne while her murdered husband lies in state.

Kris was made stage manager, while I was given several small roles that popped up throughout the play. I had lots of time to kill backstage and spent much of it with her. We spoke easily and freely. She was beautiful, self-confident, cosmopolitan, and more intelligent than I. She had a strong testimony and a deep knowledge of the gospel. More importantly, she had a good sense of humor, was fun to be with, and was unattached. She had given up on dating for a while, so there was no pressure on me to be anything but a friend.

Kris had everything a young returned missionary could want. I just didn't want all she had to offer.

Around that time, a dear friend and his wife asked me to serve as a witness for their sealing in the Salt Lake Temple. After their ceremony I found myself in the celestial room with time to contemplate the event. Suddenly, I was filled with the Holy Ghost. It was as though some unseen person said to me, "You are supposed to marry Kris."

I felt absolutely no doubt: I had received a message from God.

While I enjoyed being with Kris, marriage had not crossed my mind. As much as I liked being with her, there was no sexual attraction—I hadn't even kissed her. We'd never remotely discussed marriage or my sexual orientation—it was the 1960s, when a guy could be expelled from BYU merely for admitting to being gay. And I was too naive to even imagine how being gay would affect our marriage.

A few days later, as Kris and I took a quiet walk around campus, I worked up the nerve to share my experience. "In the temple Wednesday, I was meditating in the celestial room," I began, "when suddenly I was filled with the Spirit and received an impression: 'You are supposed to invite Kris to be your eternal partner.'"

Kris didn't say a word. Embarrassed, I stammered, "It was as clear as if someone said it out loud."

She just looked at me. Finally she asked, "When exactly did that happen?"

"After the sealing, so I guess around 8:30."

Kris took me by the hand. "I was doing my Doctrine and Covenants homework around the same time," she said, pausing to take a deep breath, "and I had that exact same experience."

Rather than celebrate our joint spiritual witness, we became extremely awkward around one another. Neither of us knew what to say, how to behave. One evening at dinner I presented her with a safety pin around which I'd tied a red ribbon, a substitute for the fraternity pin a boy gave a girl when they were officially a couple. "Now we're pinned," I said. We tried to be excited about the message we'd shared, but emotionally, we couldn't take the pressure. The next weekend, we broke up. For the rest of the semester, we could barely look at one another.

I spent the next summer touring Asia with a BYU variety show designed to foster goodwill. One night after a performance near the Korean Demilitarized Zone, on the bus back to the resort where we were billeted, I fell into quiet contemplation while the rest of the group sang familiar songs. I was filled with the same Spirit I felt in the temple—and I realized that I loved Kris. I wanted to spend my life with her. But I still had never considered what it would mean for a gay man to marry a woman.

Back at BYU, the following semester, Kris and I had become comfortable enough for me to ask her out. We went to a performance by a professional magician and had so much fun that we knew we were an item again. By Christmas break I knew I had to propose. Driving to her apartment late one January night, I wrestled with how to bring up marriage—it had been such a disaster the last time we discussed it. Finally, to break the silence, I asked, "What are you planning to do this summer?"

Casually, Kris answered, "Laura and I are going to Jackson Hole to perform in one of the summer theaters."

"What . . . ?" That she had plans of her own surprised me. I had naively assumed that as a couple, we would naturally do something together.

"I thought you'd be on another BYU tour somewhere, and Laura and I didn't want to waste the summer," she said.

I didn't know what to say but finally stammered, "I thought we'd find something to do together."

"We never have before," Kris said. "Why would this summer be different? I figured we'd see each other back on campus fall semester."

"I was kind of hoping we could go to Oregon and work for my father," I said.

"Why would I do that? I don't know anyone there! Where would I stay?" she asked.

Beaten, I quietly mumbled, "I thought we could share our first apartment."

Everything went quiet. Kris realized this unplanned, unromantic invitation was a marriage proposal. Exasperated, she blurted, "Then I guess we'd better get busy planning a wedding." We agreed on a temple wedding immediately following her graduation. It did not dawn on me that sex would be expected.

As my wedding day approached, it had been five years since I'd engaged in any sexual activities. I was doing what was right. I'd had many spiritual experiences on my mission and learned to receive personal revelation and be guided by the Spirit. To me, that was evidence that the Lord couldn't care less about the teenage sex I'd had. Add in the fact that I wasn't chomping at the bit to have heterosexual sex when married, so I just didn't think about the ramifications.

The big night arrived, and there was my new bride, in bed, with me, and we were naked. At first it was kind of exciting, but she lacked the right equipment. I had no idea what I was supposed to do. Fortunately, a young man has no problem getting an erection, and the marriage was consummated. During the act all I could think was "I can't believe I'm doing this." Not only did I have no idea what to do with her, I discovered that I didn't want her doing what I'd done with my boyfriend. She was female and had no idea how to do anything *right*. So there we were, two inept, unprepared Mormon kids doing little more than inserting Tab A into Slot B. I hate to admit that I wearied of the attempts even before the honeymoon ended. I also discovered that I couldn't climax without thinking about guys. As you can imagine, *that* affected our marriage.

We moved to the Midwest for graduate school and engaged with a variety of bright classmates from diverse backgrounds. I soon noticed several openly LGBTQ+ individuals in the theater department, as well as three other closeted gays at church, but I managed to make it all the way through my PhD without coming out. I almost succumbed one night when a guy I'd met made a pass at me. He was gorgeous, and it had been so long since I'd been with a man. Instead, I promptly confessed the incident to my bishop. He congratulated me for not giving in and regaled me with his own college experience of resisting temptation. At home, days and even weeks elapsed between sex, and I couldn't get an erection without running a mental film of one attractive guy or another.

After graduation, I took a job in an eastern city. Our ward had almost twenty PhDs, and we quickly acquired friends with similar interests. I loved my wife, and we continued our symbiotic relationship. Everything was perfect—except in the romance department. The first time I strayed was on a business trip where I hit it off with a young man I met. As a teen I had mastered the art of a double life, maintaining my relationship with Joe while acting straight with everyone else. It was second nature. Returning home to Kris from my business trip, I slipped comfortably back into double-life mode. It was as though nothing had happened—except that I had some fresh memories to help me through the obligatory marital relations, which perked things up in bed.

But after the second time I strayed, I knew I better see the bishop. For an errant gay Latter-day Saint, this was tantamount to facing a firing squad. Making that appointment to confess my transgression meant that I expected excommunication from the church and divorce from Kris. It was most likely the end of life as I knew it, but I had to reconcile myself with the church. As I left for the appointment, Kris said, "When you get back, I want to know what's going on."

My bishop listened to my tale and said, "I'm not going to lose you." It was a miracle. He made an appointment for me to see LDS Social Services and went with me to talk to Kris. Of course she felt angry, hurt, and betrayed, but she was surprisingly calm and explained, "I had figured out Scott's homosexuality before we got married, but the church always promised that if we married in the temple, he would be blessed. I assumed he'd been cured."

Kris and I wanted to preserve our marriage. We had adopted children together and were not just a couple but a family. We had earned undergraduate and master's degrees in tandem, and she supported me while I finished my PhD. When she won a national competition and got her first job at a major theater festival, I gave up my summer gig and supported her during her first big break. After graduation, the same university hired us in different programs. We even worked together in the church's youth program. We loved being together, and we especially loved working on projects together. We made each other want to do our bests. We truly had become soul mates.

The bishop accompanied me to see a psychologist at LDS Social Services. Thereafter, I went alone, once monthly for three months, until the psychologist proclaimed, "Scott is not gay. He's artistic, and as such he has an aesthetic appreciation of both the male and female forms. He'll be all right." My wife and bishop were ecstatic, but I knew that the psychologist didn't know what he was talking about. But he provided the cover I needed to go happily back into the closet—where I stayed for over a decade.

On the outside we appeared a regular couple. But I was still a gay man married to a straight woman. Eventually, it became clear that our relationship could not endure if we continued to pretend we had a normal relationship. We tried counseling, but it never worked. When I went for marriage counseling, the only solution entertained was "Get a divorce, free your wife to marry someone else, and establish yourself as a gay man." When she went for counseling, the only recommendation was "Get out of this dreadful marriage. You must save yourself." Couples counseling was even worse because I ended up revealing more details than Kris could handle. Following our sessions she would cry for days and once told me that she needed time to mourn what she was losing.

That was when she realized that our marriage could not endure unless the issue of coitus was eliminated. I was greatly relieved; it removed such a heavy burden from me. But we still didn't know how to navigate our relationship. Finally, a sympathetic stake president made it his business to help us find a way to stay together in a loving but sexless marriage.

Of course, Kris and I always remember that we both received personal revelations that we were supposed to marry. Furthermore, during blessings from two different church leaders who didn't know one another, I was given this explicit message: "You knew in the preexistence that one aspect of your journey on earth was to be homosexual." Far along in this process, I was blessed with a calling from the Quorum of the Twelve under review of the first presidency. "You do realize I'm gay," I said in response to the call.

"Yes, we do," was the answer. "But we ask you not to mention it for the duration of this calling. There are church leaders who would refuse to work with you, and you could not succeed."

Kris also had an amazing priesthood blessing that informed her that she and I had been best friends in the preexistence and covenanted to make this journey together. We believe that our lives, as unique and difficult as they have been, follow the path we're supposed to take.

But just as that belief didn't make things easy before I came out of the closet, it didn't make things easy afterward. Life isn't a checklist of absolutes; it's a complex mix of variables, and there are choices and obstacles at every turn. My sexuality has always been a challenge, and at times I behaved even more badly than I've admitted here. Of necessity, Kris and I have continually discussed our relationship, its inherent blessings and problems, and whether we should stay together. We realized that we would rather be with one another than with anyone else. We loved each other's companionship. We loved raising our adopted children together. It helped when we discovered how many heterosexual married couples simply stop having sex after a couple of decades but still stay together. Ultimately, we realized that there are many reasons people marry—and only one of them is sex. We've learned there isn't just one kind of love, and we have found *our* kind of love.

I was also blessed with the knowledge (and I'm perfectly aware that this is an inflammatory premise) that God does not concern himself with sex nearly as much as our temporal church leaders do. I believe I've been inspired by the Spirit with direction regarding what my personal parameters are as a homosexual priesthood holder. My understanding of this concept was bolstered by my realization that when instituting polygamy, Joseph Smith often behaved sexually in ways that would not be tolerated today, but God overlooked it. Each time I've approached my church leaders in confession, I've been told, "You're not supposed to be excommunicated at this time. You are required to work this out." Frankly, my excommunication would have made things much easier for both Kris and me. Kris rightly felt that I was getting away with serious transgressions with only a slap on the wrist. Had I been excommunicated, my guilt would have been made public, and she would have been exonerated as the betrayed spouse. For me, excommunication would wipe the slate clean. I would have had the responsibility to work publicly toward forgiveness and rebaptism into the church. As it was, I had to work out my repentance without any visible penalty other than the loss of my temple recommend.

Once, as I worked on a project with an ex-Mormon gay author, he said, "You know, Scott, you're not really one of us. You're gay, but you're merely a tourist in gay culture." It's true: because I'm still Mormon and still married to Kris, I'm unwelcome in many LGBTQ+ circles. The church tolerates me, probably because the leaders know me personally and have seen my contributions to the kingdom. They've let me get away with a lot of belligerence and defiance, such as my active support of legalizing gay marriage and my participation in the Human Rights Campaign. This makes it all the more ridiculous that the church doesn't want me to go alone to dinner or a professional meeting with any woman but my wife, as if that were a threat to my salvation. My wife, however, doesn't want me to go alone to dinner or socialize with any man, because she sees it as a date. It is a perfect example of being neither fish nor fowl. I'm in the church, but with limitations. I'm an out gay man, but with limitations.

These are limitations I accept. But in accepting them, I allow myself no true home. Kris also is not fully at home in the world she lives in. This situation, painful as it can be, is a reminder that we were brought together by God and that it is our responsibility to endure to the end, to remain committed to one another. I'm constantly surprised that even at this advanced stage of my life, temptations come regularly, and I still must consciously work to avoid transgression.

This essay is not intended as an excuse for sinning or breaking covenants. It's a testimony that each of us is required to work out our own salvation. Kris and I continue to love one another and to find joy in the home, family, and partnership we've created. We cherish our testimonies of God's love, the atonement of Jesus Christ, the restoration of the gospel through Joseph Smith, and that this gay man and his wife can still, after all these decades, travel the road of life together.

Hiding in Plain Sight

DAVID NICOLAY

I've never experienced sex without an all but invisible paradigm: a patchwork of scripture, things my parents told me, their body language when my body was uncovered, things I'd seen on TV—and who knows what else. It's all there, whether I'm aware of it or not, no matter how I wish otherwise, a dense web that colors and contextualizes my experience of sex. After the contributing images, ideas, experiences, and words are forgotten, the web lingers—a mix of feelings that flash through me the moment I'm aroused: hesitation, like weights around my ankles, and curiosity, fear, dominance, aggression, anticipation, strength, shame, in varying degrees. Unless I work at it, it's all but indistinguishable, just how sex *feels*.

I'm still getting used to acknowledging the existence of this paradigm. Maybe if I'd been taught early on to pay attention to the vast nuance of my own sexual experience, things would be different, but Mormons aren't taught to see sex with much complexity. Or at least we weren't in my little culture growing up, and I doubt we were unique in how narrowly we thought about it—or tried not to think about it, except to caution ourselves against it. During the October 1998 General Conference, Apostle Jeffrey R. Holland quoted historians Will and Ariel Durant, who wrote in *The Lessons of History* that "sex is a river of fire that must be banked and cooled by a hundred restraints if it is not to consume in chaos both the individual and the group." This river of fire was primarily for procreation, we were told, though occasionally it was mentioned as a means of expressing love for one's spouse. Who can blame us for seeing it the way we were taught to see it, as verboten and sinful in all but very specific, limited contexts? The upshot, of course, is that you can't really explore or understand a dimension of your humanity if you're supposed to avoid thinking of it.

I was eleven or twelve when it started. I would get home from a difficult day at school and crash on my bed. I'd find myself lying facedown with the hardest erection possible, not thinking really, blissfully adrift in a wonderful and mysterious sea of chemicals I didn't want or know how to escape. I'd stay like that for half an hour or so, until the sensations subsided.

Then one day I crossed over, as if I'd been swept down the rapids of a river I'd been peacefully wading in moments before. I'm not sure how, but lying that way I had my first orgasm: a flash of intense heat and light, like seeing God. I came to my senses, sat up, looked down—and discovered to my shock the physical evidence of what had occurred. I rubbed the viscous liquid between my fingers in curious wonder. I'd had it described to me many times in the biological sense, but to experience it was alien and new. Nothing had prepared me for the intense explosion of pleasure that had swept over me. In fact, a few years earlier, after my mother explained how fertilization works, I asked how the man's body knew when to release the semen. "It just knows," she said. I pressed, confused at how the body could know the future and identify the exact date and time to release semen so that pregnancy could occur. She insisted again, "It just knows."

Up to that moment facedown on my bed, I didn't know that semen was released through stimulation. In fact, I didn't associate the "sex" I'd learned about during the talks with my mother and from pictures in medical encyclopedias with pleasure of any kind. Oh, but how quickly I learned.

For some reason I've always had an acute sense of shame; as far back as I can remember, I've never felt quite worthy of other people. Instead, I've always felt the need to prove myself or justify my existence or value—and even when I was successful it felt like a sham, like any moment the rest of the group would figure out that I was beneath them. Now, take that feeling and multiply it by the pressures of middle school, and maybe you'll understand how when I discovered this amazing, euphoric sensation I took to it like a fish to water. I escaped into a secret world of arousal whenever I was in pain, and I was often in some sort of pain. No one needed to tell me it was wrong. As a Mormon I understood that I must "neither commit adultery, nor kill, nor do anything like unto it" (D&C 59:6), and masturbation was like unto adultery in that it involved sexual gratification outside of marriage. I also knew that adultery and killing were paired, because LDS prophets have repeatedly said, beginning at General Conference in October 1942, "sexual sin . . . stands, in its enormity, next to murder."

So there I was, a budding next-to-murderer trying desperately to hide how reprobate I was. But somehow, of course, my father knew. One day in the kitchen he stopped me and told me so. I don't remember exactly what he said, but I remember where we each stood, across the table from each other, and that I wanted to disappear. I was astounded and appalled. *How* could he know? But *how* didn't matter so much; *that* he knew was enough to drive me deeper into hiding. Eventually, I chalked his knowledge of my secret up to the fact that he was a bishop and therefore, as I understood it, had special powers of discernment granted to him. After that he rarely brought it up again. It was as though he felt as shameful as I did about it.

My religious life became defined and measured by bishop interviews, which I quickly came to dread. As a Mormon teen I was expected to submit routinely to a one-on-one discussion of my worthiness with the bishop, whoever he might be. Each time the only thing I could think about was how I'd masturbated recently. Every bishop would carefully dance around the question; uttering the correct but crude term "masturbation" was like unsheathing a dagger or pulling a sheet completely off a body. My skin crawled when I heard it, and I got the distinct feeling theirs did too, so they would use euphemisms like "stimulation" and "self-abuse" to ask about it. They knew to ask, and I knew I had to fess up—they could read my mind, after all, just like my father could.

I haven't told many people about this aspect of my life, but when I do, I'm surprised how often people respond by asking me, incredulous, "Why didn't you just *lie*?" It never occurred to me. Instead, I believed the whole point was to fess up. In fact, a member of the stake presidency once jokingly told my father that my problem was that I said too much in interviews. What he failed to understand is that I didn't want to get away with anything—I wanted to repent, and I believed repentance began with complete honesty before the Lord. "What I the Lord have spoken, I have spoken . . . whether by mine own voice or by the voice of my servants, it is the same," Doctrine and Covenants 1:38 tells us. I believed that those chosen men were vicars of Christ and that by virtue of the office they held, when I sat across the desk from a bishop it was as though I sat across from Jesus himself, so I would spill all the beans every time. In response, they would usually explain that what I was doing was wrong, as if I didn't know, and, awkwardly, suggest strategies for overcoming the habit, then schedule a return appointment to check on my progress, usually two weeks out.

Despite the kindness and good intention of these inspired men, I dreaded the return appointment, as I never managed to last the full two weeks. Often I wouldn't show, convinced that I could simply keep fighting my battle and pop in once I went two weeks without backsliding. But the elusive date at which I would be able to announce my triumph was always pushed further and further into the future.

Dodging the bishop became part of my regular church life. I simply couldn't bear the thought of confessing, again, that I'd failed and have them reset the clock of worthiness—again. So I ran. There was a time when I was called as the leader of my youth group and was asked by the bishop to prayerfully choose two counselors from the quorum, but I knew my unworthiness would prevent me from receiving revelation on whom to choose, so I procrastinated. Weeks would go by, and the bishop would ask if I'd chosen my counselors yet. I always had some excuse ready and a promise to get right on it, but I never did—I *never* actually did. I knew that if I simply picked a couple of guys, they'd be my choice, not God's, so I kept trying to go two weeks clean. That was the magic duration: if I could go two weeks, that would prove to God and myself that I was worthy, and then I would be able to pray and have access to real revelation. After about six months the bishop finally chose my counselors himself; he never did ask me about my procrastination. Maybe he believed my excuses. At the time I assumed he didn't. I figured he knew by the gift of discernment exactly why I was procrastinating and that I was just too ashamed to say it. When my leaders themselves avoided the subject of my unworthiness, I took it as further evidence that I was in fact as unclean as I suspected and that we all felt equally uncomfortable about it. As a result, silence about my sins brought no comfort at all.

As the time to serve a mission approached, I spent most days with my nose in the scriptures, teaching early morning seminary, teaming up with the local missionaries, proselytizing my friends and coworkers, and on my knees in prayer. I was so devout that I made my younger brother take down a band poster he'd hung in our room, as I felt it wasn't conducive to the Spirit. I think of that period now as my monastic phase; I was throwing all my chips in, believing that if I could do enough good works and fill my life with enough light and love, the purifying powers of the Holy Ghost would root that wicked spirit out of my breast.

But I never could leave it long enough to be declared worthy to receive the Melchizedek priesthood and my temple endowments or to serve a mission. My bishop at the time wanted me to go a full year as proof I'd overcome my weakness. In my mind I had proven so completely incapable of true repentance that I began to think of myself as an addict. When I explained this to my bishop, he suggested I meet with an LDS therapist, adding that the church would cover the expense. I jumped at the opportunity and over the next six months attempted to treat my problem like a genuine addiction. My roller coaster of brief success followed by failure was so distinct that I began to wonder if I was bipolar. I didn't know much about the condition, and my therapist had never actually treated anyone for it; still, he thought it worth a shot to try out a medication used to treat that particular disorder. As far as I could tell, it had no effect on me.

I continued working toward worthiness and freedom from my addiction, going on team-ups with the missionaries several times a week and meeting with my bishop or branch president regularly until age twenty-four, when I was told that I was no longer eligible to serve a mission. It was devastating news. But I was determined to serve the Lord in other ways. I just wanted to be clean, finally, to be free.

I moved to Utah and focused on becoming an Institute teacher. So much of my life had been concentrated on the gospel and repentance that I couldn't imagine doing anything else for a career. I'd keep my nose in the books and my knees on the ground and, most of all, my shoulder to the wheel of my struggle. Serving the Lord was a given. Just how I would serve was up to me. In the process of enrolling at the LDS Business College in Salt Lake City, I learned that I needed an ecclesiastical endorsement. As I hadn't transferred my records to a local congregation yet, I decided to take a trip home to the Midwest to visit friends and have the president of the singles branch I'd attended sign the endorsement. During our interview he asked if I still struggled with masturbation. I said yes. He explained that he couldn't sign my ecclesiastical endorsement "in good conscience." I was surprised—I didn't think an endorsement for attending a church school would merit the same gravity as a temple recommend, and when he saw my surprise he volunteered to call the stake president on my behalf. I said that wouldn't be necessary, but when he did it anyway my stake president explained that he also couldn't sign my endorsement as long as I struggled with that particular weakness. I was in tears, but I knew it was the will of God and was therefore right even if I didn't understand.

I returned to Utah demoralized but determined to keep clawing my way toward worthiness. Nothing, after all, could separate me from the love of my God. I had to regroup and figure out where to continue my education, but as time went on I couldn't get that interview out of my head. I began to think that surely there must have been a misunderstanding. I thought the endorsement was more like a character reference from someone spiritually minded and in good standing with the church, simply affirming that to their knowledge the person being endorsed was serious about being good and not a philanderer or a criminal or a compulsive liar.

Mind you, this was the first time in my life that I'd doubted the divine decree of my church leaders. During my decade-long search for a solution to my horrible habit, I'd combed through church books and magazines, through devotionals and conference talks. Eventually, I found my way to histories and biographies written by faithful but rigorously honest historians more concerned with academic and historical integrity than whether a story fit the traditional narrative. Also, considering it a kind of training for my future career, I had enrolled at the University of Utah Institute of Religion for a full day of classes, including a history class where the teacher presented the most realistic portrayal of figures from church history I'd ever encountered anywhere outside a book. He was careful to explain that while God is perfect, man is not, though we try, though we give all we have. Slowly, and for the first time, these giant men from Mormon history began to look a little like me, well-meaning but often failing and always struggling to get it right. I learned that sometimes those failures and weaknesses spilled into the lives of others—that their most earnest and compassionate struggles to understand and communicate the will of God did not always mean they succeeded.

As this new perspective solidified, I found the courage to try again to get an ecclesiastical endorsement, this time from different leaders. As a member of a student ward in Salt Lake City, I sat with a counselor in the stake presidency and told him as much of my history as time would allow. I wanted to make sure he had the same picture my old bishops and stake presidents had. When I was done he took my papers and, with a twinkle in his eye and a grin, signed them, saying, "I find you worthy to go to college."

I was actually a bit torn about this—happy that I could proceed with an education at a church school but skeptical that I was truly worthy. I almost felt I'd pulled the wool over this man's eyes, even though I'd taken great care not to, even though his reaction was what I initially expected in the interview with my branch president back home. But my ambivalence faded as I pressed forward. It was in the Lord's hands, after all.

A few years later, I went through the same basic process with another bishop, a profoundly loving and Christlike man who'd served as a mission president and understood the sexual struggles of young people. In our interviews I told him everything, holding nothing back, recounting even my inner struggle and disgust as I knowingly broke the laws of God.

I'll call this particular man Bishop M. He didn't seem to think masturbation was a big deal. I still did. By then, however, I was struggling to keep from slipping into sexual immorality with one particular girl (a good friend actually, lest I make her sound like some random hookup). In a moment of weakness what began as a kiss escalated until we had our hands down each other's pants. In conversation afterward she and I discovered that we shared an almost identical story in terms of masturbation, guilt, and shame. It was an eye-opener: I'd always associated my inflamed sexual drive with my gender, believing that men were more naturally carnal, while women were naturally purer and closer to God. After that discovery we had a hard time keeping our hands off each other.

Being with her felt almost as freeing as it did wrong—which is often true of sexual discovery. On the one hand, I could finally explore this part of life without dragging someone else down, because she and I were on the same level, but I always felt incredibly guilty afterward. The fact that we were both unclean in the same way didn't release me from my obligations. It was all part of the same failing: the masturbation and what I'd done with her were each an expression of what I considered my sexual addiction.

I confessed every mistake—usually right after it happened. I would go to the bishop in shame because I wanted to be rid of my sins more than I wanted the temporary comfort of avoiding repentance. One day I met with him to explain that I'd fooled around with this girl yet again the night before. I told him that I left her place and headed straight home, where I fell to my knees and asked God why I kept failing. I remained on my knees in tears until I had a flash of inspiration where I realized that all sins of the body start off in the mind and that if I could simply more rigorously check my wandering mind, then my body was sure to follow. I was hopeful—and fearful. I feared that if the opportunity presented itself, I wouldn't be able to say no, and *that* bothered me. I wanted to actually have faith in myself for once that I *could* walk away.

He could see that I was sincere. There was zero pretense in me. I was meeting with him to tell him what I'd done more out of respect for policy than to receive direction—I knew that God already knew what I'd done, and I knew what I needed to do, but I would keep confessing immediately every time I failed. He listened, his eyes shining with unshed tears, and finally said, very directly, "David, I find you worthy to hold the priesthood."

I can't begin to describe how that felt, sitting across the desk from him and hearing words I'd sought my entire life. He must have picked up on this; he said I would probably need to sit with it awhile before I proceeded, and he was right: it needed to sink in. I remember feeling simultaneously jubilant and sober, humbled that God finally saw fit to lay a greater responsibility on my shoulders. However, I was cautious in my celebration, because I didn't fully trust myself. I feared I would fail God as I'd failed so many times before. But I knew that if I did, I wouldn't hesitate to crawl back to the bishop to confess all and jump back into the fray.

That experience made an indelible mark on my soul, deep enough that I stayed clean awhile on the momentum of my faith alone. But eventually I returned to my habits and continued with them right up to my marriage years later—and beyond. In the months before my wedding, I again met with a sexual addiction therapist, paid for by the church, once again a Mormon who'd struggled with the same weakness in his youth.

Long before any rings were exchanged I warned my wife-to-be, first revealing only that I had a problem, too afraid to actually tell her what it was. She would guess all manner of horrors, and I would set her mind at ease explaining that it was none of those things. "Then what?" she would ask, as she could see that whatever it was, I felt painfully guilty about it.

I knew I would eventually tell her, though it was months before I mustered the courage. She was, after all, the woman I would marry. I knew that as well. She was charismatic and easygoing, witty, curious, creative, and genuinely funny, but most of all, she was kind. To this day she looks directly at things that scare her and makes her way quietly and carefully toward them. She wants improvement from herself and others, but isn't frantic or demanding about it. That kindness was part of what won me, and while I believed she would accept me, I didn't think she would comprehend the sheer depth of my brokenness. I didn't know how to articulate it—not that I really wanted to. I mean, imagine a guy saying to his fiancée, "I feel like you don't understand just how much I suck."

When I finally told her what I struggled with, she accepted me, as I'd hoped. But a lifetime of shame surrounding sexuality takes a very real toll, and the secret habits I'd constructed were agonizingly hard to break, even with her kindness and mercy. Again and again I confronted the fact that sex for me was an exercise in emotional seclusion, strictly shaped over many years into an act of solitary escape. It never felt vulnerable or connective, having been hammered into a tool of hiding rather than one of connection. Even the few sexual experiences I had had with women before marriage were emotionally distant, cloaked in an appearance of intimacy but lacking any real vulnerability or connection. Of course I understand that sex doesn't always need to be connective in that way—it can be purely for pleasure, a release, but I think that healthy sex should be able to be different things at different times, especially with a spouse. It should be able to be profoundly connective at times, an act of deep sharing, one that pushes beyond the physical boundaries of my universe into another's. For me, it's never this. In fact, that kind of sex didn't even occur to me as a possibility, a thing others may experience even, until fairly recently.

Don't get me wrong—it always feels good in the strictest physical sense, but it's hard to even get to the "feel good" of it when the old numbness settles in, when the walls go up, when my mind responds to arousal by reflexively establishing emotional distance. This is what I do with sex, after all, what I've always done. I can't reach orgasm without putting some mental distance between myself and my partner. For me, sex isn't about people, it's about sensation, about accessing a feeling strong enough to sweep me away, to drown out this overwhelming world, even if just for a moment. Could it be about both sensation and connection? Possibly, hopefully, but right now it's not. I imagine that learning to experience it in that way, as I feel I must if I'm to salvage this part of me, will be like learning to walk after a lifetime of crawling—a long and difficult road.

When it works the way it always has, when the unpredictable and frightening world around me disappears behind a veil of pleasure, it pulls with it a wife who deserves to see and be seen, to not just *feel* intimate and connected with me but also *be* intimate and connected, to have me reaching and stretching across the divide toward her as much as she is toward me. I can tell that sometimes she does feel intimate during sex—I've read that maybe it's the oxytocin, the rush of a chemical cocktail spilling into her blood as she climaxes. She speaks words of intimacy, stares into my eyes, but I don't feel it myself, not like I think

I should, like I think she does. I'm too busy running away. It's as though the physical sensation of arousal starts a chain reaction in me, a mental and physical cascade that plunges me into solitude. I can have pleasure or I can have intimacy, but never, it seems, both at once. I hide that from her, because I don't want my emotional absence to hurt her. But I can't hide it from myself. It shows up as the one feeling I have never experienced sex without: guilt.

It took me a while to stare this in the face, to come to grips with the fact that something was missing. It is, after all, my invisible backdrop, the air I breathe, the gravity binding me to the only world I've ever known. A person doesn't easily notice something invisible, a something they've never been without, or feel the absence of a thing they've never possessed to begin with.

This is where I am now and what I must deal with. Did Mormonism make me this way? It would be convenient if it did, as if dishing out censure and culpability could ever fix me, as if I could erase some of the pain by blaming my struggles on a church filled with people who in the end are just like me, people who don't know what they don't know, who do the best they can with what they have. No, I don't blame the church, though there are some aspects of Mormonism that exacerbated my pain, giving divine sanction to my preexisting condition of shame, my sense of unworthiness and the resulting perfectionism I believed would make me worthy. After all, I now know men who masturbated as boys, confessed it to bishops, and still managed to advance through the priesthood and go on missions—where they also masturbated. This means what I faced isn't something all Mormon boys encounter; there was something about the particular recipe of me, my tendency for perfection and guilt, and the ways my leaders understood their obligations that caused me such trauma.

While I can't blame the church, it's important to point out what we could have done better, then try to do those things better myself. For starters this would include less black-and-white thinking, less talk of how stepping one inch onto the devil's territory puts you in his power. It would include abandoning the idea that returning to a sin you once repented of returns all the previously atoned-for and expunged guilt of your past right back onto your eternal rap sheet. Instead, we need much, much more talk of getting up and dusting yourself off, of knowing you were built to win and believing you will. As committed to trying as I was, I believe that if my leaders had told me I was well on my way to goodness, told me not to sweat it so much when I stumbled because it wouldn't set me clear back to square one, if they'd been more thoughtful and open, more positive and realistic, less hard on themselves, if they'd talked openly about their own struggles with sexuality, thus stripping it of its shame and power, well, I think I would have left those interviews brimming with confidence and hope instead of shame and despair.

I'm continually working to see my sexuality in a healthier light, but I worry about how my old paradigm might slip through my filters and influence my children, how it possibly already has, and how it has certainly affected my wife. I want my children to experience this side of their humanity without shame. I want them to know and trust their bodies and be free to experience the richness of their sexuality with confidence that it won't diminish them. And if it's not too much to hope for, I'd like that myself as well.

7:06 A.M.

KELLAND COLEMAN

I looked out the aircraft window, the Rockies sprawling below me, the sun before me, working its way to the horizon in the west. It was September 2011; I was flying back to Salt Lake City after a work conference in Denver. I'd been away for three days, away from home, away from *her*, away from perhaps the grandest adventure of my life thus far. I could barely contain myself, shifting in my seat as I thought of being in her arms again, her body entwined with mine, her giggles and sighs of pleasure a balm to my soul. I was experiencing it! I had long ago given up on *this* ever happening to me, and to finally sit in this 737 and contemplate the possible realization of my fondest desire made me feel my life was expanding into a huge, bright space of endless possibilities. I leaned back and breathed deeply. Tears blurred my vision of the majestic landscape below.

I was forty-five years old, and it was the first time I'd been in a sexual relationship with a woman who was physically attracted to me and *enjoyed* being intimate with me.

My mind went back a few weeks to a family gathering on the Twenty-fourth of July, a Utah holiday commemorating the arrival of the Saints in the Salt Lake Valley in 1847. Marnae, my wife of twenty years, our five daughters, and some neighbors had shot off aerial fireworks in front of our home in Bluffdale, Utah. I'd spent over a thousand dollars on the fireworks. It seemed excessive, but for months I'd been facing the dissolution of our family as I knew it, and I spared no expense on experiences we could share. After the noisy confetti showers were cleaned up and everyone had gone back in the house, I sat on the porch's front steps and wept uncontrollably, as I had many times over the previous months. Though I had known for two decades that my wife was not attracted to me, the pain of it had become acute since our separation and she (at my urging) started dating women a few months before.

"She's not attracted to me!" The sadness and pain welled up from deep within. "She doesn't *want* me! She never has!" I felt deeply betrayed, but I knew even then that I had not been betrayed by Marnae. I had betrayed myself, trained masterfully to do so by my parents and the church I'd been raised in.

My parents' marriage was not a catalyst for happiness for either of them. They rarely fought, that I remember, but there was no vitality between them. Energetically, they were dead to each other. I knew from discussions with my mother while I was in college that she wasn't sexually attracted to my father. My father felt this deeply—if not consciously. I didn't see this growing up, but in the context of my marriage experiences, as I look back on his heavy demeanor as we discussed sexuality, I recognize a man who felt the sadness and self-doubt of not being wanted.

I was set up to repeat the same pattern. Touch was not part of my family when I was growing up, and sexuality was never discussed without shame attached to it. Once, when I was four or five years old, I was in the bathtub playing with a toy car, driving it around the tub and my body. When I innocently drove it over my penis, my mother snatched the car away, shouting angrily that I must *never* do that again. I was frightened and shocked.

From this and similar experiences I absorbed the message that my genitals were "dirty" and that my sexual desires were also dirty and had to be rejected and repressed except within the confines of marriage. The teaching that looking upon a woman lustfully was the same as committing adultery in one's heart weighed heavily on me, because I frequently and naturally would see a young woman and feel those urges within me without any conscious choice on my part. I took the church's teachings literally and seriously and never acted on those urges, but still, the shame I internalized about my body and my sexuality harmed and endangered me both physically and emotionally.

The seeds of my self-betrayal were sown in other ways. While in college I read an article by Elder Boyd K. Packer called "Eternal Love," in which he tells young men that many elements of attraction are "essentially unessential. The question is, do you want her as the mother of your children?" Though this logic violated my emotional and sexual interests, it still worked in my subconscious as I began dating seriously after my mission in Korea.

Having no role models for healthy acceptance and expression of male sexuality, feeling shame around my sexual feelings and my need to release through masturbation, and being very afraid of "damning" myself, I was fearful and timid in my associations with young women. I didn't kiss a woman until college, and I unconsciously found ways to mess up every dating relationship I entered. It wasn't difficult to find women I was attracted to, and there were plenty of young women who were attracted to me. But I didn't know how to deal healthily with the intense sexual desires I'd felt since age twelve, and so I unconsciously chose the safe way out: I unknowingly married a lesbian.

* * *

"Hey, Bill!" I blurted to my friend at ballroom dance rehearsal one morning during my first year in graduate school at BYU. "You know that thing we talked about yesterday?" I proudly gave a thumbs up. "It's not a problem!"

The day before, I had confided a few details about my relationship with Marnae, to whom I had recently gotten engaged after only two months of dating. Bill, Marnae's longtime friend, expressed concern about the lack of passion between Marnae and me. Now, "passion" in an engagement between two devout Mormon kids usually didn't mean much more than vigorous making out—but my reported lack of even that concerned him.

Growing up, I heard horror stories about couples who "crossed the line" before marriage and weren't allowed to marry in the temple, their desires and passions having overcome them. I hadn't experienced that challenge with Marnae. "Were we just really good, righteous kids?" I would ask myself. At one level, I was relieved, but at another, I was deeply disappointed, and I knew something was off. This grand thing—marriage and the associated *permission* to have sex—was finally approaching, yet there was no strong passion with my wife-to-be.

So, having heard my friend's concern, I talked to Marnae. It wasn't easy to discuss sex with my fiancée—a red flag right there. Having been raised in a prudishly devout LDS family herself, where sexuality was not openly discussed and where it was not even *conceivable* that she might be attracted to women, she also had no context for understanding why she felt no *zing* when we kissed. "Don't worry about it, it'll come," she said, shrugging it off. And so I dropped the conversation and reported to Bill the next day that everything was fine. I was in love, and I had every rationalization I needed to go ahead with the marriage: passion would come; if it didn't, sex wasn't *that* important for a healthy marriage; the most important thing was that my wife be a good mother. Factor in my unconscious fear of sex and the inherited shame over my body, and the conditions were right for me to marry a woman who couldn't love me back.

And so, about six months after our first date, when I was twenty-five and Marnae was twenty-four and we were both inexperienced, repressed virgins, we got married. Unsurprisingly, our honeymoon was a major disappointment. This was finally the opportunity to *legally and lawfully* express all those passions I had pushed down and demonized since I was twelve years old! And unlike some of my friends, I had actually waited. I had "done it right."

After three days alone in a forest cabin in eastern Arizona, we were ready to return to civilization and be around other people.

It took only a few days to see that Marnae was not into sex nearly as much as I was—that she was hardly into it *at all*—and only a few weeks to determine that this was how it would be going forward. We tried: We bought and read a book written by a pastor on healthy and wholesome sexual practices within a Christian marriage. We talked about it. We both had open attitudes. But we inevitably ran into two major pitfalls of forgoing sex before marriage.

The first is that we discovered after taking our vows that we were not sexually compatible. In the same way that some people don't have good conversational chemistry or lack compatible interests, we had no sexual chemistry. It wasn't a fun, fulfilling part of our relating. For two people who looked forward to experiencing this mysterious and exciting part of life together, this was immensely disappointing.

The second pitfall is that the entire nature of our relationship changed after the wedding ceremony. Even between two people whose relationship is stable before introducing sex into the equation, this new dynamic can create challenges. But when there are significant expectations that sex will be a big part of a marriage, and then after the vows you discover that sexual connection *doesn't even exist*, the effect is devastating. I didn't see it then, but I now see that since I couldn't have sex with Marnae until I married her, the main focus of getting married was to have sex. The anticipation distracted me from what should have been the real focus: building a *complete* relationship based on knowing as many aspects of my dating partner as possible.

With the lure of naive anticipation gone, our incompatibility emerged and our marriage struggled. We rarely fought, but instead of vibrancy there was a vacuum. We couldn't find much to talk about. We had few common interests. But we had covenanted to stick together, so we each found ways to live our separate lives. Together.

Hearing the experiences of others who abstained from premarital sex but won the sexual-compatibility lottery was disheartening. The friend who'd been my best man had married several months before I had. In a conversation not long after my wedding, he shared that his wife liked to have three orgasms each time they had sex. My heart sank. I knew this wasn't the experience of every married couple, but in our several months of lovemaking my wife had not had an orgasm. Nor would she until almost twenty years later.

Over time I internalized this. I thought I was just a horrible husband and lover. I felt unattractive and incompetent. Childhood worries around "not being enough" and teen insecurities about being "terrible with girls" became realities. I felt I wasn't a part of the human race, that I was missing out on something special and powerful. And because I had made a commitment to stay married "forever," I sank into the realization that I would *never* have sex that was passionate and enjoyable to me and—most devastatingly—pleasurable to my partner.

As the years passed, Marnae and I did develop a close friendship—one that exists to this day and is the basis of a close, happy family even after years of divorce. Our emotional connection grew, and we learned to truly love each other. For this I am deeply grateful. Using repression and distractions such as work and hobbies, I learned to soothe the pain from my platonic marriage, and not once did I consider taking my sexual energy outside it. But the psychological and physiological damage of infrequent sexual expression—about once every six weeks—kept building.

In 2007 we decided to leave the church. We spent many nights connecting deeply, sharing our feelings and changing viewpoints. As our minds opened and we truly explored the depths of who we were and what mattered to us, our friendship grew stronger still. I began to *appreciate* Marnae for who she was. I no longer saw her through the eyes of what she *should* be (in order to please "God"); instead, I saw her through eyes of curiosity and wonder.

We made new friends (most of our former friends would have nothing to do with us), and new mind-opening and heartwarming adventures came our way. We took classes, some together, some individually. We had a lot more to talk about. Though there was still very little sex in our relationship, the depth of our marriage increased. For the first time since we were married, I saw that I actually *liked* Marnae as a person. My patience with her increased, and criticism almost completely disappeared. It felt to me that we became soul mates—though certainly not twin flames.

But it still didn't occur to either of us that Marnae might be lesbian. I thought she just wasn't attracted to *me*, and I often wondered, very sadly, if she might be happier with another man. As my love for her deepened, especially after leaving the church, I fully embraced her differences, her unique viewpoints, and the choices she made for her self-care and happiness. I felt a growing desire to support her on her authentic life path, wherever it took her, and to love her no matter what.

And then, on February 20, 2011—a date I will never forget—as I was finishing up in the downstairs bathroom, I could hear my daughters talking to Marnae just outside the door. She was waiting for me, which was unusual. "Can you come upstairs for a minute?" she asked as I entered the hallway.

"Sure." I followed her upstairs and into our bedroom. She had a hesitant, solemn air about her. We often had serious discussions, usually about the children, but something seemed heavier, more foreboding. I felt fear.

We sat on the bed facing each other, and tears began streaming from her eyes. She wanted to share something but seemed scared. "What is it, honey?" I asked, taking her hand.

After a few moments of silence, she looked up at me and began: "You know Dreya, the life coach I've been working with?"

"Yes," I replied.

Again she hesitated. "Well, I was at a session with her a couple of weeks ago, and as I was listening to her and looking at her . . . something inside me burst open. It was as if my whole world changed from black and white to color. At first I didn't know what was happening, but over the past two weeks as I've thought about it and talked to her about it, I've discovered . . ."

"You're gay!" I blurted out excitedly. It had come to me in a flash of understanding. I could not contain my pleasure. In that moment I knew she had discovered an authentic part of her being!

"Yes . . . yes . . ." She began to weep. I leaned forward and embraced her, and for the next few minutes we laughed and cried together. This was a moment of solidarity, of truth, of love, of genuine concern for the well-being of the other.

After several minutes, when she had calmed down, Marnae continued: "I didn't know what 'falling in love' meant before. I thought it was sort of like that feeling you have when you think a little child is cute. But when that moment came with Dreya . . . I knew it was something entirely different . . . something so *powerful*. So much passion and desire arose in me. I was so taken aback I needed a few days to process it all."

As was common between Marnae and me during that period, we got into a stimulating conversation and decided to continue it over dinner. We drove to our favorite restaurant, Log Haven in Mill Creek Canyon. We had fun with our new understanding and perspective: at one point we discreetly picked out some of the female servers and "compared notes." My mind was blown by the idea that she and I could find the same woman attractive!

Given my love and adoration of Marnae, it was natural that I would be pleased and supportive about this huge breakthrough she'd had, one that would lead to so much joy in her life. We went to bed feeling peaceful and relieved.

But it all changed when I awoke the next morning. I remember very clearly that it was Presidents' Day, so I didn't have to go to work. I began to realize the implications of Marnae's discovery. I hadn't conceived that the best path for Marnae might mean *divorce*. The thought terrified me. Never in my life had I felt so much fear. I lay in bed all afternoon, and as it all sank in I began to cry until my head ached. I couldn't breathe. My mind was a whirlwind. The future had suddenly become a frightening cacophony of disturbing images. What would happen to my daughters? How would I live without my wife and dearest friend? I didn't want life to change! I was happy! I was comfortable! It was my first ever panic attack.

We had numerous discussions over the next few days. Though Marnae's coach had gently counseled that her orientation could lead to divorce, we decided to make the marriage work anyway. We sought the answer to one question: How could Marnae express her newfound sexual desires *and* keep our marriage intact? We talked with friends, we considered options that—especially having been devout Latter-day Saints for so many years—we would never previously have dared imagine: Open marriage? Threesomes? Polyamory?

We signed up for a class on tantric practices and read a book together that focused on healthy interactions between the feminine and masculine. And for a very short time, we experienced a limited degree of the passion I had wanted to experience with Marnae for our entire marriage. For the first time in her life—at age forty-four—she experienced sexual pleasure in a relationship.

But even as we worked to save our marriage, my anxiety intensified daily. I had never experienced such intense discomfort in my body. I slept little. My stomach churned constantly; my mind was in constant chaos. I knew what was coming, and my resistance to it exhausted me.

After only a few weeks, our enjoyment in sex together faded. It became clear that our sexual connection was the result of the massive release of Marnae's pent-up sexual energy. Our relating no longer brought her pleasure.

About two months after Marnae came out to me, on a Sunday in mid-April, I awoke and looked at the clock. It was 7:06 A.M. I noticed the correlation to our wedding date, July 6. I looked at Marnae, still peacefully sleeping, and I knew this wouldn't work. Both of us were explorers in life, wanting to experience all we could. We would not stop growing, ever, and this important energetic element that did not—nor ever would—exist between us would remain a roadblock to our personal fulfillment.

I'd learned some things about myself over the past few years, and I knew my desire for connection in a relationship was deep. I wanted connection on all levels: emotional, mental, physical, and spiritual. I understood that without the physical aspect, there would always be a block to full connection in other ways. And I knew she felt it too.

My mind raced. What about our five daughters? How would this affect them? How could I support two households? How would I *live* without this most wonderful woman as my partner? I had no answers. I just knew what the next step was. That Sunday morning, we decided to separate.

Words cannot describe the sadness and pain I felt watching my daughters cry as we told them of our decision to separate. And there was a growing rage in me: How had I found myself in this position of having children with a woman who was sexually incompatible with me and now having to choose between a dissatisfying marriage and causing my daughters such distress?!

Though I was a willing participant in the choice to separate, my mental health declined. The trauma threw my brain into chemical imbalance, and I fell into acute depression. For the first time in my life, I *knew* what it was to experience depression, and I knew what it was like to live in the valley of the shadow of death—almost every day became a choice between living and suicide. It was a struggle to accomplish the most basic tasks. I lost all interest in hobbies and activities. I don't know how I kept my job, and when I was home I mostly lay in bed and cried.

The strength of the friendship between Marnae and me showed its colors during this period. We never fought, and we supported each other as best we could. I loved her and wanted her to walk the path that would lead to her greatest happiness. After decades of dull grays, her life burst into Technicolor as she began dating women she was attracted to. She was very compassionate about my struggles and listened to my cries and sat with me through many panic attacks over the next months. In her sweetness she offered to go back to how it was and repress her sexual instincts, but we both knew it wouldn't work.

In time, through the help of a dear friend, a therapist, and medications, my mental health improved and I returned to a happy life. And in late August, I met and started dating Kathryn, with whom I shared a strong sexual attraction. No longer did I feel envy when I saw couples holding hands and laughing together. I was finally part of it—the great adventure of human sexuality.

But my healing continues. Even now, I struggle with insecurities that became deeply ingrained patterns during twenty years of sexually dysfunctional marriage. I learn and grow and increase my capacity for that deep connection to another that I always knew I wanted.

And what of my daughters? In ways I couldn't see from within my trauma, all has turned out well. Marnae and I remain close friends; we're still committed partners in loving and supporting our beautiful daughters. Our family is very much intact, and though we live in separate households, we still come together and share moments of love and connection. In reality, the relationship between Marnae and me is as it always has been: friends deeply committed to each other's happiness and the happiness of our daughters.

* * *

Occasionally, someone will ask me, "So, what do you teach your daughters about sexuality?"

I teach them that they are at choice and the masters of their own body and sexuality and that no organization or person has either the right or sufficient wisdom to tell them how to express their creative and sexual energy. I explain that along with this freedom comes the need to understand the risks of sexual contact with another without proper precautions and also the need to understand that bringing a child into the world—accidentally or purposefully—is a serious obligation that will change their lives forever.

I teach them that human sexual energy is a powerful force that, if harnessed respectfully and authentically, creates the impetus for deep connection with another human being that no other power known to humanity can.

Finally, I make very clear that sex is as important in an intimate relationship as any other aspect and that it should be freely and responsibly explored with potential partners before vows or commitments are made. When sex before marriage is prohibited, couples may rush into marriage in order to have sex and—because of their ignorance about their own or their partner's true nature—discover on their wedding night that the seeds of divorce have already been sown.

Unsealed

DAN SMITH

Considering my quasi-military upbringing in communities with few Mormons, the Missionary Training Center in Provo was the biggest culture shock I ever experienced. I naively thought that all good Mormon boys my age shared a certain work ethic, maturity, and orthodoxy. At the MTC, I quickly learned that was not true. My companion constantly talked about how many wet dreams he had every night and commented on how attractive or not he found sister missionaries' boobs and butts. Other missionaries bragged about masturbation, which I'd been taught to avoid entirely. And still others confessed that they hadn't even read the Book of Mormon and were serving a mission because their parents would reward them with a car or an education or some other desirable thing. And here I had worked for three years, saving every dime to afford a mission. "How is it that God chose these nincompoops to serve him?" I wondered. "They're not just unworthy; they're idiots." Even the MTC teachers were wrong, from what I had been taught. They would reward you with a two-liter bottle of Pepsi for reading the whole Book of Mormon within a specified time frame (which, in my opinion, should have been a prerequisite for being there). Where I grew up, caffeine was tantamount to alcohol, a major Word of Wisdom offense. Yet it was OK at the MTC, where God was preparing a new generation of leaders. I thought, "I know why I'm here: to bring people to Christ." I concluded that people from Utah and its surrounding states were all Jack Mormons and the only real Mormons were people like me.

I was sent to Central America and was thrilled to become more fluent in Spanish, having studied it throughout high school. But within my first month in-country, I'd lost over thirty pounds and had every type of parasite from ringworm to tapeworm. Upon finally admitting myself to the hospital, I was told that if I'd waited one more day to seek treatment, I would have died. My mission president's response was to tell me, "Elder, you just need to have more faith. That's why you're sick."

I wanted to ask why he didn't have the faith to simply heal me. Didn't he hold the mantle of authority over us missionaries? Instead, I buried my anger and frustration at him, at God, at myself. I prayed and determined to continue my course straight as a holy arrow. Although I remained ill my entire mission, I forced myself to survive. I carried toilet paper with me everywhere, knowing God would help me even if only through toilet paper. I grew to love the people, and I sincerely wanted to help them. I served faithfully, even when I found the assistants to the president baptizing children below the age of eight, which violates church doctrine and which led to another confrontation with the mission president—he almost sent me home for chastising the "Lord's anointed," as he called his APs. Regardless of our different values, I attained his average goal (what he termed the "Lord's goal") of baptizing ten people a month; by the end of two years, I had baptized over two hundred people. I felt worthy of anything and everything. Having avoided romantic love up to that point, I was ready to let it into my life and begin my life as an adult.

I enrolled at BYU, though I felt like a fish out of water. Despite my contempt for Mormons west of the Mississippi, I knew I was more likely to find a Mormon wife at BYU than in Florida, where my parents lived. I wanted the sort of intelligent, righteous wife I'd come to believe I was worthy of thanks to my chastity and the sacrifice and devotion I'd shown on my mission. I felt I deserved the peace and happiness the church promised as a reward for righteous living.

I made friends, went on lots of group dates, and, after I'd been home from my mission for more than a year, finally worked up the nerve to kiss a girl. And then I fell for June, certain she was *the one*. Her intelligence and strong charisma both challenged my self-esteem and compelled me to overcome my reserve. She was from an affluent family with pioneer roots and seemed extremely devout. I thought we shared both similar ideals and certain concerns about LDS culture and doctrine.

But there were warning signs. I had to propose three times before she accepted. Also, June's family was from the West, which I didn't like. That should have been enough for me to know it wouldn't work—I probably shouldn't have married someone whose family I disapproved of in crucial ways. But in other ways, I admired June's family. Her parents were generous and caring; they seemed to share a beautiful relationship. I assumed that would somehow translate into my relationship with June. We were married in the temple a few months after she finally accepted my proposal.

We both read up to prepare for our first sexual encounter, and it was a beautiful first-time experience. I was finally living the Mormon dream; I was a returned missionary, BYU student, temple-married priesthood holder. But the dream was short-lived. Mere weeks after marriage, I felt abandoned emotionally and physically. June had little interest in doing things together or learning about each other. We had sex, but only to conceive children and pretty much only on her terms—I was lucky to have sex with her once a month. I had an idea of what love should look like—and it wasn't what I was living.

Whenever I shared my feelings, June would shame me in some way. "You're questioning my behavior?" she would say if I asked to spend more time together. "I'm right with God; are you?" If I asked to have sex, she would say, "You're just being carnal." I had to acknowledge the doctrinal support for some of what she said, but I didn't know what to do about how horrible it made me feel, like there was something wrong with me for wanting to have sex or spend time with my wife. I didn't realize I was being gaslighted.

With a baby on the way, we decided to buy our first home. The day he was born was the day we got the keys. After a morning at the hospital with my wife and child and then hours of moving furniture, I crashed on the floor of our new house and wept. This should have been a happy, joyful day, yet I was distraught, confused, and angry. Angry that I wasn't in love with the person I'd just bought a house and had a baby with! But I didn't have time for self-pity, so I shrugged it off and, as I had done so often before, buried it.

I taught full-time at a technical college, covering the absolutely horrible 3:00 A.M.-to-noon shift, an evil necessary to accommodate people trying to get a degree while working a day job. Aside from the hours, I loved my job, but I came home exhausted and felt like a single parent with a female roommate. I knew June took care of the baby while I was at work, but it felt like she was 100 percent off duty when I got home. I could rarely take time for myself, nor would June find time to be with me. Instead, she talked with family or friends on the phone when I was home. I had no meaningful interactions with her and no social life, except what occurred at work or church.

I wasn't in love. I couldn't understand why I felt so alone. I'd done everything the church taught but wasn't getting what the church promised in return. Why wouldn't I see that my wife wasn't in love with me either? I didn't want to attribute my loneliness to her lack of attention and affection. I didn't see the neglect as anyone's fault—except my own. Whenever I tried to discuss my unhappiness with June, she would say something like, "If you're unhappy, it means you need to get right with God in some way."

I resolved to stick to the approach that had sustained me through my life to that point. A good marriage was about manning up and sacrificing myself and my needs and desires for the greater good. Since Christ had sacrificed himself, I could only follow his lead and sacrifice myself, too. I thought I was being Christlike when I took the blame on myself. My unhappiness was no one's fault but my own. Yet sometimes I blamed my unhappiness on a bad employer and felt justified—so I made a lot of career changes. But even in a job I liked, as I advanced in skill, pay, and ability, I wasn't happy, and it couldn't just be that I was wrong with God. I kept trying to find what I was doing wrong, and June provided no answers that made sense, though she encouraged me to find the underlying issues that made me so unhappy and such a disappointment.

Over the next decade, I moved further and further from what I knew love should be. My efforts to demonstrate love, care, and affection for my wife weren't reciprocated or appreciated. I felt neglected in all ways. I was responsible for all childcare at family gatherings, even though she stood aloof from conversations except to complain about the weather. I was constantly told I was too carnal for wanting sex even once a week. I eventually stopped trying to include her in my life.

Eleven years and a few children later, June was pregnant with our last daughter. As we talked one night in bed, she told me, "Dan, I don't feel sealed to you. I never have." I don't remember what prompted it, probably because it hit me so hard that the rest of our discussion was obliterated. Perhaps she'd grown tired of telling me to "get right with God" when I hadn't changed into whatever she thought I was supposed to be.

I had always believed that being *sealed* = *love*. OK, maybe not crazy infatuated erotic love—I'd given up on that—but certainly I believed in a kind of compassionate devotion to your partner's happiness. Of course I "loved" June—I was sealed to her! For her to say that she never felt sealed to me was to admit she never loved me. And she'd done it so casually, so callously, clearly unconcerned with the pain this announcement would bring me.

Overwhelmed by shock and betrayal, I silently slipped out of bed and spent the night on the couch. I cried all night. I wanted to die. I'd wasted a dozen years with someone who didn't love me yet bore my children.

I thought about leaving, but I couldn't step away because of the children and the celestial commitments I believed I'd made. I had to endure to the end, just as I'd done on my mission, just as I'd done with everything. After that night, I don't know why June stayed. I expected a request for a divorce, but it didn't come. I know I asked why she felt the way she did, but she had no response. The lack of reason only dug at me deeper, even though nothing she could have said would have comforted me because I was already so wounded and emotionally walled off.

The kids weren't just my reason for staying; they were my lifeline. I contemplated suicide, but the thought of my kids kept me alive. I trudged along a few more years and managed to find happiness within myself despite knowing my wife didn't love me. Besides, as I watched other men at church, they weren't happy either. Some looked more miserable than I. So I immersed myself in my kids when I was at home and in work when I was at work.

Also rewarding was the friendship we cultivated with Bill and Laura, a couple from church with kids our age. Over the years we took vacations together, and on weekends I helped Bill at his freelance construction job without any expectation of remuneration or compensation.

One year, as my birthday approached, June told me that Laura wanted to offer me a massage. I'd become a licensed massage therapist and given both Bill and Laura massages in the past, so I gratefully accepted this thoughtful gift. The day came, and I set up my table in the master bedroom while June entertained the kids downstairs.

I relaxed into the massage as Laura followed a routine like the one I used. She worked shoulders down to toes while I was face down; when I turned over, she worked from toes up to my neck. As she progressed up my legs, she asked, "Are you OK? You seem really quiet."

"I'm just enjoying the massage," I replied. "You're doing great."

As she massaged along my inner thigh, the touch aroused me slightly. I looked at her as if to say, *Careful.* She placed her hand directly on my draped groin and said, "It happens."

It's true that it happens, but out of both personal and professional ethics, I had always backed way off from anything I thought would make a client uncomfortable. That Laura had crossed a line I wouldn't left me stunned, speechless, and concerned. It's true that I was attracted to Laura, but I respected our friendship and was afraid to jeopardize it—or my professional standards. To my relief, Laura continued as if nothing happened, working on my stomach, pecs, and arms.

Shortly before Laura finished the massage, June knocked and came in. I watched as she sat nearby but was confused when she said something very low to Laura that I couldn't catch. Laura answered, "It's going well, but I think Dan isn't relaxing like he usually does."

This confused me even more. How would Laura know how I usually relaxed during a massage? I rolled onto my side to tell June, "She said I'm quieter than usual, but I don't know how that means I'm not relaxing." At that moment, I almost told June what her best friend had done moments earlier.

June shrugged. Laura pushed me down before I could say more. "We're not finished yet," she said. I couldn't tell who she was talking to or how to respond. They both seemed intent on Laura completing the massage. To this day, I'm not sure why I didn't fully recognize the huge red flags waving at me.

June stood up. "OK," she said and promptly left.

In short, Laura attempted to seduce me, telling me that June knew about her love for me. Laura nearly had me convinced that June fully approved. We kissed, and I touched her breasts but went no further. I wanted to trust Laura completely, but something was off. I sat up with the sheet wrapped around me, asking a million questions, which Laura evaded. Suddenly June returned. I wrapped the sheet more tightly around me and watched their interaction quickly devolve into some disagreement that resulted in Laura's departure, followed quickly by June leaving too. June wouldn't answer my questions, either. Instead, she made it sound like we had done something against her wishes—even though she admitted to knowing what Laura intended to do. I was stunned and confused. I got dressed, called Laura, and demanded, "I thought you said this was what you both wanted?"

"We did nothing wrong. It'll be fine," she responded. She confirmed that June knew and had given her permission for us to have sex if I wanted to. Laura claimed she was as confused at June's reaction as I was.

"None of this makes any sense," I said. She just repeated that it would be fine and hung up.

I called June. She was still upset. Rather than discuss what happened, she said we needed two weeks apart. It wasn't negotiable. I was dazed, confused, scared, and angry—especially since I was blamed and kicked out of my house for what had happened, though I didn't know if my crime was succumbing at all to Laura's attempt to seduce me or putting the brakes on before she succeeded.

Two weeks of sleeping on sofas at the homes of family and coworkers became three. During that time, I missed three of my kids' birthdays, but I had plenty of time for deep, anguished reflection. After the three weeks were up, I returned home and confronted June. "Someone is lying to me, and none of this makes any sense. Did you know about what Laura was going to do or not?" June confirmed that she did know and had arranged it with her.

"So why was I in trouble, then? What's this about?" I asked. "I've felt for a long time that there's something deeper going on between you two."

June confessed that she'd been "sealed" to Laura and had sex with her; a week later June was also "sealed" to and had sex with Bill. My immediate reaction was not surprise. It was rejection, betrayal, and anger at her unfaithfulness and deception. But in those weeks I was gone, I reached a place where I didn't want to hide anymore. I wanted everything out on the table. So I asked questions about their relationships and what their intent was for me. It made some sense that June was bisexual, leaning more toward women, since she had never really been interested in sex with me. Then she also admitted to being "sealed" to another man during her last pregnancy—I suppose that was what she was comparing our marriage to when she said she "never felt sealed" to me. More hurt and betrayal—but at least I was getting the truth.

I didn't judge anything June said. I didn't want to make her too angry or upset to continue talking to me. I'd just gotten out of the doghouse and wasn't about to be thrown back in it. I felt so abused and devastated, but I did everything I could to stay calm and learn as much as possible. What else could I do?

She told me they had used the last three weeks to be together and plan their futures. June looked me right in the eye and said, "God showed us that you would be removed from the picture." In fact, they were all very surprised when I returned from the three-week hiatus alive! They felt sure I would be hit by a truck and die during my traveling. When I came back, things started falling apart for them.

June and I "made up" and resolved to be more honest to each about our wants and feelings. Weeks passed. Suddenly Bill and Laura became upset with June. When I asked June about it, she told me that she had promised she wouldn't have sex with me anymore, that I still had to be out of the picture at least in that way, so they were unhappy to learn that she'd been intimate with me. The relationship unraveled further somehow when June visited them later that week. After that, they were done with her. I never did discover the details of why Bill and Laura ended their relationship with June.

With Bill and Laura out of the picture, I did my best to move forward. Pressed by LDS culture and my upbringing to fight for my family, I wanted to avoid divorce at all costs. It's true that the church doesn't completely prohibit divorce; I'd known several couples who'd divorced because of infidelity, but I also knew that many Mormons frowned on anyone who divorced, no matter the reason.

June had become more and more attracted to the doctrine of polygamy and had an elaborate explanation for why Joseph Smith was right about it. She believed that if we accomplish all that the gods (she believed there were many) require of us and prove ourselves worthy through our actions in this life, we will join the gods in the highest of heavens after we die. In that celestial realm, we are as gods, omniscient and omnipotent. We will have no need for shelter, clothing, or food and are able to create anything we do need. Because we won't need clothing to protect our bodies from the elements and because we know so much about others' bodies, we can be naked without care. We are capable of the most profound love: we share each other's thoughts; nothing can be withheld from our view, and love "seals" us to one another for eternity. Since there are no barriers, since we are all naked, and since we are all sealed together, why would we be denied the communion and intimacy of sex with anyone and everyone?

June felt that since I had stayed with her and supported her through her breakup with Bill and Laura, I had shown myself worthy to have a second wife. Because I wanted to save my marriage, I agreed. The first woman June approached was not interested. Then June approached her cousin, who accepted. We lived polygamy, as June believed Joseph Smith established, but it lasted only seven months and caused nothing but trauma and heartbreak. June pushed her cousin to seek other men, and it felt like a continuous attempt to minimize this person's importance in our marriage and, at some point, her importance as a human being, period. Though I did all I could to reassure June's cousin that she didn't need to find other partners if she didn't want to, she couldn't ignore

June's persistent directives to find additional husbands, and eventually she collapsed mentally and attempted suicide. Nothing I said or did seemed to help. I was devastated and grieving, thinking that June had destroyed this person I had come to love.

We moved to a different state, changed jobs, and tried to start fresh. June was recuperating from the "divorces" of her prior "sealings." I was recovering from the dramatic loss of the second wife, and honestly, I was still recovering from being excluded, cast aside, lied to, manipulated, and betrayed by June.

Two years later, June met another LDS couple, Elijah and Anna, and expressed a desire to be "sealed" to them. They were willing to live an unorthodox life, and June still felt I was worthy to be part of it. We performed our own ceremony and began our honeymoons. At first, we kept separate households. Then Elijah made the mistake of telling Anna's cousin, who told Anna's parents, who owned the house Elijah and Anna lived in and promptly evicted them. June was angry at the judgment, while I was furious because I had warned Elijah to stay silent. It was a horrible upheaval, but we did our best to roll with it. I paid to move them in with us, and all four adults stayed in the master bedroom together.

Initially, it seemed to work. But Elijah and June soon began to distance themselves. They moved a bed into the garage already crowded with bicycles, boxes, and tools. They also removed Anna and me from their social media accounts and insisted we "focus" on our new relationships. So we did. Anna and I had no problem being together. We had fallen deeply in love. We tried to maintain connections with Elijah and June, but their words and actions communicated clearly that they didn't want us. So focus we did, and we did it so well that we moved out and divorced them. When the divorces were final, Anna and I were married. Like, right after. We couldn't wait. We were single for the whole of twenty minutes—the time it took to get married at the courthouse after the divorce was final!

The divorces exposed a great many lies: about finances, about other relationships, about ridiculous and petty things that weren't worth lying about. In fact, we continue to uncover lies. I'm sad that it took me leaving before I could realize how thorough June's dishonesty was, but a couple of decades of being gaslighted can make you doubt your judgment. I had to be out of it completely to see how abusive June (and Elijah) were and how very different their ideas of love were from mine.

I still struggle with guilt and disappointment in myself that I stayed in that toxic environment for so long. I stayed because I felt obligated because of my temple vows and because I loved my children, but I think now it would have been better to remove them from it sooner. Anna and I petitioned for and were granted primary custody of both my children and her children. Our exes are not currently in positions to provide for children, whereas we'll do whatever is required to care for them. We're grateful that we're able to raise them in an environment more wholesome than what they were used to.

To me, love isn't about how many people you can be "sealed" to or proving your worthiness. I knew many members who lied about their worthiness—if not to their bishops, then to themselves. In my perspective now, we begin life already connected to everything. Trying to prove otherwise is futile. Our goal shouldn't be to separate from each other but to seek ways to show our love to as many people as we want. I'm not suggesting swinging or justifying one-night stands. I'm talking about the fierce loyalty of people to love with all their hearts and be true to their way of loving. In other words, be honest about what you want and with those you have relationships with.

Perhaps it's unnecessary to say that I no longer believe in many if not most of the things I grew up hearing at church. Anna and I do believe in love, and our concept of it has origins in LDS belief. I think the people from that culture, like most individuals, desire a profound, deep love. They want to believe in something that connects and makes them part of something larger than themselves. The love we have has grown exponentially since our marriage. We've been able to express our love more fully and honestly and have found ourselves empowered by it. Where we were repressed, we now have the freedom to express our love and the freedom to explore our own interests and ideas about it and grow together and as individuals. I can only hope the same for everyone.

PART III

In Sickness and in Health

Figure 7. Joseph Broom (*left*) and Mark Koepke, August 2013, Holladay, Utah

Joseph writes, "This photo from the commitment ceremony in our backyard in Holladay perfectly reflects us 'resting in' and 'holding' the love between us, as well as the joy and contentment we each felt in this love. The white katas we each wear around our necks we presented to each other during the ceremony, a token of the love and respect we each held for the other as a teacher, guide, companion, and lover through the remainder of the days we would share together."

Fear and Trepanation

TED SMITH

"You have a serious condition, so you won't be leaving the hospital today," the emergency room doctor said gravely to Tina, my wife. Tina reached for my hand, her grip trembling, her eyes wide. I tried to project calm as I returned her gaze, cradling her hand in an attempt at reassurance.

"You have a subdural hematoma," the doctor continued. "It's a pool of blood under your skull yet outside the brain. The symptoms you've noted—severe headaches or difficulty judging distance while driving and bumping up against the curb—are no doubt a result of this condition, all caused by the accumulated blood's pressure on your brain. Left untreated, a subdural hematoma the size of yours can be fatal."

The waiting room was empty except for us three, sitting amid generic office furnishings with out-of-date magazines on tables. It was indistinguishable from a waiting room at, say, an auto dealership, a place where the most shocking news you might hear is "I'm sorry, but you need a new engine," not "your wife might die."

In another, more private room we saw CT scans showing a cross section of Tina's brain from the top of her skull, like a walnut in a shell. The pool of blood was visible at the top left corner, pushing into the brain, as if a pebble had become lodged inside the shell and the walnut meat had grown as best it could around it.

Tina rocked in her chair, moaning slightly. "What's the procedure to treat this?" she asked.

"It's called burr hole trephination or trepanation," the doctor said. "Two small holes are drilled in the skull over the subdural hematoma, and the blood is vacuumed out with a small catheter. I can assure you it's a common enough procedure, perfected over the years by treating people who've had concussions in car accidents. We need to get you prepped now."

My mind raced. I had to text the kids at school, let them know without worrying them, make after-school ride arrangements. How did this happen to Tina? I had to make sure things at work were covered. Thanksgiving was in two days—what would we do about that? Could Tina actually die from this? I felt a rush of blood to my gut, panic. Then I thanked God I had not left my wife the previous spring—what the hell had I been thinking? "I have things I need you to handle," Tina said to me.

"Sure," I replied. "OK."

* * *

A year earlier, in November 2009, Tina had realized something was wrong with me. I'd been emotionally distant for a couple of weeks, so she thought I was mad at her. I have the tendency, learned no doubt from my mother, who was prone to this behavior, to give people who've upset me the silent treatment. While this seems like a form of punishment—a purposeful tactic in an overall strategy to win a fight—for me it's more the defensive measure of a quasi-introvert to avoid more discomfort, a retreat rather than an attack.

One morning as I sat in bed, staring out the window at the darkness before sunrise, Tina asked me point-blank, "Are you mad at me? What's going on with you?"

I hesitated, then said, "I feel dead inside." It was both the truth and a surprise to me, something I hadn't known until I had to voice it.

"Why?" she asked.

"I don't know." I didn't know what else to say. She attributed my situation to professional burnout, chalking it up to my perennial end-of-the-year/fiscal-quarter work schedule. We needed to talk about it, she said, and I said, "How about after the holidays? I promise to not be so withdrawn."

Yet by early February 2010, even though work had slowed to more manageable proportions, nothing had changed for me, and we hadn't talked about it. Then I had lunch with a lifelong friend who surprised me with the story of his recent recovery from a midlife crisis. "I had this overwhelming urge to leave, to start all over again," he told me. He had taken concrete steps in this direction, slept with another woman, but still managed to salvage his marriage. "Things started falling apart until I decided to see a therapist," he said.

I had never considered a therapist for myself, but I admitted to him that I had recently felt the urge to stray as well. While I hadn't acted on the impulse, I said I was afraid I might, that I would not be in control, that I was confused, that my eyes recently had been drawn to the eyes of other women rather than glancing away out of marital habit. "How'd it go with the therapist?" I asked.

"He's great. He helped me see through my own bullshit. That's what it is. Bullshit. And testosterone. Bullshit and testosterone. Testosterone makes men crazy, so we start believing our own bullshit. You should visit him. He's abrasive as hell, and you'll need just that. A lot of straight talk." We were eating at our favorite Thai restaurant, but neither of us seemed interested in the food.

"What you're going through is pretty normal, but no one ever talks about it—except to ridicule the men who blindly dive right in, turning their control over to their hormones," he continued. "And no one adequately warns you about it either, until voilà!—when it happens to you, you think something's wrong with you, that you're a sinner, but it's natural to feel this way, and knowing that is your best defense." He smirked. "It's your genes trying to replicate one last desperate time, an all-hands-on-deck assault on your system to devote all resources toward our species' mission: create offspring in as many nests as you can! It's comical, or pathetic, or something. Why a God would ever program us that way is a mystery to me."

"So things are good now?" I asked. "Like, more than just bearable?"

"Things are now authentic between us, real, which means they are better and should be very good," he confirmed. "I got lucky and saved my marriage, I think, because my marriage is worth saving. Way more valuable than what I was prepared to throw it away for."

I stalled a few weeks, waiting for I don't know what, before I made an appointment with his psychologist.

* * *

Tina was taken upstairs for surgery prep in a wheelchair by a chatty nurse, me following behind. Once in the hospital room we filled out more insurance forms, made more phone calls. Nurses came in and out in hurried succession. I called each of the kids, brought them up to date. Apparently my text messages did not strike the balance I had hoped: of course they were panicked about their mom—seems there is no truly reassuring way to say, "Your mother is having unexpected surgery, but she should be OK." Finally, two neurosurgeons arrived to talk with us. One was the older partner in the physicians' practice and did most of the talking. He wanted to know more about what might have caused Tina's condition.

"I've always had headaches since moving to Atlanta in 1994," she said. "But what really set this one off was a roller coaster ride on a school trip last August to Six Flags. It was one of those wooden ones, all rickety, a lot of sideways shaking going on. That's when it felt like something inside my head just exploded."

"That sounds like the cause," the neurosurgeon said as he looked over Tina's records of headaches and the medications prescribed to treat them. "I suspect that was it, and your headache meds themselves, unfortunately, likely made the bleeding worse."

The neurosurgeons assured us that this procedure, while serious, was common, that his team of surgeons had performed hundreds of them, and that Tina should recover nicely. In more dire situations, something called a craniotomy must be performed, he continued, this more extreme procedure requiring part of the skull to be opened in a flap in order to remove the hematoma. While this was likely intended to make us feel better about a mere burr hole trepanation, it no more succeeded than had my own explanations to our children.

His calm, professional affect didn't change as he said, "After consulting with our team, we've decided that based on your stable condition and the minimal staffing and travel schedules at the hospital over the holiday, we should wait till after Thanksgiving to perform the procedure." I didn't understand. Tina was stable? Hadn't she recently taken a turn for the worse, the hematoma affecting her driving, suggesting she was not really stable, whatever that meant? I looked to Tina, who also seemed puzzled, but we both went along, nodding in agreement with the doctor.

After a long pause, Tina finally asked, tentatively, "You mean we can't do it earlier?"

"No," he said, smiling a little to soften our inevitable disappointment, yet still too businesslike to acknowledge the fear behind her statement. "You'll have our phone numbers and access to a nurse here on staff if things get worse, such as your fever, pain, or ability to walk. If you rest in bed, you should be OK at home until the surgery next Monday."

And so, despite originally being told we wouldn't leave the hospital that day, Tina and I headed home.

The next day, Wednesday, Tina's many friends got the message through social media and marshaled forces to deliver food, company, and care. Although we no longer attended our local LDS ward, friends of ours there organized themselves to assist. Over the next five days someone was always at the house with food or to sit by Tina's side as she rested, while I juggled work and kids, with one neighbor—a nurse at our hospital and a friend from the Methodist church we often attended—coming by periodically to check her temperature, blood pressure, breathing, and pulse.

*　*　*

When I sought treatment for my own mental condition the prior spring, it was my friend and the psychologist who tended to my care, with the psychologist drilling holes into the workings of my mind every two weeks, while my friend and I had Thai food every other month.

The therapist's office resembled a cozy, dark den from the 1970s, with books on the walls and a large Persian rug in the middle of the room surrounded by a desk, a couch, and a lounge chair. My first visit there was a nervous affair.

I didn't know how to explain what was going on and was embarrassed that I needed help controlling my thoughts. When the therapist asked the purpose of my visit, I used my friend as an example of what I'd been feeling but said I had not acted on my feelings.

"Your friend is a good man. And it's a good thing we caught you so early," the therapist said, as if what I had were cancer and could spread. "Feelings can ruin your life!" he said, flourishing his pad and pencil in the air. He had a thick Boston accent, reminding me of the subway drivers when I attended Boston University, and his conversation was as direct as the line from Boylston to Kenmore. "It's all a bunch of nonsense, feelings."

"What about the feelings I have for my wife?" I asked. "I still love her; aren't those good feelings? Yet I feel the urge to leave. How does one know which feelings to respect?"

"Yes, of course. Loving your wife is a good feeling. And we're lucky, because we can control our feelings. Your feelings brought you and Tina together, but there was something else that got you two in particular to get married, not just feelings. And there's something else still keeping you together. Call it commitment. And your children. Even your finances, your 401(k). All good reasons that should trump feelings. Why wreck all of that over some idiotic feelings?"

From my therapist's point of view, how this watershed era in my life began sounded absolutely textbook, a cliché even. I was turning fifty the next month; I had purchased a convertible; I had an ongoing, panic-attack-level urge to leave my marriage, something I knew my rational mind didn't want, but that mind had had its lid blown off. I suspect all spouses can come up with a list of problems in their marriage that could constitute an argument for quitting, but for many, somehow just enough satisfactory moments keep gradually happening, surrounded by safe routine, so all that seems to keep people together, contented. For others, the rut of contentment is a dead end when they hit the barricade of a midlife crisis. This is what happened to me. I said it sounded like some kind of malware in the male genetic code. *Male*ware.

"Is there something I can do to make this go away?" I asked.

"Probably not. But you can keep your head screwed on straight until these feelings go away. That's what I'm here for. Every two weeks you'll come visit me, and together we'll keep you from doing something stupid."

On my second visit, the therapist spent a lot of time getting to know me. "You're not an easy person to get to know," he said after about twenty-five minutes. "You talk a lot about ideas, but that's just a smokescreen. You'll need to tell me how you feel and what you're thinking about that. Your feelings need to be uncovered and examined in the light of reason and, should I say, common sense."

"You sound a lot like my wife," I said. I didn't point out that he'd asked me to explain my feelings after first telling me feelings were nonsense.

"Excellent!" the therapist said, smiling. "Your wife sounds pretty smart to me, and that's a good sign for you getting through this with her."

* * *

By Thanksgiving Day I worried that Tina was out of bed, moving around too much. We were having dinner that evening with neighbors up the street, and Tina insisted on preparing some menu items. I told her there was no need. In fact, we could take some items delivered to us by her friends, like ridiculously delicious macaroni and cheese made with Gruyère, a broccoli casserole, a pumpkin pie or two. We had an enjoyable evening out, but I could see by 9:00 P.M. that Tina was fading, so we went home.

Sunday, the day before the burr hole trepanation, some of our Mormon friends came over after church, including the bishop, who asked if Tina would allow him to give her a blessing. I joined the other men in a circle around Tina; we all placed our hands on her head as the bishop blessed her that she might be healed. Afterward, tears filled our eyes as Tina assured us she would be OK. Then, one of our neighbors suggested Tina sign a living will, which the hospital had suggested as well. Her eyes glistened with tears as she signed her name to the form.

* * *

On my third or fourth visit with the psychologist, we explored some of my LDS upbringing and its effect on me. He asked if I had any women who were my friends or if all my friends were men. Other than a few colleagues and clients I worked with, I had no female friends. "Do you think my current urge to engage more with women is in some ways a backlash against a Mormon teaching to avoid being friends with women after marriage?" I asked. "I would think I've outgrown most of that in my spiritual journey."

"You never outgrow things like that," he said. "You have to unlearn them, and, yes, perhaps there is benefit in you having more women as friends, within reason. Left as a forbidden zone in your life, that seems unhealthy, susceptible to fixation, perhaps." I decided to channel my feelings toward friendships with women.

* * *

Monday morning we arrived early at the hospital. Tina had an additional CT scan, was dressed for surgery, and then was hooked up to anesthesia. Moments after Tina went unconscious, the younger neurosurgeon entered the room, his face stiff with concern. "Mr. Smith, it appears the hematoma has grown over the last few days. As a result, we'll need to do a full craniotomy instead of a burr hole trepanation. May I ask you to sign here to consent?" As an attorney I understand why spouses can give consent in situations like this, but it still hurt me to substitute my consent for hers. She would wake to something she had been told not to expect.

I sat in the waiting room and picked up a copy of the Bible, flipping to Genesis, my favorite book. I thought I might find comfort there, reassurance, since it contained so many stories about husbands and wives and their many troubles. And although I had long ago stopped looking to the Bible for the easy lessons one might find in a Sunday school manual, I did find the commonality and kinship in these stories speaking across time to me inspiring, that the Hebrew Bible envisioned our first stories about relationships, marriages.

About an hour later, our nurse friend who had visited Tina at home dropped in and sat with me. Noticing the Bible, she asked if I wanted to pray. Growing up Latter-day Saint, I can't remember when women had ever asked me to pray together, other than my own mom. I said yes. She held my hands and said some beautiful things, very specific things, almost as if she were giving directions to a blind person on how to prepare a meal, as if God were so far away that he could benefit from what she saw here on the ground. She used the biblical phrase "fear and trepidation" at one point in her prayer, with "trepidation" meaning "trembling," reminding me of "trepanation." I also noted how different it was from the blessing by the Mormon bishop the day before. Yet I also understood they were really the same, both of them an expression of hope cast toward an unseen God and a direction of comfort to those listening to their words.

* * *

By the end of April I felt I no longer needed to visit my therapist, not because my feelings had gone away or because my marriage had been restored to its honeymoon bliss but because I had bumped up against the curbs of the wider road I was on and was comfortable that I could stay on the pavement. I had also sought wisdom in movies that dealt with marital problems and men leaving their wives. One in particular, *Hannah and Her Sisters*, by Woody Allen, helped me realize how idiotic men can be (including, it turns out, its writer and director). In this movie, Elliot (played by Michael Caine) has an affair with his wife's sister, Lee (played by Barbara Hershey), who ends the affair after about a year. Elliot eventually reconciles with his wife, and when he sees Lee at Thanksgiving years later, he notes with wistful fondness that Lee seems happy. He wonders how he could have been so stupid as to pursue his infatuation with her, all of it seeming so hazy, so long ago. I had seen this movie in the 1980s when it came out, but I was too young to understand it. Yes, I said to myself, all of what I was feeling would seem foolish in a few years.

One evening in April I told Tina I would no longer see the psychologist, and she asked, "So are you going to leave me?" Tina rarely cries, but tears coursed steadily if silently down her cheeks as she spoke.

"No. I'm not going to leave you," I said. "You can count on me staying here with you."

Her voice trembling, she confessed that she had been looking for a cheaper home, thinking she and the kids would have to move out, wondering how she would make ends meet, how she might reenter the workforce. I was crushed to hear her say this, but why should she not have feared all that? And how Tina-like to quietly prepare for the worst. "No. That won't happen. I'm not going to leave you," I reassured her—and myself.

* * *

When Tina awoke from the anesthesia, she was dazed at first, but within the hour she became hyperverbal even as she struggled to find the right words. It frustrated her and led her (and me) to fear that this state of mind and speech might be the new normal. I tried to calm her down, but she was frantic. She told me to call several people and what to tell them, having forgotten that I had already done so the day before. I would step outside of her room and return minutes later, telling her that her concerns had been handled. She began another list of people for me to call, giving me very specific things to say, and then insisted, very emphatically: "And I need you to stay right here next to me so I can correct you when you're wrong!" Later, we would look back at this moment and laugh, but at the time it was no comic relief.

A couple of hours later, I finally remembered she didn't know that her surgery had been more extensive than anticipated. "Tina, I need to tell you something," I began, my voice wavering. I held her hand. "The hematoma was larger than they expected, possibly due to the delay in the surgery, possibly due to physical activity, no one knows. But they had to perform a craniotomy rather than the burr hole procedure." She didn't seem to think that was significant, yet it wrecked me, because I had agreed to the procedure without her consent.

The young neurosurgeon soon came by to check on Tina. He mentioned that she would experience a day or two of trouble speaking because her brain had been released from the pressure of the hematoma and was expanding outward toward the skull. He said this caused temporary neural disruption, with resultant speech problems for a couple of days, and that the nurses would be monitoring her progress. It was good to know the condition was temporary.

The kids came to see Tina that evening. She sat in her chair, a large turban hiding bandages on her head, afraid she would not be able to speak correctly. I told the children in advance to just tell their mom about their day, what was going on, bring some normal into the room. I spent the night in her room, afraid to leave her side. Once when she was awake, I got up and sat beside her on the bed and held her hand. "Tina, I'm sorry that I put you through so much pain early this year, last spring. I'm really sorry."

"Thank you," she said. *Thank you.* Usually this phrase is a mere pleasantry, a polite thing to say when someone opens the door, perhaps. But for me, in the darkness of that cramped hospital room, in the shadow of her mortality, her present pain, and the past pain I had caused, I don't think that phrase had ever meant so much to me. It meant that she was grateful for my regret, for my loyalty, for the comfort and love I offered her at that moment and what it all promised for the future. She was grateful *for me*, and that was something I needed.

"And I love you," I said.

"Thank you," she said again.

Today, Tina still has occasional headaches and concerns she'll develop another brain bleed, but so far she remains incident-free. Instead of worrying, she has focused her mind and body on becoming a Pilates and yoga instructor to heal herself and others. I have developed real friendships with several women we both know who have helped me better understand the challenges women face and to listen, learn, and support them in facing those challenges. Tina and I have formed new routines together, such as discussing the *Wall Street Journal* and the *New York Times* on weekend mornings, often reading aloud excerpts from articles one of us thinks the other will like (or possibly hate), as well as laughing at the fashion pictures in the style sections and sometimes saying at the same time: "Who would ever pay that much for that?"

We also discuss retirement while reading the travel sections, both of us unsure when or where we'll be ready and able to retire, but both of us certain we will do it—and everything else that follows—together.

I'm Not Who I Thought You Married

JOHN B. DAHL

It was a Friday in February 1994. I'd spent the week worrying about my sales position at IBM, that my job would be eliminated as part of massive layoffs. After a pleasant dinner out with my wife, Mylie, and her mother, I flopped down on my bed without bothering to so much as take off my shoes and promptly fell asleep. Mylie came in at 10:35 P.M. and saw me snoring away, fully clothed, with the lights on. "You going to get ready for bed?" she asked as she took her nightclothes from a drawer.

You know the feeling you get when you glance away from the road for a moment, then look back only to see brake lights right in front of you, and have to slam on your own brakes so you don't ram the car ahead of you? That feeling where your heart jumps into your throat and a wave of anxiety fills your entire body? That's how I felt as I came to on my bed, still wearing the shoes I'd put on at 5:00 A.M. I don't know why being startled awake by a simple question would leave me shot through with anxiety, but even as I got up, changed out of my work clothes, and brushed my teeth, my panic would not subside.

I was thirty-one years old that night. I'd been raised in a faithful Latter-day Saint family that made me feel loved and supported. My siblings—three older brothers and a younger sister—were among my closest friends. My upbringing provided standards and expectations that I believe make me a better person and help me be a positive influence for others. I found it easy to obey injunctions against drinking, drugs, profanity, and dishonesty. I had a little trouble with pornography in high school that caused me some grief, but I was able to work through it long before graduation. Mylie and I each served a full-time mission (me in Minnesota, Mylie in Paraguay) before we married in 1986. I began working for IBM even before I graduated from the University of Arizona in 1988.

By that night in February, Mylie and I had been married eight years; we had four sons and were expecting a daughter in July. We lived in a quiet neighborhood in North Phoenix next to a park, a school, and Little League baseball fields. We were active in our ward and had developed close friendships through it. My life was "perfect" until Mylie casually woke me that Friday night.

The anxiety grew and grew as I climbed in bed. Mylie quickly fell asleep beside me, but I was wide awake. I watched TV for an hour or so in the living room while the feeling intensified. Going back to bed brought no relief. The more I thought about it—whatever "it" was—the worse the pressure in my chest became as cold chills ran down my back and my despair deepened. It was so dark inside me. I didn't want to wake Mylie—I didn't know quite what to tell her, and I knew anything I said would concern her. Hour after miserable hour, I struggled to understand what was happening. I prayed, and still all was dark. I didn't think I was having a heart attack or a seizure or any other physical trauma. Instead, I believed I was losing my mind—totally and completely losing my ability to cope. It hit me very fast and very hard, and I was terrified.

At first light, I was relieved, hoping the darkness inside might abate as night did. As the sun rose, I went for a run. I used to run a lot. The running helped for the thirty minutes I was running. It made the darkness recede, and that made me relax. It worked until I stopped running. Then I began thinking about the night, wondering what on earth had happened. Suddenly and ferociously, the anxiety returned.

What was happening to me?

It was Saturday. That morning, Mylie and I attended our son's basketball game at a local school. Silently I watched my six-year-old son run up and down the shortened court and shoot at a lowered basket. Somehow, as I watched the game, the anxiety spiraled even further out of control. As head of the family, I needed complete mastery of myself so I could lead. Whatever was wrong meant that not only would I suffer, but so would my family.

"Mylie," I finally said on the way home, "something is not right with me. And I really don't know what it is."

"What do you mean?" she said. "You seem fine. Maybe a little tired, but fine."

I tried to steady my breathing and sound reasonable. "I'm very anxious about something," I said. "I'm just not sure what."

Mylie looked at me, baffled. This wasn't like me. Up to that point, when I was anxious about something, I would inventory what was going on in my life, figure out the source of the problem, address it, move it to the side, and move on. My education and upbringing had given me a good set of tools, tools that enabled me to diagnose the source of stress and treat the problem, so any anxiety always went away. With faith, prayer, and trying harder, things always worked themselves out for the better.

"I don't know what's causing it, which just makes it worse," I said. "I've never experienced anything like this." I could hardly breathe. Then the tears started. Of course, I'd cried before, but it was the occasional tear or two when I saw a touching movie or listened to a heartfelt story or read an article in the *Ensign* or felt the Spirit during a church meeting. I knew the difference between tears of joy and tears of grief. This was completely different. These were tears born of terror and dread. I had no idea what it was to experience debilitating panic firsthand. I'd heard of panic attacks, but I figured the attacks were somehow contrived, a way people described their inability to cope with their lives. Was this a panic attack? Were they real? Was it the first sign that I was losing my mind? I could clearly envision my fate, having seen it on the big screen: I'd be admitted to an asylum and wear white clothes like Jack Nicholson, Danny DeVito, and Christopher Lloyd in *One Flew Over the Cuckoo's Nest*. Mylie and the kids would visit me every Sunday after church, and she would wipe the drool from my chin. The inevitability of that future made the present even more intolerable. I was doomed. My life as I knew it was over, and I had no idea why.

I dreaded the night; I feared it would be as sleepless and solitary as the previous one. Sure enough, it was exactly as I had expected. Despair isn't a rational place where you think about your family or friends or Heavenly Father or Jesus Christ, the people and relationships who would typically bring me comfort. I never thought a place existed where it might be impossible to think of them. I always thought prayer, faith, and making good choices would bring peace. Always. The feelings did not fit where I was in my life with God. Where was peace? This was the darkest, coldest, scariest place I had ever been, and I would do *anything* to escape it. Well, not *anything*. Disturbing thoughts about how to get relief from these feelings crept into my mind. Horrified, I realized this must be the place people go when they consider any means to escape; this is where people are at when they decide to die. I didn't imagine my suicide, but I empathized with people in such terror that they would flee it by taking their own lives. This realization exacerbated my panic. I didn't want to escape mortality. I wanted to figure out how to make everything go back to normal. I needed a reset button.

I lay in bed, trying not to disturb Mylie, though she awoke repeatedly, wanting to make sure I was OK. But I wasn't. She sat beside me as I sobbed, leaning against me with her arms around me. Before that night, I would have thought that of course an embrace from the woman I loved would improve things, but it didn't. Mylie's inability to comfort me scared us both. Up to that point, I'd been a confident, funny, outgoing, loud, sarcastic guy, often obnoxious, and almost always happy. There was no explanation for the change.

It was impossible to sit through three hours of church the next day. I was very close to our bishop at the time; I pulled him aside and told him I was not all right. He listened in his office at the church as I cried and tried to explain the situation; he then gave me a priesthood blessing and a hug. Even with that kindness from my friend, I left the church with no relief and no hope. I didn't doubt God, but he didn't seem to be in my neighborhood providing relief.

I tried to fake it with my kids and enjoy Sunday afternoon with them. It helped, but I knew that the dark of night was coming and I would endure it alone. I hadn't slept or eaten for two days and felt no appetite or desire for anything but escape from the terror I felt.

Sunday night was another desolate night, but on Monday morning, I decided to let someone else into my dark place: my father. My dad had a PhD in psychology with an emphasis in family and marriage; he was a licensed therapist who also taught at LDS Institute facilities on various college campuses for over forty years. His service to the church included being a bishop, a stake president, and a patriarch. It concerned me that I might be one of the people my dad used to help as a therapist when I was growing up—people I referred to as "whack jobs," people who couldn't solve their own problems and needed to pay someone to help them.

It wasn't easy, but with encouragement from Mylie as she sat beside me on the bed, I called my dad in Hawai'i, where he and my mother were serving an education mission for the church. I couldn't make it through the call without sobbing. Mylie handed me a small towel to dry the flood of tears as I listened to my father. "See your doctor," he said, instantly in therapist mode. "Get a thorough workup. Let's see if there's a physical cause for this. It's always a good place to start."

The next day, Tuesday, I saw my physician. An EKG showed nothing of concern, while other tests revealed that I was even healthier than I'd been a year before, my weight and blood pressure down. The doctor handed me a prescription for something called Xanax. "It'll help with the anxiety," he told me.

"I don't need medication to deal with this," I said to myself. "This isn't a mental problem." I frowned and shoved the prescription into my wallet. Driving home on Shea Boulevard, I wept as I admitted that a mental problem was exactly what I had: I had lost my mind and was destined for the mental hospital. I don't know how I made it home.

"Maybe it would help if you went to work," Mylie said after hearing my bitter account of my glowing bill of health. "It might distract you or remind you that you're good at your job."

I had been a field sales rep with IBM for about five years. I liked the people I worked with; I liked my job and was good at it. But when I reached the IBM office, I couldn't bring myself to go inside. I sat in my car in the parking garage for at least an hour. Even more defeated, I returned home.

The next morning, IBM held a fancy sales recognition event at one of Scottsdale's many resorts. I and a few peers were honored for reaching an ambitious sales goal. The prize for each of us was an expensive set of PING golf clubs. I loved golf—playing it with clients was a real perk, even with my inferior set of clubs. On any other day, I would have been dancing in the streets at winning a set of name-brand clubs worth almost a thousand dollars, but I knew they wouldn't do a darn thing for me once my family fell asleep and I was alone in the dark.

I went home, told Mylie about the clubs, took off my suit, and climbed into bed. It was Wednesday. I'd been in a panic since Friday night. I'd eaten next to nothing for five days. I had hardly slept and didn't expect to sleep even as I pulled the covers up around my face. But bed is where you go when you want the world to leave you alone, so that's where I went.

"Call your dad," Mylie said, sitting beside me. "Tell him what the doctor said."

I was a dutiful husband; I knew Mylie's suggestion was completely reasonable. So I did it. And sure enough, my father made the suggestion I'd been dreading: "Find a psychotherapist," he said. "You need to talk to someone."

There it was, from someone I loved and trusted, someone who knew me: confirmation that I'd somehow changed from a strong and stable person into a weak-willed "whack job" unable to cope with normal situations. The worst thing about it? I was desperate enough to take my dad's advice.

"I don't know who to call," I said. "Any recommendations?"

I heard him draw a deep breath, the way people often do when they're thinking. "I'm sorry," he said finally. "It's been ten years since I lived in Arizona. I'm out of touch with the therapist network there."

A rare moment of clarity broke through my fug of dark confusion. "What about Ed? Do you remember him?"

Ed was on our stake's high council. Shortly after I moved to Phoenix I stopped to talk to him at church one day because he looked so familiar; it took only a few moments to establish that I'd met him as a boy when he was getting a PhD in psychology at the University of Arizona and very active at the LDS Institute of Religion my father directed.

"Yes!" Dad said. "He's a great guy."

"He's got a practice here," I said. "Really close to our home."

"Call him. He's one of the most kind and sensitive people I've ever met. He'll help you."

It was still hard to make the call: it was an admission that I was no better than the pathetic people who had filled my father's office all those years. But since I had no other options for help, I dialed the number and left Ed a voice message. Within minutes he called me back, and just like that, I had an appointment to see a psychotherapist at 8:00 P.M. that very night. He must have recognized from my voice how urgently I needed help.

Mylie drove me to the appointment. I was concerned about what she might hear about my condition when I met with Ed, so for some strange reason very uncharacteristic of our relationship, I asked her to stay in the waiting room.

There in Ed's office was the stereotypical couch. I chose to sit in the chair. I summarized what had happened since Friday night. Ed listened to my three-minute explanation, then stood and wrote the following list on a white board:

1. Feelings of helplessness or despair
2. Change in sleep
3. Paranoia
4. Change in eating
5. Loss of interest or pleasure in activities
6. Persistent sad or empty feelings
7. Suicidal thoughts
8. Difficulty concentrating
9. Fatigue and decreased energy
10. Feelings of panic or anxiety

"These are the symptoms of clinical depression," he said.

"Luckily I only have nine out of ten," I said. "No paranoia here."

He smiled. "You only need to have four of the symptoms to be diagnosed with clinical depression," he said.

For some strange reason it was a magical sentence. Hearing the two words "clinical depression" calmed me and flooded me with relief strong enough to make the anxiety abate. My living hell had a name. It had a diagnosis. It had a treatment. I had friends who'd suffered from depression, and I knew they managed to lead productive lives, so I knew there was hope for me. I would be OK. No Sunday visits in that mental hospital.

"There are many ways of treating depression," Ed said. "Medication often helps. . . ."

"I don't need medication," I said. "Now that I know what's going on, I can handle this."

On the drive home, I told Mylie that with relaxation therapy and a new approach to handling problems in my life, I could manage my anxiety and prevent panic attacks. I slept well that night, and while I woke with some anxiety, I was able to return to work. Deciding that medication in the very short term was all right, I filled the prescription for Xanax and took it for a few days; it helped the anxiety recede even more. One ironic thing: I calmed down enough to notice that the one symptom I'd insisted I didn't exhibit was in fact part of my life. Every day when I went to work, I was terrified IBM would let me go in a series of job cuts—even though I'd just won a fancy award. I was paranoid.

Ed helped me see that one misconception complicating my life was my need to keep everyone happy and have them like me. "Some people are just unreasonable," he said. "There are people you just can't make happy." Not until he said that did it sink in that you can't change someone who doesn't want to change. After that, I no longer felt it was somehow my duty to fix things every time something was amiss with a friend, client, church member, Little League parent, or family member. This realization helped a lot.

The other expectation I had of myself was perfection. Somehow I had twisted the standards I had lived by as a Latter-day Saint into an expectation of perfection, and when I failed to meet that expectation, I felt profound guilt and anxiety, which weren't healthy for me or my relationship with Mylie. Mylie was very patient and did not hold me to those unrealistic standards. I had brought this on myself. And I understood my relationship with Jesus Christ better when I realized he had complete and total empathy for me and everyone who has ever lived on this earth. He expected me to *try*, not to be perfect. That was also a healthy adjustment in my spiritual beliefs.

Eventually, I was diagnosed with dysthymia, a less extreme but more long-lived form of depression. Stress makes it worse, but it's not a result of a major trauma such as a death or divorce or some other upheaval. Nope! It's a gift from birth. I know my mother and her mother had it. Thanks for the genes, Grandma Johnson.

Over the next two years, I exercised, lost weight, and did relaxation therapy via a forty-five-minute recording that coached me through relaxing my body. It was effective but time-consuming. Occasionally, maybe three or four times a year, the panic would hit me, but in a matter of minutes I could calm myself and it would pass. At work I was promoted, my successes recognized with awards and prizes. My kids were healthy and happy and did well in school. I loved being home, was involved in church, and coached Little League.

In June 1996 I watched a video by Dr. James Dobson of his interview with serial killer Ted Bundy. I don't remember where I got it or why I watched it, but I did. Dobson asked Bundy what had driven him to murder so many women. Bundy said it came down to pornography and an insatiable appetite for more extreme images and experiences to meet his needs for arousal. This video disturbed me; thoughts of my adolescent experience with pornography rushed back to me. Soon I was obsessively frightened that this issue could arise anytime in my life—and I would do something terrible. I was terrified that, despite every inclination I had to protect myself and my family, I would be compelled to do something that put us all at risk. These obsessive, irrational fears brought back the darkness I thought I had learned to expel from my life.

One evening my nine-year-old son, Brad, misbehaved. Angry, I grabbed him by the arm, squeezing so hard it left a mark, pulled him into his room, and threw him on his bed. I left him alone in his room, knowing he was upset and hurt by my actions. I went to my room, where it hit me: I was an abusive father. My temper was out of control; I was sure to do something truly terrible.

I had a two-year-old daughter; who knew what I would do to her? I "knew" my temper would get the best of me. I was headed to prison for child abuse.

On top of that, I'd had a month or two at work of less than stellar performance. I hadn't made my quota goals, so no commissions were coming my way for at least two months. I couldn't support my family; I "knew" that we were headed for bankruptcy and financial ruin.

One night during a family road trip as the kids slept in the back of the minivan, I finally confided to Mylie my certainty about where I was headed, holding nothing back as I confessed my crimes in the dark, even the ones I had yet to commit. Mylie didn't laugh at me, but she did smile. "John, you're an amazing father. You're not abusive. These thoughts aren't real. We haven't missed paying one bill. You've had lean months before, but we've always been blessed. These thoughts are *not* real." I was too busy absorbing what she said to respond. "You need to call Ed again," she said after a moment, "and talk to him about the way you feel."

The next week I met with Ed and explained my two major issues of impending prison and bankruptcy. He asked about my upbringing, trying to uncover any real issues of abuse. There was nothing. As we discussed my financial situation, it became apparent to me that things were fine there as well.

"I think managing your depression has gone beyond relaxation therapy exercises and an occasional Xanax," Ed said. "It might be time to try an antidepressant."

"No," I said. "I don't need medications like that. They're for people with mental problems. Not me."

I couldn't help thinking of my mother, Shirley, who had dealt with anxiety disorders for twenty years. She suffered from severe insomnia and was continually exhausted. As she aged, she was also afflicted with arthritis and fibromyalgia. "You know who needs antidepressants," I said suddenly, startled by the insight. "My mother. I wish someone would tell her this."

When I got home, I realized the person who should tell her this was me. I called her and wasted no time cutting to the chase. "Mom, have you ever considered taking an antidepressant? I think it might help with the problems you're dealing with."

She laughed. "I've been taking an antidepressant for a year."

"Really," I said. "Well, how do you feel?"

"I still hurt like hell, but at least I don't cry about it all the time." I was astonished to learn not only that my strong-willed, no-nonsense mother used to cry because she was in such pain but that an antidepressant had helped her stop. That demolished any remaining stigma the medications had for me.

Getting a prescription for antidepressants required seeing an MD, so I went to the Mayo Clinic, where my doctor wrote me a prescription for Prozac. "How long does it take to work?" I asked.

"Four to six weeks."

"How will I know if it's working?"

He smiled. "Your wife will tell you. She'll notice before you do." Sure enough, within two months of starting the medication, my anxiety fell, my energy levels rose, my concerns and obsessions left, and I felt in control of my life for the first time in a long time.

The one thought I had when I started down the road in February 1994 was: How do I get back to normal? Eventually, I realized I could never recapture my naivete about depression, anxiety, and frustration—nor did I want to. The new "me" began with an understanding that many of my frustrations, discouragement, and even phobias started when I was a child. I'd had many of these symptoms most of my life, but I'd been able to manage the lows with music, activities, food, friends, and family. But eventually the stresses exceeded my ability to manage them. I needed help and was grateful I found it. It has brought strength to my family and to me. My being vulnerable and candid with Mylie is a blessing that has brought us much closer together. She is not burdened with depression, but she is very sympathetic.

Since my diagnosis in February 1994 and beginning medication in June 1996, I've been open about my experience. I've helped family members not only identify their own depression but understand that help is available. When I served as a bishop, I told my story many times and helped people realize that clinical depression is not a character flaw but a medical condition that can be treated successfully.

My "gift" is lifelong. After two and a half years on Prozac, I weaned myself off meds and tried going without. For eighteen months I was a raw nerve. My stress increased, I had difficulty managing my anxiety, and I sometimes cried to a degree that did not match the situation. So I went back on medication—Lexapro this time—and have taken a white pill every night since.

Sometimes when I tell people that I have clinical depression, they'll say, "You don't seem depressed."

"Yes!" I say with a smile. "That's what happens when you get help."

Figure 8. John B. and Mylie Dahl, Christmas 2018, Phoenix, Arizona
John writes, "Mylie is my best friend and the most understanding of who I am."

Holding On and Letting Go

JOSEPH BROOM

People used to sit in awe as they heard our story. I was a convert. She was a convert. We met in November 1983 in Ohio, where she was a sister missionary. I was twenty-five and had joined the church six months earlier in New Orleans, returning to Ohio to live with my nonmember parents while I prepared to serve a mission myself.

I'd been a "golden" investigator—someone who seems thoroughly prepared for the gospel and accepts it readily—and became a zealous convert. That I was able to help in the rapid conversion of my family only enhanced my self-perception as someone special, chosen by God to do great things in the church. I was receptive to, looked for, and believed in personal revelation—the power of God in my life and my ability to discern his will for me.

The day I received my call to the France Paris Mission, Sister Joan Anderson, a missionary in my ward, was notified of her transfer to a town thirty miles away. Over the previous four months, Sister Anderson and I had seen a lot of each other as she and her companion assisted me in the conversion of my older sister, my father, and my stepmother. During those months, I'd become attracted to her.

What I never admitted when we later told our "story" was that I had struggled with same-sex attraction since puberty and that one of the main reasons I joined the church was that it purported to show me a path away from those attractions. I didn't want to be gay. I wanted to have a home and a family, and the church told me I could.

Once in the Mormon world, I bought into all its concepts of marriage. I romanticized love and courtship—two concepts I had no experience with and knew little about. I'd never been in a long-term relationship and rarely even dated. I convinced myself that the reason I'd never fallen in love with a woman was that I hadn't met the right one. "The day I meet my companion," I wrote in my journal, "is the day I will truly begin to live. She holds the keys to my heart, and I will never truly love, feel, or know until she turns the key."

So much could be said about this passage now. It reflected my belief, common among Mormons, that there was a special someone destined to be my eternal companion. Beyond this, however, was the belief that once I met this woman, everything would fall into place and my whole life would change. Homosexual thoughts would be banished forever, and I would become complete. She would be the other half of my heart, and fulfillment would replace the emptiness and longing I had felt for years.

This fulfillment didn't include any grand passion. I accepted the notion sometimes preached from the pulpit that marriage wasn't so much about finding someone with whom one could fall deeply in love but more about finding someone compatible, who shares one's religious values, and with whom one could have children. This approach let me believe I could marry a woman and have a happy life. I might not be able to romantically love a woman—whatever that meant—but I *could* be a mate, a companion, a collaborator in the work of creating an eternal family. I convinced myself that God had led me to a point in my life where I could meet "the one." That belief in divine providence let me make God responsible for finding me a mate, which I sincerely believed he would do.

It wasn't long before my belief in providence seemed justified: I met Joan. "Sometimes," I wrote, "I wonder if my eternal companion has already come into my life. There are times when I feel things toward Sister Anderson, and I wish I could date her, but know I can't because she's a missionary. Sometimes, when I look into her eyes, I see eternity. . . . I don't know. I've never been in love, so I don't know what love feels like. I just pray that Heavenly Father will continue to guide me and show me the way."

As had become typical of me, I placed my faith and fate in the hands of a third party—my sister, Karen. She had delved so much into spiritual things after her baptism that she became almost mystical. In early April 1984 I confided to her some of my feelings about Joan. Had I not done so, my life would likely have turned out very differently.

Karen proceeded to play matchmaker. Before long she told me that, based on a "revelation" she'd had, she'd already told Joan that "she would someday be sealed to our family forever." So simple, so naive, so complete was my faith that, after hearing this, I wrote in my journal, "I have complete faith that if Heavenly Father intends for us to be eternal companions, he will provide a way for us to get to know each other better."

What I didn't write was that, in my heart of hearts, I was grateful to God for finding my eternal companion for me. If I'd had to go looking on my own, I doubt I could have done it. I sincerely believed God was blessing me in exchange for my faithfulness in keeping homosexual thoughts out of my mind and for my complete sexual abstinence, including refraining from masturbation, after my conversion.

Joan, for her own reasons, embraced this celestial matchmaking as much as I did. This belief that God had brought us together became the Central Myth of our marriage and our lives—a myth that relied on and was sustained by another myth: that the Mormon Church was true. Joan and I corresponded while on our missions, then engaged in a tumultuous on-again, off-again, long-distance courtship once I got home. We had little in common; our backgrounds were different; our interests were different; our temperaments were different. The only things we shared were devotion to the church and our belief that God wanted us together.

I told Joan of my attraction to men during an "off-again" period in that courtship, and at one point I wrestled mightily with whether I could or should marry her. I ultimately decided to commit myself wholeheartedly to marriage and doing my best to live the Plan of Happiness. I wasn't in love with my wife when we married, but I believed this would come in time.

Though I grew to love my wife, I was *never* "in love" with her, something I didn't fully appreciate until years later. Had I been in a serious relationship or experienced true love before our marriage, I likely never would have married Joan. Similarly, had I experienced the fulfillment of gay sex—particularly in a loving relationship—I likely would not have married at all. As it was, I was a virgin in both senses: I'd never been in love, nor had I ever had sex.

The thing that brought us together—the Central Myth—kept us together. Joan and I formed more of a partnership than a marriage, the whole of which was greater than the sum of its parts. We started having children. We did everything we were supposed to do. I went to law school so I could better provide for my family. By the time I graduated, we had two children and a pile of student loans. She stayed home while I worked. Within four more years, we had two more children and even more debt. We were active in church and fulfilled responsible callings.

Like many Mormons, we believed that the daunting obstacles in our relation-ship were confirmations of God's will rather than indicators that we'd made a mistake. This belief, that we can tell how "true" or "right" something is by how difficult it makes our life—that there is virtue in pain—infuses a certain Mormon worldview. Life is intended to be a struggle. Diamonds in the rough, we must be polished by life's buffetings for our true beauty to shine. We must be tried and tested in all things, and the greater the trials, the greater the glory afterward.

Joan and I believed that the challenges and obstacles we faced were simultane-ously signs that we were on the right path and refining experiences that would, in the end, help us overcome "baggage" from our respective pasts, ultimately making us better people. I firmly believed that the fact that I was intensely un-happy throughout most of our twenty-five-year marriage (as, I think it could be said, was she) was confirmation that I had done the right thing by marrying.

We faced many challenges in our marriage: Graduate school. Welcoming children. Financial stresses and strains present from the very beginning that never ceased to plague us. Cultural differences. Cross-country moves. Career changes. They took their toll. At times, we both felt we couldn't go on. But the Central Myth somehow sustained us. We believed that true happiness would come from confronting the challenges we faced (including my inner homosexuality) and forging ahead on the path before us. We couldn't deny the Central Myth, because that would mean that our marriage was based on fraud—a thought too horrible to contemplate.

It was precisely these challenges that (deceptively) united us. I later realized that transitory challenges deflected attention from the chronic problems of our marriage. Thus, when certain hurdles had been cleared, their unifying effect dissipated, and we faced stark realities we had swept under the rug for years.

In the final years, our marriage was in serious trouble. A major problem was that Joan and I never experienced true intimacy as a couple, though I think neither of us realized it at the time. We limped along, having good days and bad days, more bad than good, sustained by the belief that, since God had arranged our marriage in the first place, we just had to find the way out of the maze and everything would be fine. But we were wrong.

During the October 2010 General Conference, in his sermon about moral purity, Apostle Boyd K. Packer made this statement: "Some suppose that they were preset and cannot overcome what they feel are inborn tendencies toward the impure and unnatural. Not so! Why would our Heavenly Father do that to anyone?"

As a heavily closeted gay man, I was cut to the heart by these sentences. Packer's highly coded words evoked the days of my young adulthood, when the church railed vociferously against the "abomination" of homosexuality. I felt dragged back to a very dark place of self-loathing, shame, and despair. Not only had Packer called me and those like me "impure and unnatural," he had poured salt in open wounds by saying, essentially, that God never could or would make such a depraved person as me, nor could he love me for who I am.

These words caused a tectonic shift within me. In the moments, hours, and days that followed, I realized that I was no longer willing or even able to repress who I am and that my homosexuality was and is fundamental to who I am. Furthermore, I was done feeling guilty and dirty about it. I finally accepted that I am and always have been gay.

Only after coming out did I realize the degree to which my repressed homosexuality had affected our marriage from day one. Joan and I had been wrong to ignore the warning signs, wrong to view life simply as a challenge to endure, a cross to bear, a vale to pass through. We had sacrificed so much to an ideal, and in the end, we discovered, we had sacrificed ourselves.

* * *

What I know of romantic love and of true emotional and physical intimacy I learned after meeting Mark Koepke, the man who became my husband. He was an emergency room physician in Salt Lake City and had ended a long-term relationship about the time that Joan and I separated. In August 2011 he contacted me through a gay dating site. Looking at his profile, I saw pictures of him skiing, cycling, and swimming. I couldn't believe that someone like him, so handsome and athletic, was interested in someone like me (since at the time I saw myself as decidedly unathletic).

Mark invited me to lunch at the Oasis Café in Salt Lake City. I parked behind the building, entered through the back door, and walked down the stairs. I saw a tall, lean, blond man at the base of the stairs, and as I approached, he turned and looked at me, a huge smile on his wonderful face. I was smitten.

Over the following weeks, I fell deeply *in love* with Mark, and he with me, as we saw each other almost every day. I felt a connection with him unlike anything I had experienced; it seemed I had known him for years. "Every person," I wrote in my journal, "should have the opportunity to feel these feelings I am feeling, to be able to 'get it' when they listen to a love song on the radio, to feel the excitement that comes from hearing my beloved's voice, from being in the same room with him, from holding him."

Yet despite my happiness in discovering what it means to fall in love, waves of melancholy and deep, painful sadness sometimes washed over me in the weeks after I met Mark. I'd imagined that I had weathered quite well the process of coming out and separating from my wife, so I was surprised, disturbed, and frightened by the grief that sometimes consumed me.

I finally concluded that the unconditional love Mark gave me was so rich and powerful that it made me mourn everything I had not experienced previously. I was overwhelmed by grief for relationships in which I had not felt such love—my relationships with my ex-wife and my parents being prime examples. Of course, there was also the relationship with myself. I had unconsciously imposed so many conditions upon my love for myself (and believed so many negative messages about myself from others) that I basically rendered myself unlovable.

Then, along came Mark, who loved me unconditionally. And through the process of sorting and sifting, of mourning the love I'd been denied, I came to a self-knowledge and self-awareness I'd never before enjoyed. I wrote, "It's like there is this little person inside of me, rushing from door to door in the prison that was my soul, unlocking them and flinging them open. I am free to be me, free to fall in love, and free to finally start loving myself."

From the very beginning, I saw my relationship with Mark in counterpoint to my temple marriage to Joan. Somehow I never thought of myself as being in a *relationship* with her. Mormons think in terms of marriages, not relationships. Young people are not taught about relationships; they are taught about preparing for a temple marriage. When young people approach marriageable age, they are admonished to date, not to form meaningful relationships. Classes are taught on "marriage relations," not relationships.

One consequence of always focusing on "marriage" instead of a relationship is that the marriage can be objectified and held to arbitrary standards. Success in a marriage becomes closely tied to things like number of children, church activity, temple worthiness, and other external factors. I certainly felt all of this in my first marriage, and I always wondered whether Joan and I would have had a more successful marriage had we not been Mormon, or at least not active Mormons. If we'd had the chance to breathe, perhaps things would have been different.

With Mark and me, there was none of that. There was just our relationship: just him and me. True, we eventually married, but we viewed this more as a legal status than a framework for our relationship. There were no external standards to which we needed to hold our relationship. Furthermore, there were no external goals imposed upon us, such as going to the temple, getting our kids to go to church, preparing them for missions, and so on. Our goal was simply to love each other, not to create an eternal family. This opened a tremendous space for love not only in our relationship with each other but also in our relationships with our children.

My perception of my role as a father changed dramatically. Freed from the concept of an "eternal family," I was able to love my children for who they are, not for who they are supposed to be according to the church. It was at times challenging to release all the "shoulds" and simply rest in loving them, but I grew more secure in this new role as time passed.

I also managed to stop tying my love for my children to my love for my spouse. In a temple marriage, spousal love and love for children are bound together in the same grand goal of creating a forever family. In my experience, this was a recipe for dysfunction. My relationship with Mark, however, was totally separate from our relationships with our children. One did not depend on the other. Consequently, the children know they are loved for who they are; they knew and saw that the love Mark and I had for each other was independent of them. They had no "responsibility" for it; they could simply rest in it.

Perhaps the greatest counterpoint between my temple marriage and my marriage to Mark is that there is no "Together Forever," nor is there any attachment to this concept. When I first met Mark and we fell in love, I saw myself living out my life with this wonderful man, secure in our love for each other and buoyed by the happiness we had found. There was no point to our love except love, no overriding purpose, no eternal goal. But it brought me profound contentment to expect that we would grow in each other's love for many years to come.

Our world changed irrevocably on April 8, 2013, when Mark was diagnosed with inoperable advanced-stage metastatic prostate cancer. I railed at the injustice: after all I'd been through, it seemed the height of cruelty to take away the love of my life after such a short time together. Eventually, the initial shock and anger cooled into a dull but painful awareness that, someday, Mark would be taken from me, and the happiness I'd known with him would end.

Fortunately, Mark was not symptomatic when he was diagnosed. He had no pain at the time, and the doctors told us that, statistically, we could look forward to three to five years. We decided to make the best of the time we had left. Mark immediately retired from his job as an ER physician; I retired as well. In August 2013 we had a commitment ceremony in our backyard in Salt Lake City, not yet able to legally marry in Utah. We left on a honeymoon to Maui and Japan, then sold our house and moved into a townhome. In April 2014 we were legally married on our favorite beach in Maui by another gay former Mormon, his husband serving as witness. A cooler served as the altar on which we signed our marriage license.

In the next year and a half, we traveled a lot both as a couple and with our children. Mark was fit and healthy but for his cancer, and in the fall of 2014 we completed a memorable two-week cycling tour in France. A few months later, however, the first pains appeared in Mark's hip, where a cancerous mass had been discovered when he was diagnosed. We rode more that spring, but by summer, Mark's cycling days were over. Then, in quick succession, he realized that his gym and yoga days were also over. With each passing week, his pain and fatigue increased.

As Mark continued his journey to the end of his incarnation here, I traveled my own journey of coming to grips with losing him. Though I never found myself wishing I still believed in a "forever after," there were times when I was overwhelmed with panic at losing him and his love. There were times when I felt I would die with him, when I could not see my life going on without him, when I wanted to cling with all my might to the happiness I experienced each day with him.

But then I was reminded of and returned to a place Mark and I tried from the beginning to keep sacred between us, a vow to always seek to *rest* in each other's love and not *cling* to it. I realized that to truly offer love and compassion to Mark and to honor our love for each other, I needed to let go of my attachment to him and his physical form. I also reached a point where I let myself try to believe that I would not die with him and that I might someday find happiness again after he had gone.

*   *   *

This resolve and belief were severely tested when Mark died on March 2, 2016. In the end, he left much more quickly than expected. He was on hospice only twelve days and experienced the quick, relatively pain-free death he hoped for, surrounded by those who loved him.

When Mark died, we had, in a very real sense, been grieving for almost three years, ever since his diagnosis. The previous November, Mark had written on his blog that "I, we, are grieving the loss of a life we could have had. Being together for many years. Watching the children and grandchildren grow up, seeing their failures and successes. Both of us having fulfilling jobs where we contribute to our family and community."

What Mark didn't mention, because it went without saying, is that we were grieving the loss of each other, albeit differently. Mark was preparing to leave this life and the emotional attachments he had made. I was preparing to let go of the person who had loved me, had been in love with me, and had taught me so much about love.

"It's important for us to do this now," Mark wrote, "so that when it gets down to crunch time we have completed for the most part being tossed around by emotions that seem overwhelming and beyond our ability to control, to leave the space huge and open for love and celebration of all things beautiful rather than the small and confined space of grief and sorrow." Mark's words proved prophetic. There was grief and sorrow when he passed, but there was so much more of "all things beautiful."

In the months following Mark's death, there were times when I felt the love we shared slipping away from me, much as Mark had. There was no altar upon which I enshrined that love, waiting as so many others do in a fervent belief that I will be reunited with Mark in the hereafter, meanwhile paying daily homage before that lonesome shrine. But sacred moments nevertheless came, moments when I realized and was reassured that the love that we shared will always be carried gently within the folds of my heart and memory. Not clung to, not worshipped. Held. After all, we never had a goal for our love but to love, and that love, while it may not be everlasting, while it may even eventually fade in memory, will never die.

Disability Check

CALEB SCOVILLE

It was the day my disability check arrived. My sons were in bed, my wife at school. I sat on the couch opening the mail. The check was a double-edged sword: I was grateful for the money and what it meant to my family (help with groceries, the mortgage, Christmas gifts, and all our other expenses while my wife went back to school), but the check was also a reminder of my bipolar disorder (a mental illness that makes me feel incredible and fearless one day and paralyzed by anxiety and major depression the next, a mental illness that forced me to quit my job teaching high school).

My parents were a typical LDS couple. Dad worked as an insurance agent while Mom stayed home and raised six kids. I'm the oldest. I can't remember when I learned that other moms had jobs, but it took a while, and when I did realize, it didn't seem right. The "ideal" situation, I was taught, was a clean division of labor: Dad was the breadwinner, and Mom made bread.

For the first eight and a half years of my marriage, I didn't know I had bipolar disorder. I just thought I was awesome, fearless, and invincible much of the time, with some irritability and explosive behavior at others (typical of someone with bipolar during manic phases). Even on my honeymoon, I realize now, it affected me. Ellie and I were married in the Manti Temple in southern Utah, then spent a few days on a cruise to Mexico. As we headed home, I told my new wife I didn't have fun because we did all the things she wanted to do, not the things I wanted. She cried and wouldn't talk to me. I don't think she knew what to say. I know she was hurt. I kept thinking, "Why am I acting this way? This isn't me. I'm not mean to people."

But the truth is, I was mean. Too often. Starting arguments and getting super aggressive with family members about politics and insignificant things. Sending emails to superiors at work that I regretted almost immediately. Intentionally making my wife and oldest son cry because not only did I have to be right, I had to convince them that they were wrong and how dare they try to make me feel like I was the one who was wrong. I knew I was wrong, but being wrong felt like I wasn't doing a good job at being a husband or father. Being wrong was failure.

Then there were the anxiety attacks. The debilitating worry over who knows what, because anything could be a trigger: my wife saying we needed to talk about finances, children screaming and yelling, or the anticipation of a difficult week at work—it was different every time. I would check out, retreat, run from everyone. This didn't stop the anxiety attacks—nothing stopped them. I was told that exercise would help, but it didn't. I was told that meditation would help, but it didn't. I was told that a healthy diet would help, but it didn't. One, two, three, four, five medications later, and the anxiety attacks and depression kept getting worse and worse. But checking out, retreating, and running away meant I couldn't hurt anyone. It meant I wouldn't yell at anyone, or throw a marker as fiercely as I could to the back of the classroom, or slam my fist down, hard, on a table. Many times at home I would lie in bed crying, literally paralyzed by anxiety while Ellie played Hungry Hungry Hippos or Operation with the boys, wondering if I was going to come out of the bedroom. I also wondered if I was going to come out or just stay in bed till morning.

I want to make clear that I'm typically a happy, positive, friendly, loving guy. I love making people laugh, and I'm pretty good at it. I can make friends quickly and easily. I'm also a helpful husband and a good dad, most of the time. When I tell people about my anxiety, depression, anger, and so on, most of the time, they're surprised. This has been one of the most frustrating things about my mental illness: knowing I'm really a good, kind person—then acting the way I do.

A common symptom of a manic phase is delusions of grandeur, and I had plenty. I worked full-time but also became engrossed with ambitious side projects. I was a successful entrepreneur, three times, or at least I thought I was. I was learning to play the guitar and writing a song at the same time, so I was the next Imagine Dragons, or at least I thought I was. I was also a professional writer, or at least I thought I was, working on a juvenile semihistorical novel about a boy recruited to be a spy. As the main character travels to different countries, I taught the reader about geography, language, culture, art, etc. I was sure to be the next J. K. Rowling, the next C. S. Lewis. Almost all my manic phases revolved around becoming famous to some degree, and rich. I really wanted to be rich and famous. These projects were an addiction for me: having the ideas, developing them, imagining the massive and awe-inspiring success they were sure to bring me.

Professional running was a consistent goal during manic phases. I never made it to the state cross-country or track-and-field championships in high school, yet I felt I had the potential to not only make the team at a Division I university but also qualify for and place high at the Olympics. I tried out for BYU's cross-country team three times and never made it, and yet I was certain that if I trained hard and correctly, I would become a professional runner. I would qualify for the Olympics. I would win a gold medal. I had everyone convinced I could do it, even myself. Confidence flowed from me like a waterfall. None of us knew this was mania, an aspect of bipolar disorder.

A few years into my marriage, I had a good job as a legal assistant at a law firm in Provo. I was studying for the LSAT and planned to go to law school. But I knew I needed to move my family to Idaho so I could train for the 2012 Olympics. It was more than an idea: It was revelation. It was a prompting. I really felt God was directing me to do this so I could fulfill my dream and achieve my potential. So we gave it all up, moved to Idaho Falls, and lived in my parents' basement. I failed to get even close to Olympic qualifying times. So I turned to ultramarathons, races of fifty-two miles. I ran longer and longer. Sometimes my training runs were longer than an actual marathon. As with most of my running ventures, I did better than the average person but nowhere close to winning or qualifying for a championship team.

Then I got a job at a running store in Utah, so my family moved back. That lasted eighteen months before I got frustrated and quit because I felt called to start my own business. That ended after two months. I went back to school so I could apply for a master's program in exercise physiology. I failed chemistry twice and gave it up. I coached a season of cross-country at Springville High School and realized I loved teenagers and coaching them in running, so I went back to school to get my teaching degree.

Almost every manic phase has felt like inspiration, revelation, a calling. I get even more attached to an idea because I've felt God is telling me to do the things I'm doing. That means if someone challenges the idea or tells me to stop, what they're really saying is "I know better than God." Or at least that's how my mentally ill brain interpreted things. I was the priesthood holder; I was supposed to know what was right for myself—and my family.

Growing up, I was taught to be a righteous priesthood holder, not one who abuses his authority. I was taught to keep the commandments, to be loving and kind. I became an Eagle Scout, and for my Eagle Project I helped build wooden locker cabinets for two homeless shelters in Vancouver, Washington, so that residents would have a place to lock their medications and valuables. I organized the people, materials, and expertise necessary to complete this project. It required planning, communication, and persistence—all of which are necessary for maintaining a healthy marriage and raising children. I served a two-year mission in Argentina, which required communication, persistence, and the ability to get along with others.

I was taught to provide, preside, and protect. I prepared for those obligations. What I wasn't prepared for was the possibility of a debilitating mental illness. They don't teach much about that at church. I wasn't taught that a mental illness could make a normal day feel like torture, like suicide was an option. I didn't expect the church to teach me those things necessarily, but I thought the training, guidance, and structure the church provided would help more than it did.

My wife was always very patient with me—it's one reason we stayed married. Before we knew about my bipolar disorder, she would talk me through my anger. She helped me set goals and make plans to be nicer and kinder. We made promises when we were married. She took seriously the notion that our relationship was eternal. She told me often, "I am not giving up on you. I promised to help you." But delusions like mine can take a toll on a family, especially on a spouse.

In 2014 I went back to BYU to get certified to teach Spanish. I was hired by a high school in Utah. I had anxiety and depression going into teaching, but I thought it was better because I was proactively addressing the issue. I had a good doctor. We were trying medications that seemed to work, but then things got increasingly stressful. I was getting less and less sleep and working much harder than I should have. Even though I was taking medications for my anxiety and depression, things still got worse. It turns out that some anxiety and depression medication can make bipolar-related anxiety and depression even worse. Which is exactly what happened. Suicidal thoughts started creeping in. At first it was just wishing a car would kill me as I biked to work. Eventually, it was wanting to hurt myself to make the pain and suffering stop. You might not think things can go downhill from there, but they can. They really can.

Sundays were the worst. "The Sabbath" was supposed to be this wonderful day of family, peace, and rest, but for me it was the day when my most severe anxiety attacks occurred in anticipation of yet another unbearable week in the classroom, trying to manage group after group of teenagers, many of whom often didn't want to be in school and definitely did not want to learn what I had to teach. I was passionate about the subject I taught, and I thought I was passionate about sharing it, but until you do it you don't know how painful it is to be treated like the bad guy all day by people you only want to help. Monday was definitely a huge trigger, and because Sunday is the day before Monday, Sundays and specifically Sunday nights became the hardest moments of my life. That's when I would weep like a small child who'd lost a beloved toy. That's when I didn't want to be around anyone. That's when I would curl up in the fetal position at family gatherings so I could make an effort to be there, but inside I was writhing with mental and emotional torment. That's when the strongest suicidal thoughts came. Sometimes I could just go to sleep, get up the next morning, and keep going. Many times I could bear the mental and emotional pain and get through the day, but as time went on that got harder to do. Finally, I started having to take a Monday off. Then it was a couple of days. Then it was a week. But time off didn't solve anything. My symptoms got worse and worse. I was breaking.

In 2017, at the end of spring break, I had an anxiety attack that landed me in the emergency room because I wanted to kill myself. I had to stop teaching. I didn't go back for the rest of the school year, and I had the summer off. I worked with my counselor and got a real psychiatrist. I met with the school administration, and we decided I should return to teaching in the fall. I felt really good about this. I'd gone to the temple and prayed and done all my homework.

But three days into the school year I had a bad anxiety attack. A couple of days later I had another that made me not only want to kill myself but think seriously about how I would do it. That was the end of teaching. I was let go, and I qualified for and was granted long-term disability. In November 2017 I was put on a medication that completely dissolved my depression and anxiety, though I still had other issues to deal with.

One week I went to a priesthood leadership meeting at church. The topic was self-reliance. The speaker reminded us that it's our duty as men to work and provide. I truly believe that God intends for his children to be self-reliant, so talks like this are well-meaning. For those with jobs, I think the sermon was encouragement and reassurance that they're doing the right thing. For others, it was a call to action to get them out the door and doing what's right. But for me, all I felt was shame. I did my best to talk myself out of it, telling myself that my situation was different and not everyone has a severe mental illness. I often asked myself, "Why do I have a mental illness that prevents me from doing what God wants me to do?" I wanted to work but couldn't. I wanted to provide but couldn't. I might not have been clinically depressed anymore, but that didn't mean I felt good.

The night before my disability check came I was helping my sons get ready for bed. My wife was at class. I can't remember what my seven-year-old did, but I was really mad. So mad that I grabbed his arm and squeezed tight so he would know I wasn't joking around, so he would take me seriously, but then my grip loosened, and I was able to calm down. I didn't jerk him out of his little brother's room by his arm. I didn't scream at him to "cut it out" or just "stop." I didn't try to make him feel worthless, like I was better and more powerful than him. I took a deep breath, pressed my mental reset button, and calmly told him to go to his bed and that I would be there soon to read to him. Such change didn't come easy. I'd been off work for months so I could focus on my mental health. I'd worked hard with my counselor. I'd tried my eighth type of medication. But slowly, scenes where I didn't lose control started to feel like the real me, and on such nights, it was easy to have hope.

* * *

Living with a debilitating, undiagnosed mental illness was an intense trial, and I was relieved and grateful beyond expression to finally feel like I would escape it. I felt like a grownup again, like a real person. I'd learned how to conquer my worst impulses and control my responses to things that once overwhelmed me. I remember thinking, "Thank you, Heavenly Father. Thank you for helping me survive that trial. I'm a better person because of it. I'm now ready to rest and live a happy life."

In April 2018 my wife told me she was having a hard time with the church. She decided to attend only sacrament meeting and not the other meetings. She would change other things in her life because she no longer believed the church was true. It broke my heart a little, but I was happy that she was doing what was best for her. It was a courageous example of being true to oneself, but it also hurt. The church was a big part of our life, and she chose to step away.

Not long after, I met with my doctor. She asked if I was experiencing depression, anxiety, or manic episodes. I said no. She reported it on a form and sent it to the disability office. I got a phone call two days later saying that my disability benefits had ended. I would no longer receive a check.

In May my eight-year-old son was destroying a jar of peanut butter with a butter knife. It made me really mad—so mad I flipped out. Then Ellie flipped out. There was *a lot* of yelling. That had happened before, many times, but this time was different. Something snapped inside Ellie, something broke. She withdrew. From that day forward, she didn't talk to me as much. She wasn't as interested in my day and how I felt. I was the one trying to start a conversation, the one extracting information from her. I noticed, but didn't mention it, thinking it would work itself out like always. Not long after, we headed to St. George in southern Utah for a parenting workshop. On the drive I asked what was wrong. She said it wasn't a good time to talk about it, that it might make the weekend really hard and unpleasant.

And she was right. On the way home she asked if we could discuss the situation. I said yes, glad I could finally help. I can't remember the details of what she said because so much was a blur, like the cars passing us from the opposite direction. What I do remember is her saying that we needed to separate and I needed to move out. Once when I was a kid I played catcher for a family baseball game. My brother was using a heavy metal baseball bat. He hit the ball and chucked the bat behind him as he took off toward first base. The bat hit me right in the face. That's how it felt when Ellie told me we needed to separate. It was shocking. It was painful. I was mad. Bad words went through my head. Only one or two actually came out of my mouth. My head started to swim. I had to rub my temples with my fingers, pressing them hard, trying to make myself feel better.

At the beginning of June I rented a room, just a room, a really little room in a big house full of people I wasn't related to. I shared a kitchen, bathroom, and laundry room with people who weren't my family. After a couple of months I got my own place, paying four times the previous amount in rent, so I would have a place for my sons to stay when it was my turn to have them.

One day for lunch I had some amazing tacos. I thought of Ellie and how I wished she was there so we could talk about how good they were. I wished she was there so we could speak Spanish to the cute Hispanic lady who took my order. I went to a theater with a friend and saw a movie. Ellie and I had seen the trailer together before the separation and planned to watch it together. I got a prescription for glasses and ordered five pairs from Warby Parker to try on. I wanted Ellie to see me wearing them and help me pick the right ones.

Ellie asked me to not show her any signs of affection. She told me, and I believe her, that it made things really hard for her. But it's hard to do as she asked. On any given day, I want to buy her flowers. I want to send her a text that simply says, "I love you and I hope you're having a wonderful day." I want to buy her not just flowers but chocolate and a card. On the card I would write, "I'm so proud of you for getting hired full-time at such a great company! You are the best wife I ever had and I freaking love you." I want to drive to her office on the way to my counseling appointment and drop it all off and surprise her at work. I want to tell Ellie that I love her now more than I ever have since meeting her and falling in love. When I'm at the house taking care of the cat while she's out of town, I want to clean the kitchen and do laundry, but I've learned the hard way that she would see it as an intrusion. One day I almost turn to go to the house to check on Ellie and the boys because the youngest is sick and Ellie has to stay home from work with him. Then Ellie gets sick, so the boys and I buy medicine and food at the store. When we drop it off, she's lying in bed, and I want to go to her and hold her hand. Another day she's emotional and looks like she might cry, and I want to hold her and kiss her forehead in the way she's always liked.

But I don't. I keep my distance and give her the space she's asked for. I miss her at church. I want to sit close to her and see her beautiful face and smile. I love it when she smiles! I want to smell her hair and feel her energy. I look at her and she's beautiful; I want to give her a hug. I think, well, I can't do that, but maybe I can text and say, "Thanks for being my friend." But then I admit that even that would cross a line she established.

For a while I didn't know if I would be able to work again, especially when things were really bad. Then I started feeling like I *could* work, but I couldn't imagine who would hire me, so I didn't apply for many jobs. One day as I was driving my oldest to a playdate, I saw a "Now Accepting Applications" sign at an upscale, socially responsible grocery store you've probably shopped at, because its products are the best in the industry. After dropping the oldest off, my youngest and I went there. He behaved very well as I filled out the application and had a first interview on the spot. The day I found out I'd been hired, after a year of being unemployable, was a great day. It was an ideal place for me to work while I figured out what I wanted to do. Management and workers were, for the most part, wonderful, hardworking people. We gave away over a hundred pounds of food every day to the local food shelter. The hours were hard, though. Sometimes my shift started at 5:00 A.M.; other days it ended at 11:00 P.M. I worked every weekend because otherwise, there was a good chance I would lose a shift during the week. That's just how things are. Grocery stores are busiest on the weekends, so they need the most employees then.

Mentally and emotionally I'm the most stable I have ever been. The majority of this essay has made my life seem really hard. Well, it has been hard, but I feel really good. I'm so grateful for medication. I'm grateful for other things too, but the medication has made it so I don't have severe anxiety and depression. I now experience anxiety and depression like a normal person would. Which is still sad and depressing, but in a normal way, even when I'm confronting the hardest time of my life. I miss my boys. I miss my wife. I miss feeling like I'm a smart guy with something to teach others. I miss being part of a family. I miss pretty much everything, in fact, except the jerk I used to be sometimes.

Ellie and I came from strong LDS households. We were both faithful and obedient growing up. We both served missions. We went to BYU. We obeyed all the rules. We got married in the temple and didn't have sex before our wedding. We educated ourselves. We had children. We prayed together every day. We had family scripture study and family home evening. We avoided inappropriate media and watched only appropriate movies. We went to church. We accepted and fulfilled our callings in the ward. We paid a full tithe and fast offering our entire marriage, and I would even say our entire lives. We did those things not as part of a checklist, but simply because those were the righteous things we were honestly striving to do, the people we were striving to be, not as part of some goal, but because of who we already were. We were Latter-day Saints, living what we thought was our best life.

Ellie told me I would receive the divorce papers. I got a note from the post office saying they had tried to deliver them but hadn't been able to find me. I guess that's what happens when you have a job and go to work. The note told me to pick up the package at the post office. I was fine until I walked away from the desk with the manila envelope in hand, knowing my marriage was one step closer to being over. I made it to my car, got in, locked the doors—and screamed as loud as I could. This is not what I signed up for. This is not how things are supposed to end.

Working weekends was tough because it was often the only time I saw my boys. I quit the grocery store and got hired at a tech company that paid more, offered immediate benefits, and gave me weekends off, all of which were blessings. But it was also a blessing to see that I could have a better-paying job despite my mental illness. I traveled to Spain for two weeks and had an amazing time. It was something I'd wanted to do for years; I finally made it happen. Now it's time to have a real career, one where I can create and build, provide for a family, and actually save money. I applied and was accepted into a thirteen-week immersive web development program where I will learn computer programming. I start tomorrow and am very excited about the future.

I know the Book of Mormon is true. I know Joseph Smith translated it by the gift and power of God. I am however a little disillusioned and disenchanted by the church's promises about happy families and everything being all right if we cling to the word of God and do all that's asked of us. Everything is not all right now. How could Ellie fall away after everything she knew and everything she was doing and everything I was doing? How could Heavenly Father let this happen? What did I do to deserve this? What could I have done to prevent this? Could I have been better? Could I have controlled myself more? Did I make bad decisions? Did I break my covenants?

And even if I did, why couldn't Ellie still want to be with me after I got help?

I don't have answers, but I have faith that one day I will talk to someone who does.

The House of Infinite Regret

SCOT DENHALTER

Seated with my children on a chapel bench, I studied my wife's dolorous face as she sat at the organ, elevated on the choir loft behind the podium. Mary's blue, heavy-lidded eyes, half hidden by the graded rose tint of glasses more than a decade out of fashion, moved from face to face, never settling longer than a moment before wandering on, as if she were searching for a reflection of her own sadness, an unspoken bond of morose fellowship. Her cheeks no longer bore the hopeful blush of youth but rather two hasty smears of lipstick, forgotten and unblended. At forty-one, her middle-aged face sagged with disappointment, pulling her mouth into a perpetual frown, while the weight of her ample lower lip stretched the frown into an open-mouthed pout. She sat still, her posture the picture of defeat: leaning slightly forward, her back bowed, her narrow shoulders rounded. Her tiny hands lay upturned in her lap like pale, dead insects, as if she were waiting without hope for the bestowal of alms from the pocket of a generous stranger—as if she had been unwillingly and undeservedly chosen to ride on the most miserable float in the parade and was refusing to wave.

In any other sacrament meeting, I would have been reading a book. But a friend and colleague of mine, the second counselor in the ward, told me that the bishop had asked him if he thought I might be abusing my wife. He reassured me that he'd told the bishop I wasn't capable of such a thing. The bishop had responded, "Well, she sure looks like the unhappiest woman I've ever seen."

Embarrassed and defensive, I told my friend that it was genetic. Most of the women in her family looked much the same in their tenantless moments absent of thought.

"I know your heart, Scot," he consoled. "I know your heart." And I was grateful for his kindness and generosity. But he did not know my heart.

Sitting in the chapel that Sunday, I saw what my bishop had seen, and shame hit me like an unexpected and brutal slap. I was overwhelmed by the sudden, autogenous knowledge of the depth of her despair—a knowledge I had too long repressed. I realized suddenly that the cruelest thing I'd ever done to her was to marry her.

As with most Mormon couples, we married too young and after an abbreviated courtship. We were a case of opposites attracting, and less than a year of dating wasn't long enough to reveal how our very different temperaments would clash over time. But many of our friends were getting or had gotten married. The couple with whom Mary and I often double-dated were engaged. It seemed like the thing to do and the time to do it. Still, I had my doubts.

I liked Mary, but I never felt for her what I'd felt for a girl I dated for two years prior to serving my mission to Peru. The intensity of the love I felt for that girl, whom I had considered the love of my life, far exceeded what I felt for Mary or any other girlfriend.

But the girl I'd loved so deeply was already married. So were I to marry, it would have to be to someone else. Still, I wanted to feel for Mary what I'd felt for the girl who had broken my heart. But I didn't. And that haunted me, making me feel anxious and guilty. I dealt with this by calling on all the informal logic I could muster. "Mary is a good person," I reasoned. "She loves me and she'll make a good mother. I shouldn't have these doubts." I pushed my worries away, convincing myself that what I'd felt for the lost girl of my youth was mere immature infatuation—something extraordinary but too intense to last. I told myself that my feelings for Mary were more appropriate for marriage and family and that, with time, we would develop a healthy and lasting partnership. While my high school sweetheart was zany and full of fun, Mary was more grounded. She would be the thoughtful yin to my carefree yang.

Furthermore, I'd been far more sexual with Mary than I had been with anyone else, and I felt obligated to do right by her. Shortly after our engagement, however, Mary confessed to me that she had been as sexually intimate with another boyfriend.

This had happened before Mary and I started dating, but as a naive young man, unsure of my sexual aptitude, I considered ending the engagement to avoid comparison. Nevertheless, I had to hold myself accountable for my own actions, and I couldn't bear the thought of hurting Mary. So out of duty, empathy, and some degree of cowardice, I decided to marry someone I believed loved me more than I loved her.

I once heard an interview with psychologist and marriage expert John Gottman, who said there were really only three traits that all happy couples shared: affability, responsibility, and emotional stability. Statistically speaking, if both partners did not share all three of these traits, the relationship was at risk.

I was certainly affable. In high school, I cochaired the Crazy Activities Committee, organizing comedic assemblies, silly contests, and extralegal (but harmless) enterprises that sometimes made the local news. In college, I was in the LDS Student Association, helping to plan dances, concerts, and retreats.

Mary's affability was limited by her reluctance to socially engage. She was shy to the point of awkwardness. In an attempt to break out of her social isolation, Mary had joined LaDioneda, a social club for college women. Many of her social sisters had attended high school with me; when they learned Mary and I were dating, they were astonished, seeing us as utterly mismatched. But it was our differences that we found attractive in each other. I was gregarious and spontaneous. She was quiet and passive, and as I had been raised by a loquacious mother who bossed around my father, I found these traits appealing. And I believed her introversion was a validation of the proverb that "still waters run deep." Nevertheless, with time, the differences we found attractive became annoying—even repellent.

Driving home from my twentieth high school reunion, I was exhausted but happy. I had performed in drag as Mrs. Blaney, one of our ancient English teachers who had long since retired. Adopting her persona, I told each member of the class of 1968 what she really thought of them. It was just ridiculous fun, and the audience laughed harder and longer than I could have hoped. I asked Mary if she thought my performance went well. Instead of answering the question, she asked, "Why do you always have to be the center of attention?" I didn't exactly want that. Extroversion exhausted me. But I wanted to be liked, and clowning around seemed to be what I had to offer.

As far as Gottman's idea of responsibility was concerned, I was a failure. I was an immature, self-absorbed dreamer—not remotely ready for marriage and family. In the autobiography she penned in prison, Mary wrote of me, "He was undisciplined, too much the 'intellectual,' and had a big problem with authority." All true.

With an unrewarding career teaching junior high English, a wife who was often silently displeased with me, and the growing burden of financial responsibilities, I spent much of my free time escaping to my books, where I studied for one writing project or another. Yet, plagued by self-doubt and lacking the requisite drive to persevere, I failed to finish most of those projects. I would set aside one only to dedicate my time and energy to another, letting Mary carry an unfair share of the burdens of home and family.

Mary also wrote that I was "an emotionally unavailable and absent father." At one time, I would have objected to this judgment as unfair. Today, after many painful conversations with my children, I know the truth of that accusation. Buried in my books and half-heartedly pursuing my dream of being an accomplished author, I did not perceive the obvious need my wife and children had for the reassurance of my attentions.

Mary, on the other hand, was far more mature and, therefore, far more respon-sible than I. She was the bright and studious valedictorian of her high school graduating class. In nursing school, she was inducted into Phi Beta Kappa and graduated summa cum laude. With the skyrocketing inflation of the 1970s, I had given up the idea of buying a home. Mary, however, did the work to get us a loan through the Farmers Home Administration for a house in what was then rural Syracuse, Utah. She maintained our finances, balancing the checkbook each month. And she was far more attentive to our children than I.

The warmth and friendliness she felt toward me soon began to wane in the face of my irresponsibility. She was seldom confrontational, and when she was, she appeared to give in. Stupidly, I interpreted her silent withdrawal as evidence that she had understood and was satisfied. I realize now that she simply got tired of the rationalizations I offered in counterpoint. Bored to the point of distraction, I didn't like going to church. Mormonism fascinated me, but not the parboiled pablum presented year after droning year in the correlated church manuals. Mary justifiably resented those Sundays when she had to take the kids to church on her own.

Though I once saw Mary as quiet and shy, I soon began to see her as naturally gloomy and prone to an unhealthy fixation on what she considered the injustices of life. Certainly, my failure to be a fully contributing partner was one such injustice, but her sense of unfairness extended far beyond that. She bridled at what she saw as the injustices of parenthood, resenting the fact that our children obeyed me but took advantage of her. She often complained, "If my children loved me, they would obey me. They only obey you because they're afraid of you." She could never see how her own behavior contributed, even encouraged their disrespect. She was inconsistent in her demands on the children and indulgent of their failure to meet those demands. On those occasions when she lost all patience with them, she pushed me to be the enforcer. Then she would criticize me as overly harsh and strict, secretly letting them out of whatever punishment I had levied, even though it was at her direction.

She envied the good luck of others. When friends inherited a substantial fortune through the death of their grandma Ghirardelli (of the San Francisco Ghirardellis), Mary lamented, "Why doesn't something like that ever happen to us?" This wasn't wishful thinking. It was a bitter indictment of the unfairness of our having to lead modest lives. She also envied the possessions of others. When our best friends bought new furniture and a huge television for their family room, I came home from work one day to find the exact same furniture and television in our family room. Along with the obscene sums she spent every Christmas, her envy-spending was the only exception to her usual fiscal responsibility.

Though I once saw her as passive, I discovered she was far from it. My brother attended a night class at the University of Utah with Mary's older sister, who had shared accusations against me so dreadful he didn't feel comfortable repeating them. He simply asked if I knew what Mary was telling her family about me. I didn't. He said, "You need to talk to your wife."

I confronted Mary about this, but she denied it, saying, "You know what a bullshit artist he is," then adding, "and if I did say anything about you, you deserved it." This was a nondenial denial, so I assumed she was, in fact, venting to others her frustrations with me in what may have seemed to her a justified betrayal.

The truth would have been embarrassing enough. But I would discover that Mary's perception of me was as flawed as her perception of the universe's willful neglect of her. She discomfited friends, coworkers, and ward members with confidences about her physically, verbally, and emotionally abusive husband. I still wonder if it was one of those reports that made it to the ears of my bishop.

She even sent a letter full of condemnations of me to my parents while they were on a church education mission in Samoa. After their return, they mentioned the letter, though (probably in an effort to spare my feelings) they claimed not to remember the details it contained. Sadly, she also felt it appropriate to denounce me to my children. Occasionally, when I would discipline them, she'd take them aside to comfort them and tell them how much she loved them—and how little I loved them. I still can't understand why she was unable to see the emotional damage she was doing. But apparently it felt like an act of righteous defiance to tell them that I didn't love them, that I never had, and that I was only capable of loving myself.

Of course, I didn't discover any of this until after Mary and I divorced. I do not blame my children for their silence, and although I understand the hesitation of the friends and relatives who kept this from me, it would have helped to know about it when I could have tried to do something, however fruitless my efforts might have been.

* * *

But that Sunday—that Sunday, observing my wife as others did and knowing little of her secret revenge, I vowed to make it right. I took the earliest opportunity to apologize to Mary and to promise that I would no longer let anything interfere with my being a better husband and father. I was unsure of all the ways I had failed her, but I knew I had to spend less time at work (having left teaching for the private sector), less time playing, and less time with my intellectual pursuits. Perhaps my efforts were too little too late, but I wanted to try.

I knew that Mary was jealous of those in our neighborhood who were moving out of their small split-level starter homes and into larger, more nicely appointed homes. So I suggested we sell our home and move to something larger, and Mary set her heart on a house on the corner of Allison Way and Antelope Drive.

With two stories and a basement, the house afforded each of our children their own bedroom. I had wanted to get out of Syracuse—to a neighborhood with a better high school. But Mary loved the house, including its décor, which was a bit too froufrou for my taste. I also didn't like the fact that it was situated on the town's main thoroughfare, which was, in fact, a state highway. It was at the time a two-lane country road, but I knew that would soon change. Nonetheless, I wanted Mary to be happy. We bought the home and stayed in Syracuse.

It was 1994 when my oldest son, Josh, approached me as I sat reading on the front porch swing. He told me that his mother was using drugs. I dismissed his concern by explaining that what he might read as her being stoned was simply her overextending herself—burning the candle at both ends. Mary worked the swing shift as a nurse in the maternity ward of the major hospital in a town north of Salt Lake City. She would come home early in the morning and wind down, sitting in the Barcalounger downstairs and watching a movie on the DVD player. I would often find her asleep there before I went to work and tell her she needed to go to bed. (I later read in her autobiography that she considered this as me being controlling.)

At that moment, his friend James drove into the driveway. Josh said, "If you don't believe me, ask James." Although embarrassed, James corroborated my son's account of Mary. I persisted in painting a less alarming interpretation of Mary's behavior. Josh waved it aside. "Rachel's seen it, too," he insisted.

I called Rachel out on the front porch and put the question to her. She informed me that she'd found bloodied syringes hidden in empty Diet Coke cans. She added that her sister, Sarah, had found them as well.

I confronted my wife.

"You know how Josh gets things wrong. I'm just taking a muscle relaxant for my hip." She had long had problems with dysplasia. She had only to move her leg in a certain way and the ball joint of her femur would pop out of her hip socket and then snap back into place. It caused her a great deal of pain.

"You would have been prescribed pills for that, not injections," I countered.

"Oh, right, Dr. Denhalter. I forgot you know everything."

"Mary, I may not know exactly what you're doing, but I know you've been hiding it. That means either you're ashamed of it or you know it's dangerous or both," I replied. "If you don't come clean and agree to get help, I'll divorce you and take custody of the kids." It was an empty threat. I believed she was the better parent and had no intention of taking the kids from her, even if we divorced. I suspect that had she been in possession of her normally clear and intelligent mind, she would have called my bluff. Instead, she caved, admitting that she had been diverting drugs from work. Her job, at the end of her shift, was to snap the necks off bottles of Demerol left over by mothers who had gone home and to pour the remainder down the sink. She had, instead, been bringing the bottles home to help with her hip pain. "If the hospital found out what you are doing," I warned, "you would lose your job and your nursing license, and you'd likely go to jail." She agreed to go to rehab.

I wanted to place Mary in an inpatient facility where she would be under observation around-the-clock. But at that time, no inpatient program was available in Utah, so she enrolled in an outpatient program in South Salt Lake.

I admonished my four oldest children not to mention their mother's situation to their two youngest siblings. Nor were they to speak of it with their friends or the extended family. Once she was rehabilitated, I wanted no one but the six of us to be any the wiser. That way, Mary wouldn't have to deal with the stigma of being known as an addict, and my children wouldn't have to deal with being pitied as children of an addict. It would be more than three years before anyone else knew.

In 1998 a man driving with his family in their minivan called 911 to report a woman driving a white Chevy Corsica erratically on the freeway. After making the call, they spotted a highway patrolman parked in the emergency lane. They didn't know the officer had received a call from dispatch to watch for a possible drunk driver, so they pulled over behind him.

Crossing lanes, the Corsica hit the rear corner of the minivan, pushing it into the highway patrol car. The impact launched the Corsica into the borrow pit below the train tracks. The highway patrolman, the father, the mother, and their two children were treated for minor injuries at the nearest hospital and released. But Mary had to be extracted from her car and was life-flighted with a badly broken femur to the hospital that had once employed her. The accident made the papers and television news.

A few days later, my friend and colleague—the second counselor who had warned me of the bishop's concerns—approached me and asked if Mary was doing what his mother had done. His mother had been an administrative nurse at the same hospital Mary had worked at. After undergoing surgery, she'd become addicted to Percocet. She was eventually caught stealing pills from the hospital, and she committed suicide at the local Ramada Inn to avoid the public humiliation of her dismissal.

The secret I had tried to keep for Mary was public knowledge.

When Mary came home from the hospital, she complained that her osteopathic surgeon, who had deduced her drug abuse, wouldn't prescribe pain meds for her. Mary's need for pain meds was so strong that she felt forced to disclose the locations of her stashes throughout the house. Upon retrieving them, I could tell by the labels that most of what she had squirreled away had been stolen from her parents. There was even one bottle she had stolen from her best friend, who was recovering from knee replacement surgery. When she tried to replace her missing prescription, the pharmacist told Mary's friend that unless she reported who stole her pills, the prescription couldn't be refilled for a month. The friend chose to keep Mary's identity secret.

I refused at first to give Mary any of the drugs I had retrieved. But her tearful agonizing prompted me to call my sister (a nurse and a recovering addict herself) for advice. She knew Mary's surgeon and called him a self-righteous asshole. She said that a broken femur was so excruciating that it was unconscionable to send Mary home without something to blunt the pain. She instructed me to give Mary a Lortab every three to four hours. That dosage wouldn't have the same effect on an addict as on a person unaccustomed to pain meds, but it would help keep Mary from becoming dope sick and suffering the harrowing symptoms of withdrawal. But Mary grew angry at how little the dosage mitigated her pain, so she called her sister, saying I was trying to kill her. Greatly concerned, my sister-in-law called my oldest daughter, who reassured her that we were following medical advice and could not give Mary the amounts she demanded.

I stayed with Mary for the six months it took her to become ambulatory. I then moved into a one-bedroom apartment and told Mary that I planned to sue for divorce and full custody of the children, but I waited four more years to file. I hoped the possibility of losing custody of her kids would make her feel her life was so fully debased that she would sincerely seek help. But an unfulfilled threat loses its teeth. In truth, I was paralyzed. My lawyer said I had little chance in Utah of winning full custody. I felt helpless and hopeless. Nothing I could say or do, nothing my kids could say or do, had any effect on Mary's appetite for opioids, benzodiazepines, muscle relaxants, or whatever she could get her hands on.

When I had any of the younger kids over to my place, they complained that their mother was still using, still falling asleep while driving them—weaving in and out of traffic lanes, hitting orange construction barrels. They often had to grab the wheel to steer the car. This would startle Mary awake and anger her. I told them to walk to school. (The elementary school was less than a quarter-mile away, and the junior high was less than a half-mile.) If they needed to go somewhere other than school, they were to ask their older siblings for a ride or call me even if I was at work. I knew this wasn't really a workable solution, but given my circumstances, it was all I could come up with.

In the meantime, the children became more and more confrontational with their mother. She repeatedly passed out at home, even during Thanksgiving dinner, her face falling into her plate of food. She continued getting into traffic accidents, the last of which broke the tibia and fibula of her right leg. Unable to deal with her children's remonstrances and their failure to sympathize with her latest injury, she moved to her sister's, and I moved back into the house I once thought would make Mary a little happier. As the only functioning parent, I had to be both father and mother, a challenge I both feared and longed for.

In 2002 I finally filed for divorce and asked the court for full custody of my minor children. My lawyer reminded me that even with my exigent circumstances, fathers rarely gained full custody of their children. I presented to the court affidavits from my two adult daughters, outlining the many times their mother had put them and their siblings in danger by driving them while under the influence. (My oldest son was trying to remain neutral, and my second son was on his mission.)

I also presented a list of drugs she had taken, how much she had taken, where she had driven after taking them. For example, on the date of one of her auto accidents, she had angrily written in her journal that I had been controlling and bullied her into leaving the Barcalounger and going to bed before her shift began. This made her too upset to sleep, so over the next two hours she took four Lortab, four Percocet, four Xanax, and four Soma but was able to sleep only a bit before driving to work. Mary had daily recorded this kind of information in journals, which my oldest daughter found. The only reason I can see for this obsessive record keeping is that Mary wanted to prove to herself that she was in control of what she took. But for me, her journals demonstrated two things: she had never stopped using, not even during rehab, and she had developed a much higher tolerance for these substances than I could have imagined.

Mary's lawyer went first and began reading Mary's complaint. It started out as a pathetic list of chores around the house I did not do, but the judge interrupted, saying he had read all documents presented to the court. He asked my daughters, Rachel and Sarah, if they had written their affidavits without coercion. They affirmed that they had. The judge said he had enough information to render a decision, banged his gavel, and left. The bailiff called for us to clear the courtroom.

My daughters moved to hug their mother, but Mary's older sister pulled her away, shouting, "Don't you touch her. Don't let them touch you, Mary. They're traitors." Because my daughters' affidavits and my reports had not been read in court, Mary's family might not have known of Mary's addiction, and their aunt continued to shout. "She's your mother, you traitors! You should be ashamed."

My daughters fled, their heads down. Their aunt continued to berate them, while the bailiff did nothing to silence her. Someone else was speaking in soothing tones. My girls met me at the door and hurried out before me. We sat down together in the hall. My lawyer came and sat beside me. "What happened?" I asked him.

"What? You won."

I broke down and wept. I wept for my kids. I wept for Mary. I wept for myself. She with her drugs and I with my books and movies, we both had wasted years striving to escape the pain of conscious self-reflection.

A year later, with a wrecked truck and two totaled cars behind her, Mary finally received her fourth DUI and was booked into the county jail. Four months later, she was released to a halfway house in Salt Lake City, where she rode the bus daily, collecting prescriptions wherever she could. One night she overdosed in her room. It was a violation of her parole; she was sentenced to serve a year in the Utah State Prison.

Still denying her addiction, she wrote letters from prison that only served to further upset her children. Sidestepping the fact that her several doctors didn't know of each other, she argued that they would never have prescribed pain medication if they hadn't believed she needed it. She minimized her DUIs as simple errors in judgment, mistakes made by forgetting what she had already taken; her children knew that her journals contradicted this excuse. She attempted to manipulate them by making them feel guilty, disparaging them for their treatment of her after all she had done for them.

I tried to mitigate my children's resentment by telling them that Mary was no longer the woman who raised them—the drugs had rewired her brain long ago, changing her in ways we couldn't understand. Even before Mary's incarceration, I firmly believed her addiction would kill her. I warned them that they would regret their tough love stance once she was no longer around and they were unable to reconcile.

Toward the end of her prison sentence, Mary joined a rehab program for addicts called Excel that encouraged her to write an autobiography. It concludes: "I lost my job when I went to jail and have probably lost my career. I lost my apartment and car. I've lost the full function of my legs. I pray the loss of my family is only temporary. My challenges are great but I fully intend to conquer them."

She was released from prison in 2005. She looked and acted better than she had in twelve years. Unable to work, she had applied for disability, but she already had an apartment, a car, and half the equity from the refinancing of the Allison Way home. I told her how good she looked and sounded, promising that if she kept trying with the kids, they would come around.

Less than a year later, she was found dead on her kitchen floor, a half-finished Diet Coke beside her.

In prison, Mary had begun corresponding with a friend from high school, indoctrinating her on how she had been mistreated and abandoned by her children. The friend became something of a caregiver after Mary's release. She stopped by Mary's apartment to take her to a doctor's appointment. Concerned when Mary failed to answer the door, she enlisted the help of the landlord.

The autopsy revealed a pharmacopoeia of drugs in Mary's system, including a substantial amount of morphine. After the enforced sobriety from more than a year behind bars, her body no longer had its previous tolerance. Forgetting this, she had taken the excessive doses and dangerous mixes she'd once been accustomed to. She had passed out, falling to the floor in a position that made it difficult to breathe. Positional asphyxia was listed as the cause of death.

Mary's addiction left her children without a mother. The sense of abandonment this instilled in them still undermines their sense of self-worth today. They struggle with their own relationships. Some struggle to one extent or another with alcohol and marijuana. But Mary's death robbed all who loved her of the chance to make peace with her, leaving us with so many regrets. Regret is the underbelly of what's left of our lives. I regret not being a better husband sooner. My children and I regret not being more loving despite her failure to kick her habit. We understand now that it didn't matter if Mary mistook our kindness for approval of and support for her choices. And we are haunted by the impossibility of ever making things right.

Denial is an ineluctable part of both living with and being an addict. But Mary's death and our living with its consequences have laid bare all our denials but one—a sense of relief too shameful to acknowledge. This is not just the relief we feel that her pain is now gone. It is also the relief that we no longer have to be witness to the slow, thirteen-year death she chose. But no one speaks those words. We do not say she is better off dead; and we do not say we are the better for it.

The house on 1729 Allison Way is gone. The state purchased it in 2007 to widen the south side of Antelope Drive. All that remains of the house is a gravel-lined depression for collecting groundwater darkened by the ghosts of infinite regret.

From Patriarchy to Matriarchy

A Marital and Spiritual Journey

THOMAS W MURPHY

About a year after my father divorced her, my mother married a man she met at church. During their courtship, my future stepfather wore a cast on his leg and moved around on crutches. This impairment, my mother said, "made her feel safe." They married when I was seven years old, but safety and security did not characterize my experience nor that of my three siblings. Our new stepfather directed his most brutal strikes against his own teenage sons, while my preteen older brother bore the brunt of the violence directed toward us younger children. My younger brother and baby sister and I watched and learned from our older stepsister, who avoided the worst blows by a diligent obedience.

The same man, who beat us for making noise at church or stabbed us with a fork for putting our elbows on the table, gathered my mother and his new family early each morning to read from scripture around that table in our home in Burley, Idaho, traditional territory of the Shoshone-Bannock peoples. This was my introduction to the Book of Mormon. I saw my stepbrothers as Laman and Lemuel, disobedient older sons in the book's earliest stories; I blamed their failures for my stepfather's violence. I modeled myself after Nephi, the book's first hero, which sometimes helped me avoid beatings. From the Book of Mormon I learned that it was my duty to obey the family patriarch and that it was better for a child to suffer than for a family to "dwindle in unbelief." The Old Testament story of Abraham and Isaac revealed that God might expect a father to sacrifice his child's life as a sign of obedience. When I turned eight, I sought peace within our home by asking my stepfather, rather than my biological father, to baptize me.

I was seventeen when we moved to St. Anthony, Idaho, where the lands of the Shoshone-Bannock meet those of the Eastern Shoshone. One stepbrother was in prison, another was in the army, and my older brother had received psychiatric care after attacking me with a knife. He would cycle in and out of foster homes before finding discipline and structure in the Marine Corps. My stepsister had married. My mother, meanwhile, had given birth to four more boys. I was the oldest of seven children still at home and a frequent target of my stepfather's abuse.

One evening, after I argued with my mom about religion, he removed his glasses and grabbed me. "Let's fight!" he said.

A senior in high school, I was finally strong enough to defend myself. I pushed him back against the wall. When he lunged at me, I parried and wrestled him to the floor, then held him there. "You see now that I can take you," I said calmly. "I'm going to release you. Next time you challenge me to a fight, I won't be so kind."

As soon as I released him, he lunged again, intending to knock me down the stairs. To save me, my younger brother pushed us both, deflecting our stepfather's attack enough that I didn't tumble down the stairs.

"Greg, let's get the hell out of here!" I hollered. My younger brother and I had walked about a mile down the road when the deputy sheriff picked us up—our mother had called the cops on us. We told the deputy not just about this particular evening but about years of abuse. Our pleas for help fell on deaf ears. The deputy returned us to a home where we weren't safe, telling us all to "sleep on it and have a family council in the morning." We never discussed the incident.

Active on a traveling debate team and employed at McDonald's, I avoided home as much as possible. At work I met Kerrie Sumner, a first-year student at Ricks College (now BYU-Idaho) in nearby Rexburg. Kerrie was charismatic and feisty, with a fearless penchant for speaking truth to power. We spent as much time together as possible during my final year of high school. I was enamored with her "blue-gray bedroom eyes" and wrote in my journal that they "can enchant you if you stare into them too long." I praised her beauty, smile, and incredible singing voice.

One night when we got off work, my brother and I were trapped in Rexburg by a snowstorm. It was past midnight; we had nowhere to go. Kerrie, who had also worked the late shift that night, offered to let us stay in her college-approved apartment. Alarmed when they found boys asleep in the apartment the next morning, Kerrie's roommates reported her to the college's honor code office, inventing lurid and false details.

Without giving Kerrie the chance to explain herself, her bishop believed the exaggerations and fantasies of her roommates, claiming to know the truth "through the power of the priesthood."

After repeatedly identifying the inaccuracies in his assumptions, Kerrie declared, in exasperation, "So truth doesn't matter to you." She left that interrogation never wanting to attend church again. The bishop withdrew his ecclesiastical endorsement, and she was suspended from school.

Kerrie's father was a director in the Church Education System; he knew his daughter well enough to know that the worst charges against her were nonsense, and as for letting two scared boys stay in her apartment, he didn't think compassion in an emergency should get her kicked out of school. He intervened on her behalf; the administration overturned the suspension on appeal—but it came too late in the semester. While suspended, Kerrie missed too many classes to pass her courses.

Meanwhile, at home, Greg and I still endured violent rages. One evening we were in our bedroom, doing homework and listening to music. Three times our parents yelled through the wall to turn down the music. We did, each time. My mother finally stormed into the room and yelled at us to turn it down. "I already did," I replied. She demanded again that I turn it down.

I simply stated, "No."

Furious, my mother jumped on my bed, arms flailing, striking me repeatedly. I protected myself but didn't strike back until my stepfather also leapt on me. "Two against one," I later wrote in my journal. I struck his temple, his glasses flew off, and blood flowed—a lot of it.

My mom turned to him. "Bill, you're bleeding!"

He looked at me and warned, "If you ever hit me again, we'll have a real fight."

After they left, I noticed that we had accidentally pushed the button for the bass on the stereo, explaining why they felt we hadn't turned the music down. But the beatings stopped.

After that, my stepfather spoke to me only through my mother. When I would reply directly to him, he would talk to her about me, as if I weren't there. I resented that my mother stood by and always took her husband's side. Her refusal to defend me hurt enough that eventually, for the one and only time, I called her a "bitch." She responded by kicking my brother and me out of our home.

We had nowhere to go. Once again, Kerrie helped us find a place to stay, this time with a mutual friend who didn't live in college-approved housing. I'm not exaggerating when I say that Kerrie saved my life. I proclaimed in my journal, "She's all a guy could ever want and I have her." We found a comfort and security in each other's presence that was absent in our lives at home. We bonded during hikes in local canyons or long walks around neighborhoods in Rexburg and Idaho Falls, sharing our feelings and intimate stories of childhood abuse, doubts about the faith of our families, and stories of Indigenous ancestors in predominantly white families. We both insisted that if we ever had children, we wouldn't use any form of violence against them. Our compassionate conversations assured me that something better than the brutal patriarchy I'd experienced at home was possible.

One evening my mother called me at work, apologized, and asked me to come home.

"Your house isn't home to me," I replied.

"You got a letter from Utah State University," she said.

"Did I get in?" I asked.

"Yes, and they offered you a scholarship. But you have to reply to accept it." Despite my pleas, she refused to provide the information necessary to claim the scholarship. She demanded that I come home if I wanted to know how to accept it. Even after returning home, though, I knew that my stepfather expected me to pay rent once I turned eighteen. It was a demand he made of all his children.

Given that I was planning to leave for college and Kerrie was thoroughly disenchanted with Ricks College, we discussed going to Logan, Utah, as a couple. Living together outside marriage was too scandalous for our families, and we didn't want to live separately. On May 15, 1985, I picked the mall of all places to look at rings and ask Kerrie, "Will you marry me?"

"Yes," she replied. We bought each other rings on credit. A few weeks later we bought our first car together, also on credit. In a strange sort of way, our decision to get married that summer, shortly after my eighteenth birthday, became our teenage rebellion. Kerrie's parents urged us to wait, but that only increased our desire to do our own thing.

I accepted the scholarship to Utah State, and we found an inexpensive apartment in Hyde Park, just north of Logan and about twenty miles south of the site of the Bear River Massacre, where the slaughter of 250 Northwestern Shoshone opened Cache Valley for Mormon settlement. I left home on my birthday, and we moved our meager belongings to our new apartment. Three weeks later, on September 5, 1985, we wed at the Salt Lake City home of Kerrie's uncle.

To pay for college, I joined the Army Reserve and scheduled my basic training at Fort Leonard Wood, Missouri, home to the Osage, and advanced individual training at Fort Lee, Virginia, land of the Powhatan Confederacy, for summer 1986. Shortly after I signed the papers, we realized Kerrie was pregnant. Her due date was in August, during my basic training. I tried unsuccessfully to change the schedule.

The expense of a child and income lost while caring for one made college temporarily untenable, so I walked away from my scholarship. Kerrie and I decided that the best thing for her needs during the pregnancy would be to return to her parents' home in Iowa while I was away at training. We moved to Davenport, traditional lands of the Meskwaki, and I worked full-time for a few months before my duty. I fondly remember our walks and talks on the streets of Davenport, where, joined by Kerrie's dog, we reinforced our mutual promises never to lay a hand on our child in violence.

Living with Kerrie's parents, we returned to church, attending regularly, and took temple preparation classes. Just before we were to be sealed, I bore my testimony for the one and only time as an adult at a testimony meeting in Davenport. I acknowledged my doubt and wayward path to the temple but also expressed faith in God and the love of my new family.

In April 1988, at the Chicago temple in the lands of the Peoria, Potawatomi, and Miami, our daughter went to a nursery while Kerrie and I each went through initiation ordinances and the endowment ceremony. It took hours. Kerrie and I were then sealed as a couple, after which Jessyca would be sealed to us as our daughter. A temple worker brought twenty-month-old Jessyca into the room. She was shocked to see everyone dressed in white but recognized Kerrie and ran to her. She noticed me and exclaimed loudly, "That's my dad!"

When the ordinance worker called us forward to kneel at the altar, Jessyca resisted, perhaps out of shyness and the strange setting. Very likely hungry, she became upset and started crying. Kerrie tried to calm our daughter, speaking soothingly and cuddling her, so the sealing ceremony could proceed. When that didn't work, Kerrie, against the wishes of the temple staff, stepped into the hall.

Jessyca relaxed enough that Kerrie thought she could bring her back into the sealing room. But Jessyca wasn't happy about returning to the strange room filled with anxious people. Again, she burst into tears. The temple worker turned to me. "Hold her down," he said.

"What? She's crying," I responded.

"We cannot wait any longer. We have a schedule to keep. Just hold her down. Let her cry," the priesthood authority instructed.

As I held her, Jessyca's cries turned to screams. I do not remember the words of the rite, nor can I explain in retrospect why I consented to the violence that disrupted the sanctity of being sealed together for time and all eternity. As the ceremony concluded, I released my traumatized daughter. "We wouldn't normally ask you to do that to children, but this is just so important!" the temple worker said as we left so another sealing could take place.

The words reminded me of childhood beatings at the hands of my stepfather in the church foyer. That day in the temple I did what I was told and thereby violated, for the one and only time, my promise to myself and my bride that I would never use force against our child. My faith in myself and a patriarchal God crashed down.

Like many young people, we dreamed of being millionaires but didn't earn enough to pay our monthly bills. Multiple low-paying jobs in the restaurant industry, retail, and the Army Reserve couldn't keep a roof over our head, feed our daughter, or pay for her diapers.

We started a small advertising and marketing business on credit, built around Kerrie's illustrious artistic talents and my unremarkable sales skills. The next big sale always seemed to be around the corner, but it didn't stop the credit union from repossessing our car. We would have lost our mobile home, too, if Kerrie's parents hadn't financed it for us. Thanks to the church's Relief Society, though, we at least had food on the table.

Desperate, we took risks we shouldn't have. We were conned by a client who offered us contract work and made big promises that were all lies. When the con artist disappeared without paying us, we spiraled slowly and painfully into bankruptcy and a profound skepticism of others.

I worked most Sundays and drifted into inactivity at church. A leader in Primary, the church's auxiliary for children, Kerrie continued to attend. I was ready to give up—on everything. I felt like a failure, unable to fulfill my basic responsibilities to my family. "I can't do this anymore. I'm done. I can't go back to church, and I want out, out of our marriage. I'm not the man you thought. I can't fulfill your dreams," I told Kerrie less than a year after our sealing.

"You *are* my dream," Kerrie replied. "You're far more important to me than the church. Maybe we should have waited to get married, but I think we both know we never would have if we didn't do it then. I just wish we could want each other that bad always."

Kerrie showed me a type of love I had never experienced before. I couldn't leave. If she could accept the failure that I felt I was, I couldn't rob her of the dream we still had, of growing old together.

I applied to the University of Iowa and received financial aid. On Veteran's Day of 1990 my National Guard unit received an alert for activation as part of Desert Storm, interrupting my second year of college. My deployment to Iraq, Saudi Arabia, and Kuwait during the Persian Gulf War devastated our finances. We needed help. Though we hadn't yet attended church in Iowa City, the bishop of our ward loaned us $500 to pay a portion of more than $1,000 in telephone bills that kept us connected during the war. To pay off our debt, the bishop asked us to set up chairs each week for Sunday school for the next six months.

We were open with the bishop about our doubts as well as our needs. Soon after we returned to church, a member of the Iowa City bishopric and a professor at the university invited us to his home for dinner. "The Book of Mormon tells a vastly different story than what I'm learning about ancient America in my anthropology and history courses," I announced bluntly during the meal.

The professor nodded. "I believe the Book of Mormon is a product of the nineteenth century, not an ancient document," he said. We were stunned by this revelation and surprised to learn that college towns had their share of doubters, even within the church. This bishopric counselor and his wife introduced us to a community of intellectual Mormons where skepticism was commonplace and to *Sunstone* magazine, related symposia, and the academic Mormon studies journal *Dialogue*.

Informed a half year later that we had paid our debt, we asked five-year-old Jessyca on our way home if she still wanted to go to church. She shrugged. "I don't really like church."

Kerrie and I looked at each other and grinned a bit. "Why not?" Kerrie asked.

"Well," Jessyca said, "my Primary teacher says Black people are dark because God cursed them. I don't think that's right. Eli isn't cursed." Eli, Jessyca's best friend at that time, was dark-skinned, of Afro-Venezuelan descent.

"You're right, that's wrong!" Kerrie said. "Some people at church might believe that, but we don't. It's racist."

"What else did your Primary teacher say?" I asked.

"She said women shouldn't work. They should just stay home with their children." Kerrie gave me *that* look. We'd had many discussions about this message from the church. Out of necessity, Kerrie had worked to support our struggling family and was going to college to gain skills and knowledge for a future career. Again, we told Jessyca that we didn't believe those things even if others did and that she could have any career she wanted.

Jessyca leaned forward in her seat. "If you don't believe, why do you go to church?"

She had a point. Smart kid, our daughter.

Our only activity in church thereafter was some participant observation while doing research among Maya, Nahua, and Zapotec peoples in Latin America. Freed from gender roles defined by the church and inspired by Kerrie's courses in women's studies, we made purposeful changes in our lives. We agreed that it was important for Jessyca to have professional women as role models and selected a female doctor and dentist for the family. We regularly attended women's sporting events and enrolled Jessyca in a coed swim team. We formally split the household duties: I became the cook, partly because I was more committed to a regular schedule of meals and had worked as a cook in the army and a chef in the restaurant industry. After I washed something red with whites and forgot a load of clothes at the laundromat, Kerrie took primary responsibility for the laundry.

At the U. of Iowa, Kerrie and I took an anthropology course about North American Indians together and joined an archaeological field school at a Paleo-Indian and Hopewell site along the Mississippi River. Kerrie descended from Peninah Shropshire Cotton Wood, a Cherokee woman often heralded as among the first Native converts to Mormonism and the first to enter a polygamous marriage. Orphaned and displaced from homelands farther east, Peninah was a servant in the Illinois household of Daniel Wood and charged with caring for his first wife. Peninah, the "hired girl," married the patriarch before moving west in 1846 to the land of the Goshute, Ute, and Shoshone, at that time claimed by Mexico, later the Territory of Utah. In Bountiful and Woods Cross, Peninah raised her own children, those of her sister wives, and three Timpanogos children orphaned in the invasion of Utah Valley. The three orphans died of disease just before adulthood.

The expectation for Indigenous converts to Mormonism was that they would become "white and delightsome," but that was easier to preach than make true. Prejudice lingers. In the 1990s, Kerrie and I attended a family reunion for the descendants of Daniel Wood and his wives. "Which wife are you descended from?" one of her relatives would ask.

"Peninah," Kerrie would proudly declare.

"Oh," the relative would gasp, as if Kerrie had exposed a family scandal. One wonders if the scandal was an interracial, polygamous marriage to a household servant or a proud woman from a matriarchal tradition living among the Mormon patriarchy and refusing to forget where she came from. Whatever it was, Kerrie never felt she met the threshold of "white and delightsome."

My family's connections to Indigenous people were more tenuous. My grandmother repeated stories from her grandfather about his Iroquois grandmother, who was refused admittance into her daughter's and son-in-law's home. My great-great-grandfather was left outside with this Indigenous grandmother, stories about whom he would later tell to his grandchildren.

We learned in our college classes that stories of "Indian princesses" in family lines aren't uncommon in America. The immediate trauma of forced assimilation and the pressure to "pass" as white led some people to become detached from their ancestral roots. These stories project European aristocracies onto Indigenous communities and are often fairly dubious, a way for settler colonists to claim indigeneity without taking responsibility for the injustices of conquest and colonization. While my family stories initially inspired my interest in anthropology and American Indian studies, I learned to keep them close to my chest until I could better understand my own identity. How could I tell such stories without invoking this settler-colonial mythos?

We began to ask more questions and seek guidance from elders and community members. We began to repair and reweave threads that had been broken, making a connection to our ancestors' more matriarchal traditions.

In 1993 I began graduate studies in anthropology with a research focus on Native America and Mormonism at the University of Washington. Tired of school, Kerrie elected to delay graduate studies. Our first year in the Seattle area, Kerrie and I both worked for the Native American Science Outreach Network, housed at UW. We began to establish deep, sustainable, and reciprocal relationships with Coast Salish nations of western Washington. We volunteered at cultural events with local tribes and in the urban Indian community as I completed an MA and PhD. These experiences helped us develop a deep appreciation and understanding of the diversity of Indigenous traditions, so grossly misrepresented in the

Book of Mormon. The more intimate our relations, the less desirable was that goal of becoming white and delightsome.

In 2002 an essay I'd written using new DNA evidence to refute racist stories about Native American origins in the Book of Mormon was published in a book titled *American Apocrypha: Essays on the Book of Mormon*. Though I was inactive, the local stake president scheduled a disciplinary council in December 2003 to try me for apostasy. "I should just resign, take the power away from them," I said to Kerrie.

"Don't make it so easy for them!" Kerrie urged. So I put up a fight using the media and, surprisingly, won: the stake president called off the disciplinary action. Within five years the church changed the introduction to the Book of Mormon to make it more compatible with DNA evidence. Later, the church amended chapter and verse headings to be less racist too.

One benefit of a Mormon heritage is the church's long-standing commitment to genealogy. Many members are dedicated genealogists—including my mother. Her genealogical work led me to probe beyond the stories of an Indian heritage. She pointed me toward an actual ancestor, Susannah Ferguson, seven generations before me. Susannah was born around 1786 in the ruins of the Mohawk village of Tiononderoge in the aftermath of the Revolutionary War. In 2015 Kerrie and I visited this place, known today as Fort Hunter, near Florida, New York, and sent my mother pictures and stories from their archives of our ancestors.

Susannah came from a matrilineal (some would say matriarchal) tradition of the Haudenosaunee (or Iroquois, a union of nations that included the Mohawk, Oneida, Onondaga, Cayuga, and Seneca). Either Susannah or her daughter Rachel was the ancestor I'd heard about, the one denied entrance to her daughter's home. By my generation, her matriarchal legacy had been smothered by decades of Christian and Mormon patriarchy.

Kerrie helped uncover that legacy. After earning an MSW from UW, she did an internship with Tulalip Tribes and the UW's Indigenous Wellness Research Institute (IWRI), which subsequently hired her as a researcher, faculty member, and community liaison. As teachers and mentors, we help Native youth strengthen their identities and connect with ancestral traditions while earning college degrees and starting careers.

When the director of the Edmonds Community College Foundation refused to sign a grant application for an annual powwow from the Native American Student Association I advised, Kerrie again encouraged me to take a public stand. "Warn them," she said, "that the students will protest at the foundation auction if this decision stands."

I wrote a lengthy, blunt email addressing student charges of institutional racism, cc'ing relevant parties. In response, I was censured by our college president.

Nonetheless, administrators found someone to sign the grant application—and the students got their powwow. In return for these public confrontations on behalf of Indigenous communities, our Native students and their families began inviting us to sweats, potlatches, and other cultural events.

Meanwhile, a family of ex-Mormons in the local Snohomish Tribe adopted Kerrie and me together in a public ceremony after we collaborated on the construction of stəl̓jxwáli, or Place of Medicine, an ethnobotanical garden in a city park. "You are sduhúbš (Snohomish), children of swakulem (the sea monster man)," cəlálakəm (our adopted sister) insists.

Through service-learning projects and an archaeology field school with my students, we helped repatriate salmon to b'ka'ltiu (Mukilteo), the site of the Point Elliott Treaty. Once exterminated from the area, coho and chum once again swim in the waters where they annually greeted our sduhúbš (Snohomish) predecessors.

In this network of reciprocal relations, tribal leaders began inviting us and our students on Tribal Canoe Journey, a regional movement to reclaim ancestral pathways on the water and revive previously outlawed songs, dances, languages, and cultural traditions. As we've traveled through the Salish Sea and North Pacific, we and many of our students have been accepted into the Blue Heron (Snohomish), Samish, Stillaguamish, and G'ana'k'w (Tlingit and Haida) canoe families.

Rosie Cayou James, an elder from the Samish Nation, has been an inspiration to us, but especially me as I've gained the courage to speak openly of my Indigenous ancestry. I'd been very self-conscious about the "Indian princess" stories in my family and their unsavory reputation in Indian Country. Rosie proudly claims her French and Hawaiian ancestors alongside her deep Coast Salish roots. "Remember all your ancestors," Rosie admonishes. "Ancestors don't see color; they only see descendants." It's important in Coast Salish country, Rosie says, to "know where you come from." DNA tests and archival documents validating our family stories also helped my confidence.

We've learned to acknowledge our English, Irish, Scandinavian, and Mexican heritages, as well as the cultures of our Indigenous ancestors, both adopted and lineal. The latter have become increasingly important, even dominant, in our lives. Kerrie and I have found spiritual healing in sweats, pipe ceremonies, Sun Dance, and Tribal Canoe Journey. The Indigenous teachings we learned in community and ceremony reinforce values of reciprocity and balance in relationships and are much more compatible with the sort of marriage we want. They validate Kerrie's feminism and provide her with greater leadership opportunities than Mormonism's patriarchy. Kerrie's powerful voice, for both singing and political activism, has earned deep respect and many invitations to participate in ceremony. Her coworkers recognized her as "most likely to pick up the sword."

We're fortunate that our jobs allowed us to participate in Tribal Canoe Journey together. I lead a community-based anthropology field school at Edmonds College that would take students as service learners on journeys that often last three to five weeks as we travel from one reservation or reserve to another, often across the US-Canada border dividing Coast Salish nations. Kerrie's responsibilities at IWRI included serving as a liaison between the university and local tribes on journey. Strong Native women play key leadership roles in our canoe families, and these women appreciate Kerrie's spark.

Jessyca has followed in her mother's footsteps. She has a bachelor's degree from Western Washington University and a master's from the New School in New York. She helped start LadyFest, a female art and music event, and Make-Shift, an art makers space in Bellingham. She sang in a punk band called Scum Eating and worked as the administrative manager for the Bellingham-Whatcom County Commission Against Domestic Violence.

After three decades in our rebellious marriage, I no longer think of Kerrie as mine or claim that "I have her." Instead, Kerrie and I have been valued partners as we forged our way out of a patriarchal religion and accepted invitations back into an Indigenous culture that values female leadership and aspires to matriarchy. The communities we participate in aren't some romanticized place free of gender struggles, prejudice, and violence, but they are a home where we can recover from the historical trauma of domestic violence and settler-colonial patriarchy. We feel safer and more at home in Native communities.

One morning after a late night of singing and discussing Rebecca Roanhorse's *Trail of Lightning*, I tried to nudge Kerrie awake. We'd spent the night at a friend's home in Olympia, not far from the Nisqually reservation, for an Indigenous women's book club. When Kerrie didn't respond I thought maybe she was just tired. I let her sleep while I went out for a cup of coffee and helped our hosts make breakfast.

I soon returned to the bedroom. "Time to get up!" I announced. "Breakfast's almost ready." She didn't respond. This wasn't normal. I gently shook her. "Wake up!" I urged.

She stirred and muttered slowly, "I . . . am . . . awake." The words were barely audible. Rolling over, she winced in pain. "My . . . arm," she groaned.

"What's wrong?" I asked.

"It . . . hurts." I could hardly make out the words.

I thought of times when I imagined I'd awakened in a dream; I would try to move my body, and it would barely respond. That's what I thought was happening at first. I Googled what to do when someone won't wake from a dream state. While the responses to my Google query weren't alarming, I was deeply concerned. I called to my friends, "Can you come help me? Kerrie won't wake up."

We tried but could not rouse her to anything beyond a mumbled response. I called the nurse's line, asking what to do. "Call 911 *now*," they instructed. Paramedics, emergency room, blood tests, CT scan, and MRI followed. I called Jessyca, who immediately drove to Olympia to be with us through this ordeal.

Because of a misdiagnosis, it was a week before we knew Kerrie had suffered a brain stem stroke. During the three days Kerrie was in a coma, the Samish Canoe Family, coworkers from IWRI, and members of the Indigenous Sisters Resistance came and sang for Kerrie, who tried to sing too. At first we could just see her vocal cords move; later her barely audible voice returned. The music seemed to bring her back.

Fifteen minutes, then an hour, then a few hours of wakefulness. Kerrie remembers almost nothing from the seventeen days and nights I slept by her side in the hospital. After sixteen more days doing rehab in a skilled nursing center, she insisted on coming home to heal. That made thirty-three days in a medical facility, one for each year of our marriage.

Brain stem strokes impact basic motor skills, the necessary functions of life. Few victims survive. Kerrie has learned again to swallow, to talk, to sing, to eat, to walk, to see . . . to remember. I took over two years of medical leave and a sabbatical to be her primary caretaker. Permanent, irreparable damage to optical nerves limits her recovery. Double vision, dizziness, bouts of vertigo, and impaired mobility linger. Nothing is more important to me than to care for the woman I love; paid family medical leave made it possible initially; online teaching and early retirement hold promise for the future.

I had already prepared to take medical leave before the stroke. My mother had called a month earlier to tell me that she had stage IV terminal breast cancer. A reoccurrence, inoperable, untreatable, final. In October her doctors told her she had less than three months to live. Kerrie's stroke came just a few days before I had planned to go to Idaho to help my sister, Suzanne, care for our mother.

We spent Thanksgiving in the hospital instead. Kerrie needed me. I couldn't be there for my mother. On Mom's birthday, December 14, we called, and Kerrie sang "Happy Birthday," her first full song since coming out of a coma. My mother and I wept. A few days later Mom asked family and friends to pray that she could "go home quickly and peacefully."

"This is the beginning of the end," the home hospice nurse said.

Christmas passed. Mom developed pneumonia. Her breathing was tortured, but somehow, she hung on. Suzanne asked Mom what was holding her back. "Tom," she muttered. Kerrie and I packed up her wheelchair, her drum, and a duffle bag and drove to Idaho at last. When we arrived, Mom could no longer speak, but she could hear. I didn't know what to say, only that I was sorry it took so long and I loved her.

"It's just a matter of hours," the nurse said as 2018 wound to an end.

Early in the afternoon on January 1, 2019, I called Kerrie into the room with Suzanne, Mom, and me. "Could you please sing for her?" I pleaded.

From her wheelchair Kerrie called upon Susannah Ferguson and her daughter Rachel, the Mohawk ancestors Mom had documented in her genealogical research. Kerrie began to sing: first the Mohawk "Water Song," then "Women's Warrior" and "Strong Women." Struggling to sustain her voice at the end of these songs, Kerrie shifted to just drumming. Turning to Suzanne, Kerrie softly said, "Let go. Let go," she repeated to both of us.

Suzanne looked bewildered. She didn't want to release Mom's hand. Kerrie offered Suzanne a rattle. My sister finally let go, and together they kept time.

"They're here. The ancestors are here," Kerrie quietly noted. She handed me the drum, directed me on the proper beat, and began to sing "Strong Women" again. While Suzanne rattled and I drummed, my mother's intermittent breathing finally stopped. By the end of the song, we knew that Kerrie had brought Mom the peaceful passage for which we'd all prayed.

Figure 9. Thomas W and Kerrie Murphy, February 2020, Point No Point Park, Washington

Thomas writes, "Each year we celebrate Valentine's Day and our wedding anniversary in September with a getaway. Our getaway in February 2020 took us to the Port Gamble S'Klallam Tribe's resort on Washington's North Kitsap Peninsula and a stroll on the Point No Point beach where the S'Klallam and neighboring Coast Salish nations signed a treaty with the United States in 1855. While celebrating our thirty-fifth Valentine's Day together required an eye patch and assistive devices for walking, the new challenges have made the experiences together even more deeply rewarding."

The Marriage Bed

An Essay and Three Poems

ROBERT A. REES

Behold, thou art fair, my beloved, yea, pleasant: also our bed is green. The beams of our house are cedar, and our rafters of fir.
—Song of Songs 1:16–17

What sign coud be so clear
as this of our own bed?
—Penelope to Odysseus, *The Odyssey*

Ruth Stanfield and I were married in the Los Angeles Temple on April Fool's Day 1961 while we were in graduate school at the University of Wisconsin, driving from Madison to Los Angeles and back during spring break. It was a crazy trip, capped by Ruth having morning sickness the last five hundred miles of the return trip. (Yes, we followed church instructions not to use birth control!)

Marriage, someone once observed, is "the school of love." Given the mortal (and moral) and eternal consequences of marriage for Latter-day Saints, one could argue that "Mormon marriage is the graduate school of love." By that, I mean that realizing that one's marriage is not just until "death do you part" but rather for time and all that lies beyond time concentrates the heart, mind, and imagination toward the necessity of getting love right. The vows and covenants made across an altar in the temple before "God, angels, and witnesses," that image of two people with clasped hands looking into the mirrors of one another's eyes, which in turn is reflected in the echoing mirrors framing the altar, are symbols not just of eternal love but of eternity itself, a symbol of our beginning when Heavenly Father and Heavenly Mother were somehow in some place joined as one.

Our marriage that began that day was indeed the beginning of my schooling in how to love. And I had much to learn! From the time my parents divorced when I was an infant, I witnessed the failure of marriage. My mother married five times, my father four. Nearly everyone in my family of origin has struggled to make marriage work. There's no question but that Ruth taught me how to love—love myself, love her, love our children, love even those few people I found it challenging to love. I think it was her clear view of the eternal possibilities of love that gave her the courage and strength to challenge my immaturity, my limitations in love. That and the ennobling teachings about love and marriage unique to Latter-day Saints constituted my schoolhouse. "In the heavens are parents single?" is one of the defining questions of Mormon doctrine and cosmology. Written by early Mormon poet Eliza R. Snow, the question is part of a poem that is one of the first articulations of the Mormon belief in both a Mother and Father in Heaven.

If one is fortunate enough to love and be loved completely by another, the possibility of which, I contend, is enhanced by marriage and perhaps greatly magnified by eternal marriage, then at some point one reaches the conclusion that this is the primary purpose and crowning achievement of life. If, as James Finley says, "infinite love is the architect of our hearts," then it is husband and wife who together, with the blueprint of love, are emboldened to construct the house of love in which they hope to spend their lives. If the house of love is built on sand, as it seems so many marriages are today, then when storms and floods come, it cannot stand. Extending Jesus's metaphor, a marriage built on the rock of commitment, sacrifice, and fidelity, while the dwelling itself is constructed out of grace, generosity, forgiveness, and other virtues, has a good chance of withstanding the storms of life.

In Book 23 of *The Odyssey*, "The Greatrooted Bed," Odysseus and Penelope, separated for so many years, finally come together in the bed that Odysseus fashioned with his own hands at the beginning of their shared life. He built the bed with a living olive tree as one of the posts, then built the bedroom around the bed and the house itself around the bedroom. Thus, their bed, both by its prominence and its symbolism, signifies their marriage. Through his wandering at Troy, his time on Calypso's island, and the thousand nights spent on treacherous seas, Odysseus dreamed of his bed and Penelope, who, through twenty years of loneliness and suffering, slept in it alone. Homer describes their reunion using an extended metaphor to reveal the intensity of Odysseus's longing and then shifts subjects in the last two lines to apply the metaphor to Penelope as well:

> Now from his breast into his eyes the ache
> of longing mounted, and he wept at last,
> his dear wife, clear and faithful, in his arms,
> longed for as the sunwarmed earth is longed for by a swimmer
> spent in rough water where his ship went down
> under Poseidon's blows, gale winds and tons of sea.
> Few men can keep alive through a big surf

to crawl, clotted with brine, on kindly beaches
in joy, in joy, knowing the abyss behind:
and so she too rejoiced, her gaze upon her husband,
her white arms round him pressed as though forever.

Not just in *The Odyssey* but in so many ways, the marriage bed is a lovely little landscape, a microcosm of the larger landscape of wedded life. So much takes place in that small space: daily discourse about the world, recountings of the day's triumphs and disappointments, laughter about things shared with no one else, back-turned-to-back stony silence, wild embraces, and always the nocturnal pas de deux, turning together in a dreamlike dance throughout the night. Perhaps the most powerful longing for the marriage bed in the English language is the cry of the anonymous Middle English poet who thinks, far from home, of his conjugal bed:

O westron wind, when will thou blow?
The small rain down can rain.
Christ, that my love were in my arms,
And I in my bed again.

The bed is a poignant symbol of marriage not only for the sheer amount of time a couple spends there but because of the deep knowing possible between husband and wife on and in that small space—knowing one another spiritually, socially, intellectually, and physically/sexually, "knowing" in the biblical sense. To retreat each night to that small retreat, to find refuge there, to nurture one another there is one reason God elevated marriage as a sacrament. It's a place to find oneself, where, with love, we recover some sense of ourselves. These thoughts underlie a poem I wrote during the last year of Ruth's life:

FINDING

We help one another these days,
finding things we have lost, finding
words we have forgotten or which don't come
readily to mind, finding our way in the dark
when winter storms bring down trees
against the light, finding our way through
the twists and tangles of our children's lives
and the labyrinths of our own. But each night
we find ourselves in the small boat we call our bed
and sail through darkness and dreams
to dawn.

At least a third of the fifty years of married life Ruth and I shared was spent on or in our bed. It was the locus of our final rituals of the day. We went to bed each night around midnight, first kneeling to say a few words "to the close and holy darkness," as Dylan Thomas would say, me on the left side, she on the right, then meeting in the middle, cupped together like spoons in a drawer, covered by a sheet or less in midsummer, electric and wool blankets in winter, the smell of clean cotton when we changed the linen together each week.

When our children were growing up, our bed (then a king size) was where our children found us too early on Christmas mornings. It was where they brought awful breakfasts in bed on birthdays and anniversaries. It was where they wanted to be when they were home sick from school. It was the place our family gathered at night and on Sunday afternoons. When they were in high school and going to parties or on dates, our children would come into our bedroom when they got home, flop down to talk. The dogs would come in too and sometimes sneak onto the bed as well. Every Sunday after church when dinner was finished, we would all lie on or sit propped against the bed reading the Sunday paper, sharing the comics, reading aloud some humorous or poignant piece we found, sharing back rubs, always telling stories. It was where we felt comfortable together.

After our children went to their own marital beds, ours shrank to queen size. Once when our two daughters were visiting, I heard them upstairs laughing. I found them happily ensconced on our bed and sat down to share the experience with them. Their mother came in and there we were, just like old times.

Later, it was our grandchildren who came in to awaken us on Christmas mornings, who sometimes slept in our bed when they visited or came in before their parents were awake to snuggle and talk. After giving our youngest grandson his bath during one of his family's visits, we would dry and dress him for sleep on our bed. He loved to scramble about on the bed like a crab, hide under the covers and then try to scare us, and be pummeled by pillows. When he awoke in his room down the hall before dawn, we got him a bottle and let him sleep between us as we did our own children so many years before. It was a sweet presence and a sweet remembrance.

And so we go on.

My father said that when he was little and his parents were in the fields working, he would climb into their bed and pull the covers over his head. He said he liked their smell; it made him feel warm and safe. Our bed has been a place where I have felt warm and safe as well, except on those occasions when earthquakes in our California home shattered our repose, or screeching brakes and the sound of metal on metal on the street outside shocked us awake, or a child's nightmare tore us from dreams.

For a time we lived by a river, and the last sound I heard at night was the water running over the rocks. It was a lovely way to fall asleep, listening to river music and embracing the woman I was privileged to love for more than five decades. We recognized that some dark night in the future, one of us would be in the bed alone, with nothing to hold on to but our memories.

* * *

Ruth passed away February 6, 2012. Her passing was peaceful, with our four children and me by her bedside. She taught us all not only how to love but how to sing. The hospice chaplain came and, knowing how much music had been part of our family culture, brought his guitar. To his accompaniment, we sang song after song—hymns, carols, anthems, chorales, folk songs, musicals. We sang "Amazing Grace," because the grace of those moments truly was amazing. The singing gladdened her heart, just as it saddened ours to know that soon we would no longer hear her beautiful angelic voice harmonizing with ours. The chaplain said he had never heard a family sing so beautifully or harmoniously. I can think of no better gift or tribute to Ruth and the many gifts she gave us through the music she brought into our lives. We were all there for her last breaths. I put on the "Rest Well" chorus from the St John Passion, a piece her choirs had sung and which she loved. I wanted her to hear that restful prayer of peace, Bach's lullaby to the Savior, sounding in her subconscious if not in her consciousness as she passed from this world to the next:

> Rest well, rest well, Beloved sweetly sleeping,
> That I may cease from further weeping.
> And let me too, rest well.

When she was finally gone, her poor body lifeless on the bed and all of us standing around, I imagined her awakening in that other place, seeing the Savior's glorious face and him seeing hers with her amazing smile.

The rest of us left the room to be with our private griefs as our daughters bathed her body and dressed it in elegant white clothing appropriate to Latter-day Saint burial rituals. As I looked at her on our bed after they finished, I thought of our wedding day, when Ruth was dressed in a beautiful white silk dress and, clothed in the robes of the holy priesthood, hands clasped, we knelt across the altar of the temple, our images echoing into infinity in the facing mirrors.

Since Ruth's passing, I have written a number of letters and poems to her. While I have an absolute conviction that individual lives, personalities, and relationships continue beyond the grave, I have no idea as to whether Ruth knows of my thoughts or has any way of knowing what I've written to her. My assumption is that, at the very least, under some flowering tree on some green hill in a heavenly sphere, she and I will sit down, and I will read to her what I've written over these lonely months and years since she went away, and I will hold her hand, look into her eyes, and tell her how much I love her—and have always loved her.

These days I sleep alone, and the bed is always too big! I'm reminded of the sweetness of sharing the bed with Ruth whenever I do the laundry and change the linen. Here are two poems that reflect the loneliness I often experience:

MAKING THE BED

After once more making the bed alone
this morning—tucking the corners
of the bottom sheet, smoothing
the wrinkles, folding the top sheet
(as you taught me fifty years ago
when we made our bed together after
that first night), adding the blanket,
needed more now that your warmth is gone,
putting cases on the pillows, only one
of which now softens my sleep
on this small, solitary meadow
of love and dreams—

I want to crawl back in
and just lie there thinking of you
and all those Saturdays we washed
the sheets and made the bed together,
you on one side and me on the other,
then together at night
with soft cotton enveloping
us and down comforters comforting us
as we enfolded one another against
everything and everyone else
in the world.

A common ritual in our marriage was my taking the sheets from the dryer, finding Ruth, and enveloping her in them. This poem describes how that ritual has changed in the years since her passing.

WARM SHEETS

Do you remember when,
taking sheets from the dryer
just as the cycle ended or on a
summer day from the backyard,
fresh and sun-blessed, I enfolded you
in that soft heat, enveloped your body
with womb-like warmth, embraced you
as I had all those mornings before we stripped
the bed and did the laundry?

I remembered you

this morning when I took the sheets
from the dryer and held them against my face, savoring
the warmth, remembering your body, remembering too
that last day when warmth left your body as surely,
as imperceptibly as it leaves mine now
standing alone in our cold empty bedroom
embracing these soft white ghosts.

I hope there are beds in eternity! I hope there are nights! I am as certain as I am about anything that there will be love.

Figure 10. Robert A. and Ruth Rees, April Fool's Day 1961, Los Angeles

Robert writes, "I was living in Madison, Wisconsin, beginning my graduate studies. Ruth was in graduate school at BYU. I made a mad trip to Provo over Christmas vacation and proposed. Ruth moved to Madison the next semester, and we planned a June wedding. As spring break approached, we thought, 'What the heck!' and drove home to Southern California to get married in the Los Angeles Temple, where the only day available for our wedding was April Fool's Day. This photo was taken at our wedding reception that evening. After a brief honeymoon we made a mad dash back to Madison, arriving just in time for an exam in my romantic poetry class—which I was and wasn't prepared for!"

Glossary

Aaronic priesthood: The lesser branch of the priesthood within The Church of Jesus Christ of Latter-day Saints. It includes the offices of deacon, to which young men are ordained at age twelve; teacher, which young men may attain at age fourteen; and priest, which they may attain at age sixteen. (Women are currently denied the priesthood.)

bishop: The lay leader of a local congregation known as a ward.

bishopric: The three men who lead a ward, consisting of a bishop and two male counselors.

branch: A local congregation too small to be a ward.

branch president: The lay leader of a branch.

BYU: Brigham Young University. The university's main campus is in Provo, Utah. BYU-Hawai'i is in Laie; BYU-Idaho is in Rexburg and was known as Ricks College until 2001. Students at all three locations must agree to abide by the commandments of The Church of Jesus Christ of Latter-day Saints.

celestial kingdom: The highest level of heaven in Latter-day Saint theology. People judged worthy of its glory will be permitted to be married for all eternity and to become gods.

celestial room: An elegant room in the temple set aside for quiet contemplation that worthy Latter-day Saints may enter after participating in an endowment ceremony.

companion: See mission companion.

correlation: Twentieth-century effort to standardize curricula and practice throughout The Church of Jesus Christ of Latter-day Saints. Before correlation, auxiliary organizations and local congregations could create their own programs and manage their own budgets; after correlation, everything is overseen by committees in Salt Lake City.

counselor: One of two assistants in most leadership units in the church. For instance, the president of any local Elders Quorum will have a first and second counselor; the president of the entire church also has a first and second counselor.

Doctrine and Covenants: A collection of writings that are purportedly revelations from God and Jesus Christ given mainly to Joseph Smith but occasionally to others.

elder: The first office in the Melchizedek priesthood. Men are traditionally ordained to the office of elder at age eighteen, and it is the title for male missionaries, who are typically in their late teens or early twenties. Thus, in Latter-day Saint culture, despite its conventional meaning, the term often connotes youth and immaturity rather than age and wisdom, even though it's also the title used for the highest-ranking senior members of the church's gerontocracy.

Elders Quorum: All men who hold the office of elder in a local ward or congregation. The term also refers to a meeting on Sunday during which elders discuss a lesson on gospel topics.

endowment: See temple endowment.

Ensign: A devotional magazine published by the church from 1971 through 2020. It was replaced in January 2021 by the *Liahona*.

family home evening: An evening, generally Monday, during which a family typically plays games, hears a church lesson, sings church songs, and eats treats. Often abbreviated FHE.

fast offering: On the first Sunday of every month, Latter-day Saints fast for two meals and donate at least the cost of the missed meals to the church as part of a welfare fund for people in need.

garments: See temple garment.

general authority: A high-ranking leader in The Church of Jesus Christ of Latter-day Saints; one of the church's few paid leadership positions.

General Conference: A semiannual church-wide meeting held in Salt Lake City and broadcast to congregations throughout the world the first weekend of April and of October.

Heavenly Mother: Female counterpart (and wife) to Heavenly Father. Also known as Mother in Heaven and God the Mother.

home teachers: Two men (sometimes a father and son) assigned to visit a set of families in their own homes. Every household that included a Latter-day Saint would be assigned home teachers by the local congregation. The practice was replaced in 2018 with a less formal system not requiring visits inside the home and allowing a husband and wife, rather than two men, to visit families.

inactive: Used as both a noun and an adjective. Refers to a person who is still a member of record of the LDS Church but who doesn't attend meetings. Participating fully in the church is referred to as being active.

Institute of Religion, a.k.a. Institute: A building on college and university campuses offering Latter-day Saint students religious instruction and social opportunities.

Melchizedek priesthood: The more advanced branch of the priesthood. Its offices include elder, which men may be ordained to at age eighteen, as well as seventy and high priest.

mission: For men, a two-year period of service that may begin when they reach age eighteen (until 2012, the age requirement for men was typically nineteen); for women, an eighteen-month period of service that may begin when they reach age nineteen (until 2012, the age requirement for women was twenty-one).

mission companion: A missionary's assigned working partner. Companions are typically reassigned every month or so.

Mission Training Center: One of several locations, the main one being in Provo, Utah, where missionaries spend the first portion of their missions preparing for missionary service. A stint there is usually a few weeks, unless missionaries must learn a foreign language, in which case they stay closer to two months.

patriarch: A formal calling extended to a man who, by virtue of that calling, is blessed with special prophetic faculties and is able to offer individualized insights and guidance to members via a one-time event called a patriarchal blessing. It's common to receive one's patriarchal blessing in adolescence or early adulthood.

Plan of Happiness: God's divine plan for human progression on Earth, according to Mormon belief. Also called the Plan of Salvation.

polygamy: Within The Church of Jesus Christ of Latter-day Saints, this term refers to the practice of men having multiple wives, described in Section 132 of the Doctrine and Covenants as a sacred law of heaven. It was practiced in secret by Joseph Smith and other men while the church was headquartered in Illinois; it was practiced openly throughout the West after the church moved to Utah in the 1840s. Under pressure from the US government, the church twice disavowed it, in 1890 and 1904. It is currently forbidden in the church; practicing it is grounds for discipline.

preexistence: The period before we are born. Latter-day Saints believe that our identities were already established in the preexistence and that we can create relationships then that can continue in this life and the next.

Primary: The church's organization for children. Children enter it when they turn three and graduate from it when they turn twelve.

promptings: Messages from God or the Holy Ghost.

Quorum of the Twelve: The church's top leadership. Upon the death of the president of the church, the president of the Quorum of the Twelve becomes the new president and prophet of the church.

Relief Society: Women's auxiliary organization, founded in 1842. Originally a self-governing organization within the church, it was subsumed during a mid-twentieth-century program known as correlation and is now overseen by the church's male hierarchy.

sacrament meeting: A Sunday worship service.

sealing: A sacred ordinance performed in the temple in which a couple or family is sealed together as a unit for all eternity.

sealing cancellation: The rendering of a sealing null and void so that a woman may be sealed to a new husband after a divorce. Also called a temple divorce.

seminary: Religious instruction on weekdays, often scheduled before the regular school day, for Latter-day Saint high school students.

singles ward or singles branch: A congregation consisting entirely of unmarried adult Latter-day Saints. One of their primary purposes is to help members find a spouse.

Spirit: Another term for the Holy Ghost. It is a means by which Latter-day Saints receive divine revelation and personal guidance.

stake: A geographical collection of wards or congregations roughly equivalent to a diocese.

stake center: A large meeting house in which stake offices are located and stake meetings may be held.

stake president: The lay leader who oversees a stake.

temple: A sacred building where necessary sacred ordinances are performed for both living Latter-day Saints and the dead. Not used for regular meetings or Sunday worship.

temple endowment or endowments: A sacred ritual in which Latter-day Saints are endowed with the knowledge of specific terms, tokens, and handshakes they believe they must offer the angels guarding the celestial kingdom in order to enter it. Receiving one's own endowment is often called "going through the temple" for the first time; worthy Latter-day Saints are thereafter encouraged to return to the temple and participate in the endowment ceremony as proxies for people who died without the opportunity to attend the temple.

temple garment: Modest underwear that Latter-day Saints begin wearing after receiving their temple endowment to remind them of the covenants they have made to God.

temple marriage: Marriage contracted "for time and all eternity" and performed only in the temple. Also known as celestial marriage or eternal marriage.

temple recommend: A small card about the size of a driver's license showing that the possessor is worthy to enter the temple.

temple recommend interview: Interview covering such areas as sexual behavior, tithe-paying and honesty in business dealings, adherence to the Word of Wisdom, belief in and fidelity to the church's teachings, etc. designed to assess one's worthiness to enter the temple.

testimony: A witness from God that the church (or one of its teachings or elements) is true and ordained of God.

testimony meeting: A meeting (often held on the first Sunday of the month) set aside for the sharing or "bearing" of testimonies.

ward: A local congregation of between 150 and 500 members.

Word of Wisdom: The Latter-day Saint dietary code, found in Section 89 of the Doctrine and Covenants. Originally intended only as advice, its recommendations included eating less meat. In the twentieth century, it was codified as a commandment and is interpreted as forbidding the consumption of coffee, tea, tobacco, alcohol, and illicit drugs. Very strict adherence could include forgoing soft drinks with caffeine, but this was never an official requirement and was explicitly disavowed in 2012.

Young Men: The church's organization for boys over the age of twelve. They graduate from it at age eighteen. Also known as the Young Men's Program.

Discussion Questions

1. The introduction opens by quoting Supreme Court Justice Anthony Kennedy's statement about reasons why marriage is so profound a union. Do the marriages discussed in this collection support or undercut his statement? Why or why not?

2. The introduction states that this volume is intended to address this question: "Given that a particular emphasis on marriage is one of the things distinguishing The Church of Jesus Christ of Latter-day Saints, what distinguishes LDS marriages for the [people] in them?" Based on the essays collected here, how would you answer that question? How is that answer different from the answer you might give based on expectations you've formed elsewhere about LDS marriage?

3. Some of the writers don't discuss their belief at all; religion seems to be a backdrop rather than a focus for the issues they want to discuss. How does this affect the overall view presented here of The Church of Jesus Christ of Latter-day Saints and its members?

4. Some of the essays discuss topics related to sex, such as cross-dressing, sterilization, erectile dysfunction, pornography, promiscuity, infidelity, polyamory, polygamy, and masturbation. What do you see as uniquely Mormon about the way these topics are treated? What do you see as representative of our society as a whole?

5. Many of the essays are straightforward chronological narrations, but some essays also play with form or focus, telling a story through a travelogue, a diary of making pies, a discussion of poems about beds, a comparison of the author's marriage with the marriages of friends and loved ones, or an alternating account of a wife's life-threatening illness and a husband's midlife crisis. Which sorts of forms and focuses did you find most effective, and why?

6. Several of the essays discuss an author's suicidal longings. What do you think the significance of this is in the context of marriage and religious belief?

7. What benefits do you think the priesthood and the obligation to preside bestow on Latter-day Saint men? What difficulties do you think the priesthood and the obligation to preside create for Latter-day Saint men?

8. Many writers discuss their preconceptions about marriage and how those preconceptions affect the marriage they actually end up in. Which preconceptions seem most powerful to you? Which seem most destructive? How common do you think such preconceptions are, not just among Latter-day Saints but our society at large?

9. Which essays do you think offer the most useful insight and guidance to couples beginning a relationship, and why?

10. What preconceptions about Latter-day Saint men do you think this volume challenges? What preconceptions does it reinforce?

Bibliography

Achieving a Celestial Marriage. Church Educational System, 1976.

Arnold, Matthew. "Dover Beach." 1867. Poetry Foundation, www.poetryfoundation.org/poems/43588/dover-beach.

Aronowitz, Nona Willis. "The Education of Natalie Jean." *Elle*, 5 Nov. 2019, www.elle.com/life-love/a29438763/natalie-lovin-mommy-blog-influencer/.

Bielski, Zosia. "The New Reality of Dating over 65: Men Want to Live Together; Women Don't." *Globe and Mail*, 26 Nov. 2019, www.theglobeandmail.com/life/relationships/article-women-older-than-65-dont-want-to-live-with-their-partners/.

Birger, John. *Date-onomics: How Dating Became a Lopsided Numbers Game*. Workman, 2015.

Blake, William. "Auguries of Innocence." 1863. Poetry Foundation, www.poetryfoundation.org/poems/43650/auguries-of-innocence.

———. "The Everlasting Gospel." Bartleby.com, www.bartleby.com/236/58.html.

Bob's Mormon Cred Scale 2.0. 2017. Proprofs.com, www.proprofs.com/survey/t/?title=kedrt.

Carroll, Jason S. "Delaying Marriage: The Trends and the Consequences." *Ensign*, Mar. 2017, www.churchofjesuschrist.org/study/ensign/2017/03/young-adults/delaying-marriage-the-trends-and-the-consequences.

Catron, Mandy Len. "What You Lose When You Gain a Spouse." *The Atlantic*, 2 July 2019, www.theatlantic.com/family/archive/2019/07/case-against-marriage/591973/.

Chambers, Claire. *Against Marriage: An Egalitarian Defence of the Marriage-Free State*. Oxford University Press, 2017.

Chen, Victor Tan. "America, Home of the Transactional Marriage." *The Atlantic*, 20 Aug. 2017, www.theatlantic.com/business/archive/2017/08/marriage-rates-education/536913.

Cherlin, Andrew J. *The Marriage-Go-Round: The State of Marriage and the Family in America Today*. Vintage, 2009.

———. "Marriage Has Become a Trophy." *The Atlantic*, 20 Mar. 2018, www.theatlantic.com/family/archive/2018/03/incredible-everlasting-institution-marriage/555320/.

Coontz, Stephanie. "How to Make Your Marriage Gayer." *New York Times*, 13 Feb. 2020, www
    .nytimes.com/2020/02/13/opinion/sunday/marriage-housework-gender-happiness
    .html.

———. *Marriage, a History: How Love Conquered Marriage*. Penguin, 2006.

Curtis, Larry D. "After Changes to Handbook Terminology, LDS Church Members
    No Longer 'Excommunicated.'" *KUTV*, 19 Feb. 2020, www.kutv.com/news/local/
    after-changes-to-handbook-terminology-lds-church-members-can-no-longer-be
    -excommunicated.

Durant, Will, and Ariel Durant. *The Lessons of History*. Simon and Schuster, 1968.

Ehrenreich, Barbara. *The Hearts of Men: American Dreams and the Flight from Com-
    mitment*. Anchor, 1983.

"The Family: A Proclamation to the World." The Church of Jesus Christ of Latter-day
    Saints, 23 Sept. 1995, www.churchofjesuschrist.org/bc/content/shared/content/english/
    pdf/36035_000_24_family.pdf.

"Fidelity in Marriage." The Church of Jesus Christ of Latter-day Saints, www.churchof
    jesuschrist.org/study/manual/eternal-marriage-student-manual/fidelity-in-marriage.
    Accessed 29 Feb. 2020.

Finkel, Eli J. *The All-or-Nothing Marriage: How the Best Marriages Work*. Dutton, 2017.

Finley, James. "Union with Infinite Love." Center for Action and Contemplation, 19 Feb.
    2017, //cac.org/union-infinite-love-2017-02-19/.

General Handbook: Serving in The Church of Jesus Christ of Latter-day Saints. The Church
    of Jesus Christ of Latter-day Saints, 2020, www.churchofjesuschrist.org/study/manual/
    general-handbook. Accessed 29 Feb. 2020.

Gottman, John M., and Nan Silver. *The Seven Principles for Making Marriage Work: A
    Practical Guide from the Country's Foremost Relationship Expert*. 2nd ed. Harmony, 2015.

Gregory, Alice. "Why So Many of Your Favorite Beauty Personalities Are Mormon." *Al-
    lure*, 11 Oct. 2017, www.allure.com/story/why-so-many-beauty-bloggers-are-mormon.

Holland, Jeffrey R. "Personal Purity." *New Era*, Feb. 2000, www.churchofjesuschrist.org/
    study/new-era/2000/02/personal-purity.

Homer. *The Odyssey*. Translated by Robert Fitzgerald Farrar, Straus & Giroux, 1998.

Hoyt, Amy, and Taylor G. Petrey, editors. *The Routledge Handbook of Mormonism and
    Gender*. Routledge, 2020.

Hudson, Valerie. "The Two Trees." *FAIR Latter-day Saints*, Aug. 2010, https://www.fairlatter
    daysaints.org/conference/august-2010/the-two-trees.

Jacobs, Becky. "LDS Church Announces It Still Opposes Equal Rights Amendment as
    Supporters Rally at Capitol." *Salt Lake Tribune*, 3 Dec. 2019, www.sltrib.com/news/
    2019/12/03/lds-church-announces-it/.

Jason Isbell and the 400 Unit, "Hope the High Road," *The Nashville Sound*, RCA Studio
    B, 2017.

Jones, Jeffrey M. "In U.S., 10.2% of LGBT Adults Now Married to Same-Sex Spouse." Gal-
    lup, 18 Nov. 2019, news.gallup.com/poll/212702/lgbt-adults-married-sex-spouse.aspx.

Kennedy, Anthony. *Obergefell v. Hodges*. Supreme Court of the United States, 26 June
    2015, www.supremecourt.gov/opinions/14pdf/14-556_3204.pdf.

Kiesling, Lydia. "The Evolution of a Mormon Mommy Blogger." *The Cut*, June 2018, www
.thecut.com/2018/06/what-happened-to-natalie-jean-nat-the-fat-rat.html.

Kimball, Spencer W. "The Angels May Quote from It." *New Era*, Oct. 1975, www.church
ofjesuschrist.org/study/new-era/2003/02/the-angels-may-quote-from-it.

———. "Oneness in Marriage." *Ensign*, Mar. 1977, www.churchofjesuschrist.org/study/
ensign/1977/03/oneness-in-marriage.

Livingston, Gretchen, and Kim Parker. "8 Facts about American Dads." Pew Research
Center, 12 June 2019, www.pewresearch.org/fact-tank/2019/06/12/fathers-day-facts/.

Matchar, Emily. "Why I Can't Stop Reading Mormon Housewife Blogs." *Salon*, 16 Jan.
2011, www.salon.com/2011/01/15/feminist_obsessed_with_mormon_blogs/.

Matsuura, Alicia. "Religious OCD: When Faith Becomes an Obsession." *Daily Universe*,
29 Jan. 2020, universe.byu.edu/2020/01/29/religious-ocd-when-faith-becomes-an
-obsession-rather-than-a-consolation-at-byu/.

McConkie, Bruce R. *Mormon Doctrine*. 2nd ed. Bookcraft, 1966.

———. Untitled Address from *Conference Report*, Sep-Oct 1955, The Church of Jesus
Christ of Latter-day Saints, 1955, pp. 12–13.

McDannell, Colleen. *Sister Saints: Mormon Women Since the End of Polygamy*. Oxford
University Press, 2019.

Mendel, Arthur, editor. *The Passion According to St. John* by J. S. Bach. Libretto translated
by Henry S. Drinker, Harvey Officer, and Arthur Mendel. G. Schirmer, 1951.

Murphy, Thomas W. "Lamanite Genesis, Genealogy, and Genetics." *American Apocrypha: Essays on the Book of Mormon*. Edited by Dan Vogel and Brent L. Metcalfe.
Signature, 2002, pp. 47-77.

Nelson, Russell M. "The Correct Name of the Church." YouTube, uploaded by General
Conference of The Church of Jesus Christ of Latter-day Saints, 8 Oct. 2018, https://youtu
.be/XORXvaNSC4I.

Packer, Boyd K. "Cleansing the Inner Vessel." YouTube, uploaded by The Church of Jesus
Christ of Latter-day Saints, 3 Oct. 2010. https://youtu.be/2C1wUI5xuhs.

———. "Eternal Love." ScottWoodward.org, scottwoodward.org/Talks/html/Packer,
BoydK /PackerBK_EternalLove.html.

———. "To Young Men Only." Internet Archive, 2 Oct. 1976, https://archive.org/details/
ToYoungMenOnly. Accessed 29 Feb. 2020.

———. "The Unwritten Order of Things." BYU-Idaho, 15 Oct. 1996, emp.byui.edu/huffr/
The%20Unwritten%20Order%20of%20Things%20—%20Boyd%20K.%20Packer.htm.

Richardson, James. *Vectors: Aphorisms & Ten-Second Essays*. Ausable, 2001.

Rumi. "The Guest House." Translated by Coleman Barks. Scottish Poetry Library, www
.scottishpoetrylibrary.org.uk/poem/guest-house/.

Samaran, Nora. "The Opposite of Rape Culture Is Nurturance Culture." 11 Feb. 2016,
norasamaran.com/2016/02/11/the-opposite-of-rape-culture-is-nurturance-culture-2/.

Sartre, Jean-Paul. *No Exit*. Translated by Paul Bowles, Samuel French, 1958.

Scott, Richard G. "The Eternal Blessings of Marriage." YouTube, uploaded by The
Church of Jesus Christ of Latter-day Saints, 3 Apr. 2011, www.youtube.com/watch?v=
QDNAZ6zXeXA.

Shellenbarger, Sue. "The Secret Benefits of Retelling Family Stories." *Wall Street Journal*, 11 Nov. 2019, www.wsj.com/articles/the-secret-benefits-of-retelling-family-stories-11573468201.

Snow, Eliza R. "Oh My Father." In *Hymns of The Church of Jesus Christ of Latter-day Saints*. The Church of Jesus Christ of Latter-day Saints, 1985, p. 292.

Stack, Peggy Fletcher. "Why Young LDS Men Are Pushing Back Marriage." *Salt Lake Tribune*, 29 Apr. 2011, archive.sltrib.com/article.php?id=51631455&itype=CMSID.

"Steps in Overcoming Masturbation." Internet Archive. archive.org/stream/STEPSINOVERCOMINGMASTURBATION/STEPS%20IN%20OVERCOMING%20MASTURBATION_djvu.txt. Accessed 29 Feb. 2020.

"Style Guide." The Church of Jesus Christ of Latter-day Saints. newsroom.churchofjesuschrist.org/style-guide. Accessed 29 Feb. 2020.

Thomas, Dylan. *A Child's Christmas in Wales*. 1952. Project Gutenberg Australia, gutenberg.net.au/ebooks07/0701261h.html.

Way, Katie. "I Went on a Date with Aziz Ansari. It Turned Into the Worst Night of My Life." *Babe*, 13 Jan. 2018, babe.net/2018/01/13/aziz-ansari-28355.

Welker, Holly. "Attempting Mormon Marriage." Introduction. *Baring Witness: 36 Mormon Women Talk Candidly about Love, Sex, and Marriage*, edited by Welker, University of Illinois Press, 2016, pp. 1–18.

———, editor. *Baring Witness: 36 Mormon Women Talk Candidly about Love, Sex, and Marriage*. Urbana: University of Illinois Press, 2016.

———. "Changes in Role of Mormon Women Can't Be Discussed—but Let's Discuss Them Anyway." *Religion Dispatches*, 4 Jan. 2019, religiondispatches.org/changes-to-lds-temple-ceremony-on-role-of-women-cant-be-discussed-but-lets-discuss-them-anyway/.

———. "Cleanshaven: No More Beards: Straight Women, Gay Men, and Mormonism." *Sunstone* 147, October 2007, pp. 44–50.

———. "From Here to Eternity: Of Mormons and Celestial Marriage." *Religion Dispatches*, 6 Oct. 2010, religiondispatches.org/from-here-to-eternity-of-mormons-and-celestial-marriage/.

———. "LDS Church Rescinds Hurtful Marriage Policy without Apology." *Religion Dispatches*, 7 May 2019, religiondispatches.org/lds-church-rescinds-hurtful-marriage-policy-without-apology/.

———. "Sorry, Your Friends Can't Come to Your Mormon Wedding." *Slate*, 17 Sept. 2013, slate.com/human-interest/2013/09/mormon-weddings-why-you-cant-attend-your-friends-lds-wedding-but-should-still-be-able-to-celebrate-with-them.html.

———. "Why I Go to Sunstone." *Sunstone* 138, September 2005, pp. 14–15.

"Western Wind." *The Norton Anthology of English Literature*, M. H. Abrams, general editor, 4th ed., vol. 1, W. W. Norton, 1979, p. 340.

Whitfield, Charles. *Healing the Child Within: Discovery and Recovery for Adult Children of Dysfunctional Families*. HCI Books, 1987.

Yalom, Marilyn. *A History of the Wife*. HarperCollins, 2001.

Yarrow, Andrew L. "Marriage, Poverty and the Political Divide." *New York Times*, 24 Jan. 2016, www.nytimes.com/2016/01/24/fashion/weddings/marriage-poverty-gop-political-divide.html.

Contributors

Kevin Barnwell grew up on a hog farm in rural Oregon. He lives in Phoenix, Arizona, where he has worked treating periodontal disease since the late 1990s. He is entranced with hummingbirds, wind chimes, and Arizona sunrises and tinkers with kintsugi, the art of repairing broken pottery with precious metals in order to embrace flaws and render them beautiful. He dreams that when the patriarchy crumbles, his three granddaughters will ring the death knell with delight.

Scott Blanding is a theater professional who has directed university, Off Broadway, outdoor drama, and independent productions for almost fifty years. He has taught theater at four universities. He has published several plays; written on Scandinavian literature, dramatic theory, and criticism; and reviewed Broadway openings.

Joseph Broom is a retired attorney living in Salt Lake City, Utah. A native of southern Illinois, he has lived most of his adult life in Ohio, British Columbia, and Utah. Besides spending time with his ten children (including three adopted from Russia) and his grandchildren, he writes and travels and assisted in the production of the 2019 documentary *For They Know Not What They Do*, a sequel to the award-winning film *For the Bible Tells Me So* that explores the interface of sexual orientation and identity with conservative Christianity.

T. Kay Browning is a stay-at-home dad to three kids currently in Sweden. Raised by a father descended from Mormon pioneers and a mother who joined the church as an adult, T. Kay served a full-time mission in Argentina and was married in the temple in 2008 before leaving the church in 2012.

Michael Carpenter has lived in California, Utah, and Idaho. He is the father of three and grandfather of four. He has worked as a software engineer for more than thirty years. He volunteered in various Boy Scout adult leader positions for over twenty-five years and is a recipient of the Silver Beaver Award. He loves outdoor activities, including hiking, camping, kayaking, and landscape photography. He currently resides in Silicon Valley.

Stephen Carter has a PhD in narrative studies from the University of Alaska–Fairbanks and is the editor of *Sunstone*, an independent Mormon magazine. He is the editor of *Moth and Rust: Mormon Encounters with Death* and the author of *Mormonism for Beginners*, *What of the Night?*, and *iPlates* (with Jett Atwood), an award-winning series of graphic novels based on the Book of Mormon. But Stephen's most recent (and challenging) jobs include managing his youngest daughter's dance schedule and learning to do her hair and makeup.

Tyler Chadwick is an award-winning writer, editor, and teacher. He has three books to his name: two anthologies, *Fire in the Pasture: 21st Century Mormon Poets* (Peculiar Pages, 2011) and *Dove Song: Heavenly Mother in Mormon Poetry* (Peculiar Pages, 2018), and a collection of poetry and essays, *Field Notes on Language and Kinship* (Mormon Artists Group, 2013). He lives in Ogden, Utah, with his wife, Jess, and their four daughters.

Kelland Coleman lives in Sandy, Utah, where he works in information technology. In his free time, he enjoys hiking, exercise, movies, reading, and spending time with his five wonderful daughters.

John B. Dahl works in the information technology field for a software company. He enjoys golf, fly fishing, and watching college sports. He and his wife, Mylie, have five married children and more than a dozen grandchildren. He has held a variety of callings in The Church of Jesus Christ of Latter-day Saints, including bishop and Elders Quorum president.

Scot Denhalter has six children and seven grandchildren. A former English professor, he is now a slave to the private sector. Scot lives in Logan, Utah.

John Doe lives in Utah with his wife, his four children, six cats, and his alter ego, Jane. John also loves playing bluegrass and Celtic music and can often be found fiddling or picking a banjo. John and Claire have celebrated twenty years together in what some may consider a complicated but fulfilling marriage.

Joey Franklin is the author of the essay collections *Delusions of Grandeur: American Essays* (University of Nebraska Press, 2020) and *My Wife Wants You to Know I'm Happily Married* (University of Nebraska Press, 2015). His essays have appeared in a variety of literary magazines, including *Hunger Mountain*,

Gettysburg Review, *Ninth Letter*, *Brevity*, and *Fourth Genre*, and he's had work anthologized in *The Norton Reader*, *Bedford Select Custom Database*, and several other collections. He currently coordinates the MFA program in creative writing at Brigham Young University in Provo, Utah, and serves as coeditor of *Fourth Genre: Explorations in Nonfiction*.

Theric Jepson is the author of *Byuck*, which he meant to be funny, and *Perky Erect Nipples*, which he didn't know was funny until readers told him so. Both demonstrate remarkably poor judgment when titling things. Luckily, his wife got final say on their children's names, or they likely would have ended up as Artaxerxes, Giogioni, Bloodstone, and Whoops. The six of them live on borrowed time in El Cerrito, California.

Clyde Kunz was born and raised in the shadow of the temple in Logan, Utah. He is a descendant of Swiss converts to Mormonism, some of whom became polygamists in the church's early years. Following several years in the California banking industry, he relocated to Arizona and now owns a successful consulting firm serving nonprofit organizations. Active in the Episcopal Church locally and nationally, he officially resigned his membership in the Mormon Church in 2008 in response to its support of anti–gay marriage legislation.

Scott Russell Morris earned a PhD in English from Texas Tech University and an MFA in creative writing from Brigham Young University. His writing has previously appeared in *Brevity*, the *Chattahoochee Review*, *Superstition Review*, and elsewhere. He is an assistant professor of writing and rhetoric at the University of Utah Asia Campus in South Korea. His essays and poetry explore themes of enthusiasm, travel, and domestic masculinity.

Thomas W Murphy married Kerrie Sumner in 1985; they have one daughter, Jessyca. Thomas earned a PhD in anthropology from the University of Washington in 2003 and currently serves as anthropology department head at Edmonds College in Lynnwood, Washington, and affiliate professor of Canadian studies at UW. Students and the Board of Trustees at Edmonds recognized him as Honorary Triton Outstanding Faculty in 2005 and with an Excellence in Education Award in 2008. The Washington Association of Conservation Districts selected him as Washington State Conservation Educator of the Year in 2011, highlighting his intercultural partnerships with Coast Salish tribes.

David Nicolay lives in Salt Lake City with his wife and three children.

Boyd Jay Petersen is the program coordinator for Mormon studies at Utah Valley University. He was editor of *Dialogue: A Journal of Mormon Thought* from 2016 to 2019. He holds an MA from the University of Maryland and a PhD from the University of Utah, both in comparative literature.

Robert Raleigh attended BYU, graduated from the University of Utah with a degree in English, and edited the short fiction anthology *In Our Lovely Deseret: Mormon Fictions*, published by Signature Books. He is currently working on another short fiction anthology tentatively titled *The Path and the Gate* and a documentary about the Mormon Church's Indian Student Placement Program. He is employed as a technical writer in Salt Lake City. He has two kids, five stepkids, and a lovely, patient wife.

Robert A. "Bob" Rees is visiting professor and director of Mormon studies at Graduate Theological Union. He is the author and editor of numerous articles, essays, and books, including *The Reader's Book of Mormon*, *Proving Contraries: A Collection in Honor of Eugene England*, *Why I Stay: The Challenges of Discipleship for Contemporary Mormons*, and *A New Witness to the World*, as well as a collection of poetry, *Waiting for Morning*. He is cofounder of the Bountiful Children's Foundation, which addresses malnutrition among children in the developing world.

Eric Robeck spent most of his career as an exploration and mining geologist, exploring underground coal mines in the western United States and mapping remote areas of Mongolia. He left the mining industry in 2017 for a job at a government mapping agency and settled in St. Louis with his wife and four children. He enjoys wildflower gardening, raising chickens, and cycling.

Caleb Scoville trains legal professionals to use case management software. He enjoys art, movies, playing the piano, singing, running, dreaming, and most of all, being with his two sons.

Kim Siever is an independent journalist specializing in political news. He has a bachelor's degree in dramatic arts and currently serves as Sunday school president in his ward. In his spare time, he tries to straddle the fence of being simultaneously queer and Mormon.

Dan Smith grew up in the East, feeling the earth breathe beneath his feet, the trees singing as he climbed them, and the ocean begging him to swim. After many years in the Southwest, he now lives in Florida, where he works as an artist.

Nicholas Don Smith is eagerly awaiting the fall of the oppressive capitalist system. He survived the coronavirus pandemic in American Fork, Utah, and is a comedian, writer, children's book illustrator, and bulldog enthusiast.

Ted Smith is a lawyer who has liberal Protestantism envy. Ted and his wife have three children in various stages of collegiate life.

Andrew Spriggs is a gay, nonbelieving, cultural Mormon. When he's not working (as a tax accountant, but not the kind who files many tax returns), he divides his free time between fencing épée, playing saxophone for his YouTube channel, discussing Mormon and other Christian theological and cultural questions online, and watching Netflix.

Holly Welker is an award-winning poet and essayist and the editor of *Baring Witness: 36 Mormon Women Talk Candidly about Love, Sex, and Marriage.* Her work has appeared in dozens of publications, including *Best American Essays, the Iowa Review, Slate,* and the *New York Times.*

The University of Illinois Press
is a founding member of the
Association of University Presses.

———————————————

Composed in 10.5/13 Adobe Minion Pro
by Jim Proefrock
at the University of Illinois Press
Manufactured by Sheridan Books, Inc.

University of Illinois Press
1325 South Oak Street
Champaign, IL 61820-6903
www.press.uillinois.edu